FAMILY SECRETS

FAMILY SECRETS

LIFE STORIES OF ADULT CHILDREN OF ALCOHOLICS

RACHEL V.

Harper & Row, Publishers, San Francisco

Cambridge, Hagerstown, New York, Philadelphia, Washington
London, Mexico City, São Paulo, Singapore, Sydney

FAMILY SECRETS. Copyright © 1987 by Harper & Row, Publishers, Inc. Introduction copyright © 1987 by Claudia Black and Harper & Row, Publishers,
Inc. Conversation with Robert Bly, copyright © 1987 by Robert Bly and Harper
& Row, Publishers, Inc. Conversation with Marion Woodman, copyright ©
1987 by Marion Woodman and Harper & Row, Publishers, Inc. All rights
reserved. Printed in the United States of America. No part of this book may
be used or reproduced in any manner whatsoever without written permission
except in the case of brief quotations embodied in critical articles and reviews.
For information address Harper & Row, Publishers, Inc., 10 East 53rd Street,
New York, N.Y. 10022. Published simultaneously in Canada by Fitzhenry &
Whiteside Limited, Toronto.

FIRST EDITION

Library of Congress Cataloging-in-Publication Data

V., Rachel.
    Family secrets.

Bibliography: p.
    1. Children of alcoholic parents—United States. 2. Alcoholics—United
States—Family relationships. I. Title.
HV5132.V17   1987   362.2'92   86-43017
ISBN 0-06-250702-8 (pbk.)

    88 89 90 91 RRD 10 9 8 7 6 5 4

*To my own children and to
the young children still suffering
in the alcoholic home today.*

" . . . story is something lived in and lived through, a way in which the soul finds itself in life."

James Hillman, *Loose Ends*

Contents

Acknowledgments

For their help and support I first want to thank my family: my husband and my children, who encouraged me at every turn, and my parents.

This book would not have been possible without the generous spirit of each and every person I interviewed. It is a collective effort to help break down the denial that surrounds the disease of alcoholism and addictions. All have told their stories with the hope that others may find feelings they can identify with and discover that there is a solution to their problem. I thank all those interviewed, many more than could be included here.

Thanks go especially to my editor, Roy M. Carlisle of Harper & Row San Francisco, whose belief in the project has sustained me all along. His vision and encouragement made the book possible.

Though Sherran B. typed the transcripts, her role in my work is always much larger as a friend and careful reader. Theresa K. kept the rest of my life functioning smoothly while I attended to this book. Jude R. helped with research. Emma F. provided good counsel. Barbara W.'s talks brightened weeks of difficulties. My sponsor, Betty S., was always there when I called. Richard L. first directed my attention to the issues of Al-Anon and Adult Children of Alcoholics and insisted that I get to an ACA meeting. I am particularly grateful to him for his suggestions. John G.'s willingness to listen helped me through the months of work. Ella's concern and generous support has been extraordinary. No amount of acknowledgment can suffice to thank her for our friendship and her help. Neltje's assistance came at a crucial moment, as did Florette P.'s guidance and steady encouragement.

Timmen Cermak, M.D., lent his grasp of the subject, and his insights to increasing my understanding of co-dependency and the family system overall.

Hera's constancy during my travels has shown me what a

treasure friendship can be. Barry L.'s thoughtful perspective provided a balance that only a brother can give. Diana and David R. provided the warmth of their hospitality during the travels for this book. Tara D.'s studies and friendship opened doors for me to this material that I never would have seen otherwise.

Lois W. and Bob S. Jr's. comments give us an glimpse into the history and development of Al-Anon and AA. Lois agreed to an interview despite frail health, and Leon S. gave assistance at every turn, promptly and generously. Al-Anon's Family Group Headquarters in New York provided their materials on Adult Children of Alcoholics, the Al-Anon and Alateen programs, suggestions, and support. AA World Services in New York lent their hand as well, guiding me through the ways to properly observe the Traditions in maintaining the anonymity of the members of AA and Al-Anon. The National Council on Alcoholism, the Foundation for Children of Alcoholics in New York, Debtor's Anonymous, the Junior League of America's "Woman-to-Woman Program," the Adult Children of Alcoholics Program in Los Angeles, and the National Association for Children of Alcoholics have all contributed information and resources to the development of this book.

Lois J., Kay Nell H., Jean C., and Patricia L. were a special help to me, unfailingly supportive. N. W. Ayers Associates in New York, who created the National Council on Alcoholism's media campaign for youth "It's OK To Say No," deserve special commendation for their work.

Joseph Campbell and Jean Erdman, James Hillman, Goia Timapanelli, and Enrique Pardo directed me at critical moments in pursuing my ideas on the symbolic value of the child. Gail Thomas and Barbara McClintock provided me with materials, introductions, and their stimulating friendship.

The illuminations provided by the conversations I had with Robert Bly and Marion Woodman were delightful and were only increased by our working together. Claudia Black took particular interest in the development of the project. The dimension added to the book through the generosity of these three is immeasurable. I am grateful for their lively participation.

Naming the Family Secret

"When an inner situation is not made conscious, it appears outside as fate."

JUNG

If you came from an alcoholic family, chances are you have married an alcoholic, work for one, or keep finding yourself in relationships with people who are chemically dependent. Your life is in a frequent state of crisis, you have trouble with intimacy and figures of authority. You may be deeply unhappy, but on the surface, no one would ever know.

Maybe there wasn't alcoholism in your family, but you just sensed that something was wrong and you never knew what "it" was. Whatever it was, you never talked about it. That was one of the rules: "Don't talk, don't trust, don't feel." It was a house full of secrets.

This book is about the new understanding we have of alcoholism and chemical dependency as a family disease that affects all members of the family. Whether you ever picked up a drink or not, having alcoholism in your family has affected you, and may be still affecting you in ways that you haven't realized.

If we are raised in an alcoholic family, we tend to take on very predictable roles in order to survive. You find them in the stories that follow, as well as in Claudia Black's discussion of the "family hero," the "scapegoat," the "lost child," and the "mascot." Though these roles are necessary for survival as children, as we grow older and move out of the family setting, they become less useful and can eventually work against us in our everyday life.

Furthermore, we now understand that there are many kinds of family systems, the alcoholic family being only one of them, that produce a similar response and problem for their members. Families in which there is any kind of drug addiction (including prescription drugs), families with mental illness, military families, families with workaholics, even families with a very religious background, just to give a few examples, can impede the healthy growth of their members. Compulsive or obsessive behavior, whether it's about alcohol, drugs, money, sex, gambling, food, you name it, tends to throw a family system off balance. The term *alcoholism* is used generically in this book and can often apply to other situations in which there is chemical dependency or compulsive behavior. Understanding alcoholism as a disease in which the family plays a major role in transmitting helps us begin to understand other compulsive behaviors as well.

Families are living organisms, dynamic, constantly shifting, fluid systems that are always seeking a balance. It's useful to think of a mobile hanging from the ceiling. If you touch one part, all the others move to readjust and create a balance. That's the way families work, too.

The stories in this book give you a glimpse of how some people have come to understand what part they played in their families and how, unknowingly, the same behavior that allowed them to survive began to defeat them later in life.

Often it's difficult to acknowledge that there was ever a problem in your family, much less alcoholism. Yet life is full of problems and every family has them. It's how problems are confronted within the family that makes the difference between a functional family and a dysfunctional family. (I avoid the word *normal* altogether as there seems to be no such thing.)

In my own situation, for example, it never occurred to me that anything was wrong in my family as I was growing up. I just thought it was me. Call it loyalty, family pride, or my own denial, I would never acknowledge that there was anything wrong; I did my best to assure you, and most of all myself, that we were all "just fine."

But in the end I wasn't fine. By my mid-30s I was an alcoholic. Six years ago I came into Alcoholics Anonymous and began my recovery. After three-and-a-half years of learning how to stay sober, it became clear that I needed to understand my part in the difficult and painful relationships I kept finding myself in. How did I get there? With alcohol no longer my anesthetic, I discovered that I was in a lot of pain. No wonder I drank. It was not nice living inside of me. Al-Anon is a Twelve-Step program of recovery modeled after Alcoholics Anonymous but focused on the needs of friends and relatives of the alcoholic who have their own needs for recovery from life with an alcoholic. A friend suggested that Al-Anon's Adult Children of Alcoholics meetings might be helpful and they were. These meetings focus on what it was like growing up in an alcoholic family.

At first I couldn't relate to the content of people's stories that were shared in meetings. The alcoholism in my own family seemed peripheral, but the range of feelings that surfaced, the grief, the anger, the fear, and the sorrow showed me that I had a lot to learn at these meetings. I identified with people's feelings completely. Suddenly my marriages into families with histories of chemical dependencies and abuse made sense. Moreover, I had three children of my own, who, thanks to my alcoholism, now qualified for this program without question. What had happened to them? Once I began to understand this disease and how it is passed down in families, I vowed I would do everything in my power to let the alcoholism stop with me. Let me be the last one. No more. Not *my* children.

But like it or not, I can't stop alcoholism in anyone else but me. I am powerless over this disease and the reprieve I've found in AA is just that, a reprieve, not a cure, one day at a time. The most I can do is educate myself and my children, break the taboo of not talking about feelings, and let them see the recovery in me. But that meant I had to begin my own ACA recovery, which meant delving back into my own childhood. I didn't like that idea. "Let sleeping dogs lie," "Water under the bridge," "All you've got is today," I kept telling myself, along with "What's done is done." Yet I could not deny the power of the feelings that swept over me in meetings. The very strength of my resistance told me that it was important to look back whether I liked the idea or not.

Finally, I agreed to write this book, knowing that only a contract and deadline could make me walk through what I've had to face going back into childhood, my own and others. Listening to people's stories, hearing their insights and grief touched my long-buried wounds. Each story was taped initially so that you hear that particular person's voice. Some of the stories are shocking. I wrote with my hands on fire.

Most disturbing of all is the fact that *today* millions of children are living these stories and much worse, over and over again. The cycle of abuse goes on unchecked. Conservative estimates put the number at 7 million children in alcoholic homes today. Do those figures include chemical dependency as a whole? Madness? Who answers the questionnaires asking if there is alcoholism in your family? The alcoholic? This is a disease of denial. I never thought I had a "drinking problem" until I was licked and willing to walk into AA. Had I been asked, or my family, we would have all said "no problem here" in all innocence, but it would have been the kind of innocence that comes from ignorance and denial. Even if we assume that a lot of people are innocently lying, still one out of every three adults in this country reports trouble with alcohol abuse in their family, according to the National Council on Alcoholism. And those are just the figures on alcohol. How about cocaine, crack, prescription drugs, PCP, speed? Where does it stop? Current estimates are that at least fifteen million people in this country are alcoholic and that that number increases by a half million each year. At least twenty-eight million Americans come from alcoholic families. For every one alcoholic it is estimated that at least four other people are intimately affected, be they family members or co-workers. Many alcoholics under the age of 45 are cross-addicted. Many drug addicts don't understand that they are also alcoholics. Cut down on the cocaine or the marijuana and the alcohol consumption goes up. Not too many people seem to understand that despite the variety of different physical manifestations of addiction, chemical dependency lies underneath substance abuse of any kind. I wonder what the figures *really* are. Alcohol is just a legal drug.

Those millions of children still in abusing homes have the voices we do not hear. Theirs are the stories, if they survive, that might make their way into a book like this thirty years from now. Read the stories in this book with the knowledge that each story represents not only one person's past, but what millions of children are experiencing today. Know that this collection is just the smallest beginning of the stories that can and need to be heard. No one is immune from this disease, not women, not Jews, not Chinese, not Italians, nor many others whom folklore has maintained don't become alcoholic. Most of the stories in this book are white, middle-class stories, but not all of them. ACA is a relatively new movement, just gathering momentum in the last five years, and at this writing it is largely white and middle class. But this is changing. The Twelve-Step recovery programs of AA and Al-Anon can work for us all, whether black, white, red, yellow, or brown.

In the process of writing this book, I went into an ACA therapy group, did ACA workshops, went to more Al-Anon and ACA meetings, read constantly, and finally turned back to mythology and fairy tales. I looked for stories of the divine child, found in every culture, and I thought again about Christ's statement that in order to enter the kingdom of God, we must become as little children. His statement that the weak will confound the strong took on new meaning.

Who is this "child" we talk about in ACA? Depth psychology has a great deal to offer on the subject. I looked back into the works of some of the major Jungian analysts such as James Hillman, Marion Woodman, Marie Louise Von Franz, John Giannini, as well as Carl Jung himself. I turned to Joseph Campbell, scholar of comparative religion, and the poet Robert Bly, both of whom have been strongly influenced by Jung as well. In his essay on the archetype of the child Jung tells us:

We talk about the child, but we should mean the child in the adult, for in every adult there lurks a child—an eternal child, something that is always becoming, is never completed, calls for unceasing care, attention, and education. That is the part of the human personality which wants to develop and become whole.[1]

In ACA meetings we often talk about the need to recover the child within, to contact that part of ourselves again, so long ago lost. But it is important to understand that the need to find the child is part of an ancient human longing. Beyond the individual past lies our cultural past, contained in myths. In myths we see that the child is often the offspring of the union of the human and the divine. It is the mythic child—the divine child—that we seek as well as the child of our own personal history. And unless we understand this dual nature of our task, we can never reach the wholeness that lies within each person's grasp.

Folklore, legends, and myths can be tremendously useful and reassuring as analogies for the process of integrating the inner child into the whole self. Joseph Campbell's classic work, *Hero With A Thousand Faces*, compares folktales and myths the world over, showing the underlying pattern and psychological meaning of the theme of this quest for integration and wholeness. The hero on this quest is Everyman or Everywoman.

The journey toward recovery that we talk about in the Twelve-Step programs is the same journey that the heroes take in the myths and fairy tales. But unless we understand the nature of this journey—the journey toward wholeness—we may well not succeed. Campbell shows us that we must go through the process of integration, or what Jung called individuation. The world of the human and the world of the divine that make up the world of myths must be understood in a very particular way. Campbell gives us "a great key to understanding of myth and symbol—the two kingdoms are actually one. The realm of the gods is a forgotten dimension of the world we know. And the exploration of that dimension, either willingly or unwillingly, is the whole sense of the deed of the hero."[2]

The human and the divine, the solar and lunar, day and night, conscious and unconscious, female and male, adult and child, all worlds are actually one, dimensions of one another. The knowledge of this, the ability to move back and forth between these worlds is the fruit of wholeness, the gift bestowed on the hero, the human being who becomes whole, the fullness of being that we all seek.

The archetypal child of mythology also represents the life of the imagination and of memory. Too often in the West we have impoverished ourselves with reason and will, relegating the world of the imagination to the realm of art, madness, and children, as James Hillman brings out so clearly in his brilliant essay, "Abandoning the Child."[3] He shows that to find this child within is to recover our imagination as well. He notes the deadly error of taking the world literally. We make everything concrete and one-dimensional. How often in this society do we reject metaphor, symbol, myth, imagination, art, any activity that demands tension, paradox, complexity, and invokes the unknown. To limit the idea of the child to our own personal history is to make this mistake of literalism.

On the hero's journey there are obstacles along the way to find, for example, the Holy Grail. And yet help comes from another realm. No one can complete the journey without help. The gods always enter. There are confrontations and battles, but before the hero's task is accomplished, there must also be for-giveness and reconciliation. This is the way to wholeness and recovery. We are not in such a new place today as we are still in an ancient one that we need to recognize.

The recurrent image of the archetype of the child in mythol-ogy gives us numerous, rich images of what we may encounter along this journey. In the myths the hero confronts the father or the mother. The success of this encounter determines whether or not the hero can continue on the journey. Sometimes there is an atonement, a reconciliation. Sometimes a death. These psychic maps tell us what we must do to become whole and reveal that the very nature of the task is heroic.

So often those of us raised in an alcoholic home have spoken of being abandoned as children. Here mythology and folklore have something to tell us again. The beginnings of the heroes are often humble and difficult: persecuted, exposed, aban-doned, solitary, lonely, without human companionship in some cases, in others raised by cruel stepparents. This can well de-scribe the feelings of being a child in an alcoholic or dysfunc-tional family. Becoming a fully realized person is a heroic task. Life is difficult, under the best circumstances. To simply survive in many cases, much less accomplish anything, is indeed miraculous.

Parents of many of the mythological gods abandoned them, tried to kill them, or left them exposed to the elements. In his essay on "The Primordial Child in Primordial Times," C. Ker-enyi discusses the recurrent theme of the god child as orphan. After examining several myths he concludes that "what, from the purely human point of view, is an unusually tragic situa-tion—the orphan's exposure and persecution—appears in my-thology in quite another light."[4] In "The Orphan Child," he discusses this theme in mythology. Kerenyi finds that "the child god is usually an abandoned foundling . . . threatened by ex-traordinary dangers: it may be devoured, like Zeus, or torn to pieces like Dionysius. . . . Sometimes the father is the child's enemy . . . or he may merely be absent." The mothers, he finds, were often already dead when the child was born or the child was abandoned by the mother at birth. In some myths, the mother shares the child's abandonment and "wanders home-less . . . lives without honor."[5]

These descriptions of orphan children in mythology can also accurately depict what it feels like being raised in an alcoholic home: abandoned, impoverished, left to one's own devices, sometimes enduring great brutalities.

Kerenyi tell the story of the child god of the Voguls (an early Hungarian tribe) who had to come down to earth without his mother. He is taken into the house of an uncle and aunt who beat him. He goes to another house where he is kept behind the door, dishwater is poured over him, and all kinds of harms befall him. He leaves and goes to another's house only to be bound to a "sleigh with an iron cable thirty rods long." The child is then beaten, almost to death, with a "club of mammoth-bone," cast on the dunghill and intended as a sacrificial victim. But at this last moment there is a turn of events. "The boy suddenly becomes possessed of snowshoes, armor, quiver, bow and sword" and goes about destroying all who tormented and abused him. "From the miserable plight of the orphan there emerges a god."[6]

"What is it . . . that affects us so powerfully in the mythologem?" Kerenyi asks. "The very thing that constitutes its whole meaning, and that is the revelation of divinity in the paradoxical union of lowest and highest, weakest and strongest."[7]

That which was weak is now strong.

Another dimension of this journey is symbolized in the tales of hags and monsters that, once kissed, turn into fairy princesses or grant us our every wish. This is a delightful way of conveying an older wisdom that tells us that we must claim our own shadow, integrate our dark side. I call it "eating the dark." That means taking back all the projections of power, for good or ill—all the qualities and behaviors of "others" that we either fear or admire—back into ourselves. The enemy is within, not without.

What does all this have to do with children of alcoholics? At a certain point in recovery there is a very real danger of getting caught in blaming one's family for whatever one's difficulties in life may be. Acknowledging what happened in our childhood, experiencing pains long buried *without* blaming others requires more emotional skills than many of us have when we first find Adult Children of Alcoholics.

To fail to understand these matters means we run the risk

of being childish instead of becoming childlike. There is a world of difference. To be childish is to be without a sense of responsibility, to be dependent—whether on chemicals, food, relationships, money, sex, or whatever one can be dependent upon. Becoming *childlike* on the other hand, is a worthwhile goal, having to do with the ability to be spontaneous, to experience wonder, joy, sorrow, trust, love, surprise, hope, creativity, imagination. Being childlike means being able to face disappointment, failure, tragedy, and betrayal without giving up love and trust. It has something to do with what is necessary to be in the presence of God.

It is no easy task to remake a personality, to take apart a defense system, a rationale, and a worldview and then start over from the ground up. It is a process that takes a great deal of time and work. Most of all it requires enormous courage. It takes humility and willingness to ask for and receive help, qualities that don't sit well with our notions of adulthood that seem to demand a kind of unnatural self-sufficiency that no other creature would think of requiring of itself.

In the stories in this book you will find the symbol of the child and the hero's journey unfolding in people's lives today.

It is this inner child that I am learning to care for, parent, and befriend. In his lecture, "Healing the Wounded Child" at the Jung Institute in May 1986, John Giannini flatly states that "the neglect of the inner child is the original sin." Mine was almost dead. I had dreamed of dying babies, one stacked on top of another. In another dream, I argued with my father over a baby girl. He said she would die; I said she would live. Then I began to work on this book, to listen to people's stories, and I began to find my own child. I had to build bridges over the ocean of grief that threatened to drown me as I looked back. It was the myths and fairy tales—stories—that formed the bridges, showed me the way back, the way across, the way home. They connected me to a larger continuum of human experience: the human past, haunted by sorrow, punctuated by the joy and suffering that shaped the human spirit five thousand years ago—or last week. I had to pray longer and harder, meditate more, seek out broader spiritual teachings and guidance in order to live with this material, my own and others'. The gift has been the opportunity to be deeply moved with compassion for us all, whether parent or child, alcoholic or nonalcoholic. The child in my dreams came alive.

There is an old saying that never fails me: "The obstacle is the path." I've found ancient meditation practices in which you visualize anyone who might have hurt you or angered you as your parent or your child whom you cradle with love. In doing this, I am beginning to use the image of family and that primary relationship as a way of transforming obstacles on my path. In my meditation, my past adversaries are the very people whom I hold as children or am held by. I imagine light pouring over and into them. I wish them peace and love and joy in their lives.

This is not an easy practice. It is a pleasure to wish joy to people I love, but I cannot stop there. Do I include those who have hurt me because I care so much? Not in the beginning. I was hardly that advanced. I began this meditation practice for all the wrong reasons. I did it out of sheer selfishness: because it made me feel better. I didn't like feeling hurt, angry, resentful, vengeful, or self-righteous any more. Slowly, slowly, over the years, with the help of many others in the fellowships of Al-Anon and AA, I've begun to change. I do this meditation and others like it because I know that unless I can also learn to love those who have hurt me, I will be a withered vine, a plant that bears no fruit. I will give no nourishment, leave nothing behind for others to carry on in this business of living, which is learning to love—everyone.

It is easy to love those who love and accept us. It is a delight. The harder part is in learning how to love those whom I am tempted to call my enemies. A difficult relationship is the benchmark of my growth, showing me where I am and where I need to go next. The obstacle becomes the path. The hardest and most rewarding people for me to do this meditation with are those I have been the closest to and been hurt by: family, former families, close friends. This is where I work on forgiveness, for myself and for them, and seek compassion for us all.

Rachel V.

NOTES

1. Carl Jung, "The Development of Personality," in *The Essential Jung*, ed. Anthony Storr (Princeton: Princeton University Press, 1983), 194.
2. Joseph Campbell, *Hero with a Thousand Faces* (Princeton, NJ: Princeton University Press, 1973), 217.
3. James Hillman, "Abandoning the Child," in *Loose Ends* (Dallas, TX: Spring Publications, 1975).
4. C. Kerenyi, "The Primordial Child in Primordial Times," in *Essays on a Science of Mythology*, ed. Carl Jung and C. Kerenyi (Princeton, NJ: Princeton Univeresity Press, 1969), 36.
5. C. Kerenyi, "The Orphan Child," in *Essays*, ed. Jung and Kerenyi, 27, 28.
6. Ibid., p. 32.
7. Ibid., p. 33.

Introduction

It's easy to be raised in an alcoholic home and not even know it. Many people don't know enough about alcoholism to identify it for the chronic, progressive disease that it is. One of the characteristics of alcoholism is denial of reality, such as calling Dad's hangover the result of "a hard day," Mom's drinking a "depression." Children in alcoholic homes are quickly taught the silent rules of "don't talk, don't trust, don't feel," making it difficult to understand much less identify the problem. They learn not to ask questions. As you will see from the stories in this book, children develop very effective coping mechanisms to survive the chaos of an alcoholic home. But as children grow up, the very behavior that assured survival can bring a downfall without our having a clue about why.

As a result of our growing awareness of how widespread alcoholism is and how it often repeats itself in families, we are now beginning to connect the problems we have today as adults with our early experiences in the alcoholic home.

Alcoholism, like people, comes in a variety of shapes and sizes. The derelicts of skid row are only 5 percent of all practicing alcoholics. The other 95 percent are ordinary people, just like you and me, from all walks of life, socioeconomic and ethnic backgrounds. Chemical dependency knows no bounds. People often don't realize how variable the alcoholic's drinking patterns can be. Some alcoholics drink daily, some do not. Some alcoholics are dry for long periods of time then go on a binge periodically. Some drink enormous quantities of alcohol and some do not. Some alcoholics drink only beer, some only wine, still others hard liquor. Some people become alcoholic early on in their drinking; in others it takes years to develop. There is an "invisible line" that separates social drinking from alcoholic drinking. Many alcoholics report that they were able to drink socially for years before losing the capacity to *predictably* control their drinking and before it began to cause problems in their lives.

In some families, both parents are alcoholics, in others, only one parent is chemically dependent. Some families are headed by single parents who are addicted. Most adult children of alcoholics had one parent who was nonalcoholic. Yet as the disease progresses, the nonalcoholic parent became increasingly preoccupied with the behavior of the alcoholic. The preoccupation is called "co-dependency" or "co-alcoholism." A child loses the nonalcoholic parent as that parent gets caught up in the alcoholic's drinking. Just like the alcoholic on whom the "co" is focused on out of genuine concern, the nonalcoholic parent becomes increasingly unable to respond or be consistently available to the children. Co-alcoholic parents can become as unstable, hostile, depressed, distant, and sick as the alcoholic. Placing unreasonable demands on the children, they often try to depend on their children as peers rather than as children who need parenting. The roles get reversed.

Michael P.'s experience, related in the pages following, illustrates this process: "The other side of the violence in my house was my mother's desperate need to deal with her feelings. I've talked to other men who had this experience, too, when it was the father that was the alcoholic—the mother turns to the son, at least my mother did. . . . She would pour out her feelings and her disappointments to me, but I was only a child."

Some people think it's a mistake to look back at our past, but professionals in the treatment field have found over and over that for us to feel good about ourselves and to regain our self-esteem, we have to go back and examine our childhood. The purpose is not to blame our families, but to come to an acceptance and peace with the past that we have never known before.

The concept of Adult Children of Alcoholics* and the issues of being raised in chemically dependent family systems did not arise until the 1970s. Until then studies were relegated largely to academic journals. Research focused on the genetic predisposition that seems to be at work in the transmission of the disease, such as the famous Scandinavian adoption and twin studies. We began to hear about fetal alcohol syndrome (FAS), the only preventable birth defect of the three most common in

---

*In some parts of the country it is called COA for Children of Alcoholics or ACOA for Adult Children of Alcoholics.

the U.S. We now know that there is no known "safe" amount of alcohol for a pregnant mother to drink. Drugs should also be avoided during pregnancy. The plight of infants born to alcoholics and addicts is tragic, the consequences lasting up to an entire lifetime. This is crucial information that the general public must understand.

The NIAAA (National Institute for Alcoholic Abuse and Alcoholism) was established by Congress in the seventies as well. Margaret Cork's pioneer study, *Forgotten Children*, came out and, coupled with the 1974 Booz-Allen and Hamilton, Inc. report on Children of Alcoholics, we began to have some meaningful information for the growing number of inpatient alcoholism treatment programs.

At the same time, Stephanie Brown, Ph.D., of the Stanford University clinic and I were developing models for group treatment for both young and adult children of alcoholics. The term "Adult Children of Alcoholics" was one that Stephanie Brown and I coined as we described our work to *Newsweek* magazine in an interview in 1979. As the article noted, the phrase in no way was intended "by Black or Brown to imply that these adults behave as children. It was meant to validate the experiences these adults had as children and in doing so, validate who they are today as adults."[1] We thought that within the adult today who was raised in an alcoholic home, there is a child that continues to need nurturing. This same child still needs to learn skills that many others learned in childhood.

Family treatment began to be developed, particularly in the Midwest in the 1970s. Vernon Johnson developed the "intervention" process whereby an alcoholic was confronted with his or her drinking problem and given the choice of treatment or loss of a job or family or both. Sharon Wegscheider-Cruse began to talk about the different roles members of the family take on in order to live with active alcoholism and the chaos that it creates. She identified the "family hero," the "scapegoat," the "lost child," and the "mascot" as characteristic behavioral responses to the alcoholic family system. About the same time I too was influenced by Virginia Satir, and I developed a model that was similar. My "responsible" and "placator" child could be Sharon's Hero. The "adjuster" easily becomes the Lost Child, and my "acting out" child is the Scapegoat. You will find vivid illustrations of each of these family roles in the stories that follow.

Sam S. is a good example of the "family hero": "I was the child who was always responsible, a high achiever who excels and whose achievements help the family feel good about themselves. The only hitch was that I didn't feel good about myself." The "hero" is often, though not always, the oldest child. They perform at a very high level and few people suspect the pain that their performance masks.

The "scapegoat" in the family is often the "identified" problem, whose escapades keep the family's focus *off* the alcoholic. In some way the scapegoat is the most honest person in the family system as their troubled behavior says loud and clear: "Something is wrong. This is painful. I need help." Marion's story illustrates the role the scapegoat plays in the family.

"I was always getting into trouble. People thought 'Poor Bill and Molly' for having to put up with me. I was the second child. . . . I was getting picked up for shoplifting, called into every principal's office . . . from the time I was in grade school." Both Marion's parents were practicing alcoholics. I conservatively estimate that over 65 percent of the young people in juvenile halls are children of alcoholics. Unfortunately, they are identified as isolated problems and not understood within the context of the alcoholic family system. They are sent back into that family, whose illness has *not* been identified or treated, and they act out again and end up back in the juvenile justice system. I call it the revolving door. Runaways are another population of young people who often come from alcoholic or chemically dependent families. We shouldn't say that we have shelters for runaways, these are shelters for children of alcoholics.

Nicholas K.'s story gives us an example of the "lost child." They cope by drawing as little attention to themselves as possible within the family. "I was the one they call the lost child. . . . I just removed myself whenever there were problems. . . . I would go off someplace . . . withdraw . . . wouldn't say a word." This is the child who tries to blend into the woodwork.

The "mascot" on the other hand is the child, often the youngest, who learns to deflect the attention from the family's problem through humor. Ashley tells us: "I was always the life of the party, the clown. . . . I could always crack a joke."

Unfortunately, the mascot never learns to take himself or herself seriously and the wit and humor eventually backfire by deflecting reality.

These descriptions are only the most general, given here to help you identify the different parts of the alcoholic family system. The way they actually work is very dynamic and fluid. Roles can shift around among family members, depending on the number of children, when the alcoholism became active in the family, and a variety of other factors. Today we know that as children, we survived in the dysfunctional homes we were raised in because of these roles. As adults, if we remain unaware of these behaviors, we tend to repeat them to our detriment.

One of the clearest indicators of a smoothly working family is consistency. In contrast, the best words to describe living in an alcoholic family are *inconsistency* and *unpredictability*. I firmly believe that whatever co-alcoholic spouses or children do while living with the alcoholic's drinking, they do because at the time it makes sense to them. Sarah's story in the pages that follow illustrates this well. As a child she would hide in the closet with her drunken mother while her grandparents searched the house for them. She wanted to see her grandparents, but as the family hero, she was also caught up in protecting her mother and maintaining the facade that all was well. Her straight A's at school proved that point: she was on top of everything, there was nothing wrong here. She assumed all household responsibilities: cooking, cleaning, and shopping.

Many of the stories in this book illustrate the unpredictability of the alcoholic home. Meals, especially dinner, seem to be problematic. Holiday celebrations and the often-violent moods of alcoholic, have a random and unpredictable quality to them that keeps tension in the air and leaves everyone tiptoeing around on eggshells so as not to set off the next explosion. As the problems surrounding alcoholism cause more and more inconsistency and unpredictability, the behavior of the nonalcoholic family members can get equally off-balance in the natural—and unconscious—attempt to restabilize the family system. Within the context of the family system these adaptations seem to make life easier and less painful. For example, everyone might want to believe Mom's explanation that Dad *likes* to sleep on the floor now because it's good for his back rather than being upset that he's passed out on the floor again in front of the television set because he's drunk.

In most well-functioning families, emotions are expressed clearly and each person has the opportunity to share feelings. The feelings are accepted by an attentive group that offers its support and understanding. Family members feel free to ask for attention and to give attention to others in return. But in a home being destroyed by alcoholism, feelings are repressed and become twisted. Family members usually do not share emotion, but sadly, when they do they often pronounce judgment and lay blame on others. Unhealthy alliances form between one parent and child against the other parent.

Families need to have fair and flexible rules that are definite and agreed upon by everyone. Observing rules such as "no hitting" and "everyone will have a chance to be heard" encourages a healthy family. But in an alcoholic family, even if there are such rules, they are not based on the healthy need to protect its members but rather on shame, guilt, and fear. Instead of spoken rules, there are more often the silent rules such as "you won't tell anyone how you got that bruise or you'll get another one."

Generally there are clearly defined roles in a family. Adults typically divide up or share the functions of breadwinner and administrator. Children raised in homes in which there is open communication and consistency usually have the ability to adopt different roles to meet the needs of the situation they are in. They learn how to be responsible, organized; how to develop realistic goals, how to play, to laugh, and to enjoy themselves. They can be flexible and spontaneous. They are usually taught to be sensitive to the feelings of others and are willing to be helpful. They develop a sense of autonomy and yet also know how to belong to a group. But children growing up in an alcoholic home seldom develop these strengths and instead become locked into roles based on their perception of what they need to do in order to "survive."

Though the data on adult children of alcoholics is relatively new, the concepts that serve as the basis for understanding children of alcoholics and their treatment are currently based on a handful of premises. Most children from alcoholic homes develop a coping mechanism that allows them to function well despite the chemical dependency in the home. Their need to maintain a facade, to "look good," is based on the denial in the alcoholic family system. If their situation isn't noticed and addressed in childhood, it will carry over and have its consequences in adulthood. Once carried into adulthood, the experiences from childhood create a delayed grief response in the adult. And as Dr. Timmen Cermak, M.D., has noted, the symptoms and consequences of being raised in an alcoholic home are similar to post traumatic stress disorder (PTSD) experienced by war veterans.

Dr. Cermak says that "the phenomenon of Post Traumatic Stress Disorder (PTSD), which is linked in most people's minds to the difficulties that some Vietnam veterans have had in readjusting to civilian life, is a helpful model for understanding many of the characteristics seen in Adult Children of Alcoholics."[2] Cermak explains that PTSD occurs when people are subject to intense stresses that clearly lie outside the range of normal human experience. The effects are especially severe if the stress is caused by a series of traumatic, human-caused events. The effects are heightened and become more severe if coping strategies are rigid or if the support system surrounding the individual encourages denial of the stress. For example, one parent tries to reassure a child that his little sister wasn't really hurt when Mommy got drunk and beat her with a coat hanger. The child who observed the beating is rightly disturbed and upset as is the child who was beaten. But then if both are told that the beaten child "wasn't really hurt," "everything's all right," "Mommy didn't mean to," they become more confused and unsure of their own perceptions of reality.

Dr. Cermak notes that it is essential for ACAs and those interested in understanding them to acknowledge that *it is not normal to grow up with an alcoholic parent*. Early childhood within an alcoholic family system creates a stress clearly outside the range of "normal" human experience. If this isn't understood, ACAs grow up believing that the unpredictable, chaotic, and destructive alcoholic family system is the normal state of affairs. Coming to understand that our childhood was not normal, healthy, or appropriate is a cornerstone in the process of recovery. The daily environment of fear, abandonment, denial, inconsistency, and real or potential violence fostered in the alcoholic home is hardly a functional, healthy environment. It creates prolonged stress and is clearly of human origin—unlike a tornado, hurricane, or earthquake—and it can produce significant distress. The symptoms of PTSD are similar enough to the characteristics of ACAs to suggest that many people are suffering from a variant of PTSD. Like the vet who, ten years after the war, reacts to a car backfiring as though it was a grenade in battle, adult children often find themselves inexplicably overcome with feelings from childhood when confronted with a situation that recalls past trauma.

PTSD also leads to a condition called psychic numbing, experienced as a sense of estrangement and detachment, often to the point of feeling that there is no place or group to which we belong, no place where we fit. Emotions seem to shut off, especially around intimacy, tenderness, and sexuality. ACAs often lack spontaneity and have an extreme need to control their feelings. Many speak of how they are able to tolerate miserable situations by maintaining a facade of being present and attentive, while mentally they have retreated and disappeared.

Post traumatic stress disorder results in a kind of generalized anxiety, excessive nervous activity, and hyperalertness. Unexpected sounds often startle people with PTSD. Many vets suffer from survivor guilt, which leads to chronic depression. The same is true for many ACAs. People with PTSD unconsciously mold their entire lives to avoid any activity that recalls the original trauma. Adult children of alcoholics do that as well. Dr. Cermak states that the characteristics of ACAs are best seen as a combination of co-dependency and a variety of post traumatic stress disorder. ACAs are not guilty of distorted reactions to normal events so much as they try to have normal responses to abnormal events. Recovery involves shifting from seeing oneself as abnormal to understanding that the experience of growing up in an alcoholic home was abnormal.

Part of this shift in ACA recovery involves grieving. Because loss is so characteristic of the alcoholic home, ACAs spend a lot of time grieving during the first part of recovery. When one first identifies the problem, breaks through the denial about what happened in the past, grief rushes up, as well as old sadness, fears, embarrassment, and anger. This is a painful and disconcerting process, but at the same time it is liberating, because the ACA no longer has to minimize what happened or deny the experience. By identifying feelings and expressing them, fears are lessened and ACAs become more able to trust others and to trust their own perceptions. This recovery is an ongoing process with no time limit.

The best recovery today seems to come from some combination of using the Twelve-Step self-help programs such as Al-Anon, AA, and ACA in conjunction with some kind of therapy. The self-help programs are free and ongoing. Therapy, while sometimes costly, can often be limited to a shorter term and is especially fruitful when done in conjunction with working through the Twelve Steps. Most professionals offering therapy today to ACAs are themselves adult children of alcoholics. Those therapists who have gone into a recovery process themselves, those who are familiar with the Twelve-Step programs and support their client's involvement in them, can be most helpful to others with their recovery.

Statistics on children of alcoholics reveal that children of alcoholics often become alcoholics and marry alcoholics. Daughters of alcoholics are twice as likely to become alcoholic as daughters of nonalcoholics.[3] Sons of alcoholics are five times more likely to become alcoholic than other sons. It is my belief that no one *intends* to become an alcoholic. Children of alcoholics who are aware that they are being raised in an alcoholic home often make the resolution that what they see happening to their parents will never happen to them. "It will never happen to me," was such a constant refrain that it became the title of my first book on this subject. Many imagine that through will power, self-control, or sheer intellect they can avoid the alcoholism they saw destroying their parents. The irony is that they feel so confident that they will be different from their parents, and yet they become exactly like them. They will drink and use alcohol for the same social reasons that anyone does, but they will discover that it allows them a way to feel good, that it numbs their pain, provides solace, gives them a sense of wholeness, power, and helps them loosen up. In fact, alcohol does more for them than for the social drinker but at the time, they don't know that, and the positive effect of alcohol becomes a reinforcer for the use of alcohol as a way of controlling feelings that other people without the biochemical predisposition don't have. Put the psychological reinforcement together with the physiological predisposition and it becomes easier to see how children of alcoholics are more prone to become alcoholic.

On the surface it is difficult for many people to understand why so many children of alcoholics marry alcoholics, but ACAs have few skills for developing healthy, intimate relationships. Like attracts like, and they tend to attract others also from dysfunctional families. Identity stays intact, the old survival skills are put to use, and the defense system is not threatened. Often if you are an adult child of an alcoholic you fall into a relationship with another alcoholic without seeing it because your new partner drinks differently from your alcoholic parent. Another possibility is that he or she is at a different stage of the alcoholism or perhaps an earlier one, so you can't see the similarities. Or you may realize that your partner has a drinking problem, but you accept it as "not as bad as your parents." Beneath this you believe that you don't deserve any better, and consequently you get into something you think you can handle, but it almost inevitably gets out of control.

Many adult children find that they were affected not only by alcoholism but also by physical or sexual abuse in the family. Research that I've conducted with Sandra Padilla and Stephen Bucky found that 66 percent of a sample of 400 adult children of alcoholics experienced physical abuse in the family, by either witnessing people hitting each other or being hit themselves. In our control groups we found that mothers in an alcoholic home were four times more likely to be violent and fathers were ten times more likely to be physically violent.

In the alcoholic home it is not necessarily the alcoholic who is the abusive parent. It is common to find the abuser to be the nonalcoholic parent or spouse. We also find more sibling abuse—kids abusing each other—in the alcoholic home. At times children abuse parents, though this is more likely when a teenaged child is chemically dependent. Another form of abuse that is more subtle is severe punishments that may not involve physical abuse but are designed to humiliate and degrade the child. Having to witness someone else being abused, even to watch self-directed violence, such as a parent trying to hurt himself or herself or even attempt suicide, is another form of abuse.

Sexual abuse is one of the most traumatic forms of abuse children are subjected to. Incest often begins under the umbrella of "normal affection." It can be extremely subtle in the beginning, very covert. The initial contacts may simply be touching or fondling, but then the contact progresses to various forms of masturbation, oral-genital contact, and in time may involve intercourse. Some people justify themselves by requiring of children all forms of sexual behavior *except* intercourse. They tell themselves that it isn't incest, but it is incest. In our study (Black, Bercher, and Padilla) we found that daughters of alcoholics were twice as likely to become incest victims as were daughters in other families. Though not as common, male incest does occur as well. Children growing up in such situations have difficulty developing healthy attitudes about sexuality. A drunken parent can speak crudely, make sexual innuendos, or tease a child inappropriately. Some children must contend with the nudity of a drunken parent. Drinking parents sometimes make no attempt to maintain discreet sex lives. Children often face these problems alone, become confused, and feel needless shame.

To look at how alcohol affects us as a society, not just within the family, we can refer to the study Stephanie Covington, Ph.D., M.S.W., did on "Alcohol and Family Violence." Using the National Council on Alcoholism's figures, she notes that in their study of robberies, 72 percent of the offenders had been drinking. In murder cases, 86 percent of the offenders and 40 to 60 percent of the victims had been using alcohol, in rape cases, 50 percent of the rapists had been using alcohol, and in assault, 72 percent of the offenders had been using alcohol. As Covington notes, "the probability of suffering abuse from someone we know *is greater* than from a stranger. The sad fact is that what is occurring within the microcosm of the family is a *direct* reflection of the violence occurring throughout our culture and the world."[4] I wonder, is the violence in our world a direct reflection of the violence in the family? Domestic violence often, though not always, takes place during or after drinking. "There is a growing acknowledgement of the association between family violence and alcohol use. While the research is still scarce and not *all* the data is consistent, studies to date [April 1986] indicate the following:

- alcohol is a factor in 56 percent of the fights or assaults in U.S. homes
- alcohol is a factor in 40 percent of all family court problems
- alcohol has an association in 34 percent of the cases of child abuse
- 50 percent of alcoholic parents are child abusers
- 66 percent of children in alcoholic homes are abused
- 67 percent of *sexually* aggressive acts against children involve alcohol use
- 80 to 90 percent of husbands who batter use alcohol
- 70 percent of battered women are frequent drinkers
- 39 percent of sexually aggressive acts against women involve alcohol use
- 35 percent of incest perpetrators are heavy drinkers
- 50 percent of incest victims are from alcoholic homes.[5]

Dr. Covington goes on to state in her report that "there appears to be a cross-generational transmission of both alcoholism and violence in families. In this generational cycle of family violence, males who were abused as children become abusive adults. Women who were physically abused as children become child abusers and/or victims of an abusive partner."[6] Alcohol and addiction in general are threads that run through a wide variety of the problems that we face as a society, and we would do well to consider them when we lament the rise of violence and crime.

On a more hopeful note, twelve states have passed legislation that provides free and confidential counseling to students at school on alcoholism in the family. Education is one of our most powerful tools, breaking the denial that surrounds this disease. Many school districts are implementing prevention and student assistance programs and are developing policies to more effectively respond to the adolescent abuse of alcohol and other drugs. Models for support groups of high risk children, specifically children of alcoholics, are available and being implemented in schools throughout the country.

In summary, here are some common problems that people from alcoholic homes notice as adults:

We have problems with personal relationships, especially with intimacy and trust. Control is extremely important. We are often not able to maintain or be happy in personal relationships.

We tend to have problems in our relationships at work and trouble with authority figures in general. We are often unable to feel successful, no matter how well we succeed in our careers. Job performance can be inhibited by our difficulty in following instructions and making decisions. We don't know how to negotiate and focus instead on trying to please everyone else.

As parents we have difficulty setting limits. Our expectations are unrealistic, and we don't trust our own perceptions.

Our health is problematic. We suffer from a variety of stress-related disorders such as ulcers, headaches, colitis, and a wide variety of eating disorders, most commonly overeating. We are prone to depression, chemical dependencies of all kinds, being abusive, and suicide attempts.

Many of us are alienated from a concept of power greater than ourselves, or else have a concept of a punishing God that we live in fear of offending.

You don't have to be from an alcoholic or chemically dependent home to have these problems in your life. Many people have them, but they are simply more concentrated in the alcoholic family environment. These kinds of problems and their repetition often provide the very crisis that make us finally willing to ask for help.

We are now able to list characteristics that typify the adult child of an alcoholic:

We became isolated and afraid of people and authority figures.

We became approval seekers and lost our own identity in the process.

We were frightened by angry people and any kind of personal criticism.

We lived life from the point of view of helping and seeking victims. We were attracted by that weakness in others when we pursued love and friendship relations.

We had an overdeveloped sense of responsibility. It was easier for us to be concerned with others rather than ourselves.

We would feel guilty when standing up for ourselves and instead would give in to others.

We were addicted to excitement.

We confused love with pity and tended to "love" people we could pity and rescue.

We blocked our feelings from traumatic experiences in childhood and lost the ability to feel or express our feelings.

We judged ourselves harshly and had a very low sense of self-esteem. Sometimes we compensated for this by trying to appear superior.

We were terrified of abandonment and would do anything to hold on to a relationship rather than be alone with ourselves.

We became reactors instead of actors.

We often married alcoholics, became them, or both.

We developed a high tolerance for inappropriate behavior. We didn't know what was normal, healthy, or appropriate.

We had difficulty trusting our own perceptions as well as in trusting other people.

Claudia Black

NOTES

1. Claudia Black and Stephanie Brown, quoted by Diane Shah and Michael Reese in *Newsweek*, May 28, 1979.
2. Timmen Cermak, *A Primer on Adult Children of Alcoholics* (Pompano Beach, FL: Health Communications, 1983).
3. J. Nici, *Journal of Alcoholic Studies* 40, no. 7 (1979): 677–82.
4. Stephanie Covington, "Alcohol and Family Violence," in *Women and Addiction: A Collection of Papers*, 1–2. Available from the author, 1129 Torrey Pines Road, La Jolla, CA 92037.
5. Ibid, p. 2.
6. Ibid.

This book accurately reflects my interviews with people recovering from being raised in chemically dependant and dysfunctional families. However, the names I have used in this account are not real names and individual characteristics and locales have been changed to protect the anonymity of those involved in accordance with the traditions of the Twelve Step Programs.

Rachel V.

1. Anne R.

I grew up in the Southwest with an alcoholic father. I was the middle child of three girls. My father and I fought constantly in the family. I was the defender of the women in my family, particularly my mother, and said everything what no one else would say. I fought back. He was very temperamental. We had a very volatile and verbally abusive relationship. He was never physically abusive; he never laid a hand on us. When he drank, he was mean and he'd say all kinds of things, especially to me. He'd tell me that I was ugly and stupid. "Everybody hates you," he'd yell on top of it all. We fought all the time when I was young. I felt terribly lonely. My older sister was very close to my mother, my younger sister was close to my father—I had no one. Over the years I have come to realize the advantages of that position: I didn't become symbiotic with either parent. I was able to separate from them much more easily than my sisters, and I was able to express the anger that I felt. Everyone else was feeling angry too, but they didn't express it. I think I was a lot better off for just saying what I felt. My older sister became an alcoholic. She was the hero in our family, the one who would never say that anything was wrong. My younger sister became a born-again Christian. That was her way of coping. My older sister is in recovery now and is doing very well. She caught her alcoholism very early and has been sober for several years now. She's very active in AA.

When my father wasn't drinking, he was a very nice man, a shy man. He did not drink in bars. He drank from the time I was very little, as far back as I can remember.

My parents were very involved socially. A lot of times he would come home drunk from parties. Very drunk. As I got a little older, I can remember him starting to drink a lot at home. As his alcoholism progressed, he began hiding his bottles; his drinking began earlier in the day. Once he'd started drinking, his personality changed and the fighting would begin. I felt pretty bad about it all. I was very much a loner and still am to this day.

I started to draw. Art became an outlet for me. I started a little theater, neighborhood style. I began that when I was very young. My sisters joined in. We all became very involved in the theater from an early age. I began to write as well, and by the age of 9 I had written a book. I began to express myself creatively at a very young age, which I attribute directly to living with an alcoholic parent. I'm at the point now where I can look back and see that. It's one of the good things that came out of all the pain and chaos.

When I was 15 years old, I began to manifest a lot of physical anxiety; for example, I would hyperventilate. I could hardly breathe I was so nervous all the time. My parents took me to a psychiatrist. My father's drinking was never mentioned.

During that time in high school, I read an article in *Seventeen* magazine on alcoholism. I remember so well bringing it home to my mother and my older sister and saying, "Look! Dad's an alcoholic. He should read this." They looked at me as though I'd lost my mind and said, "What are you talking about? Maybe he has too much to drink now and then, but he's certainly not an alcoholic."

Even though I understood that he was an alcoholic at that time, I didn't really understand what that meant or that it had had any impact on me. I understood that when he drank, he was a mean man and I couldn't get along with him. I also knew how nice he could be when he was sober. He could be sweet and funny and then so awful when he drank. Somehow I couldn't make the connection between all this, even though now I had a word to call it.

Not too long ago I found a letter that I had written in college, describing my fears that I would never be able to love anyone. The letter went on talking a lot about alcoholism and the impact my relationship with my father had had on me. I was all of 19 years old. I had quite an intellectual grasp of the problem, but it didn't do anything for me emotionally.

While I was in college, my difficulties with breathing came back. It got so bad that I had to breathe into a paper bag in order to get a complete breath. I became depressed as well. Despite these difficulties, I was very active in college and did very well.

After years of being told I was stupid, going away to college showed me that I clearly was not. I was an honor student, and that was really exciting for me after what I'd been through at home. Not living at home did a lot to improve my relationship with my father, but my relationships with friends and boy-friends were really problematical. My difficulties seemed to re-volve around not trusting or ever believing that I was loved. I just reenacted my relationship with my father over and over again. I would act with men just like I acted with my father. No matter what they did, I could not believe they loved me. They were very nice men, but there was no way in the world that they could be nice enough to get rid of my own bad feelings about myself. Nobody could do that but me, but of course I didn't know that then.

In my early 20s I moved around a lot, traveling in this country and in Europe for a year. Then I married another adult child of an alcoholic for about three years. That didn't work out, so I just kept moving, taking a "geographic" as they're called when you keep moving as a way of trying to make life better without ever dealing with your real problems. Finally, I settled in a big city and just hit bottom. I wasn't prepared at all. I took one job after another. I might have had as many as fifty jobs in a year. I would take these receptionist jobs where I would go to work in the morning, go out for lunch, and never come back. I was a wreck, and I just couldn't survive. I couldn't take care of myself. I was becoming really dysfunctional, and I was terribly depressed. The whole cycle took about two years. I kept finding other things to fill up my life with. I got very involved politi-cally, worked with a lot of good projects, but I happened to work with a group that you could give to for forty-eight hours a day and it wouldn't be enough. That was perfect for me. I never had time to think or feel.

During the years that I was going through all this, my mother had begun to go to Al-Anon, my sister had gotten into her own recovery in AA, and they had finally decided that it was time to do something about my father. His business was on the verge of ruin. He was passed out all the time at home now. Everybody knew that he was going to drink himself to death, that it was just a matter of time. Years before, I had wanted to do an intervention but no one else was willing to do it. Now the time had come. An intervention is a well-thought-out and carefully planned event in which the family or those closest to a practicing alcoholic or addict confront him or her about the substance abuse. You work with a trained intervention counselor who guides you through the process. The end result is that the alcoholic has to choose between going into treatment or losing his or her job or home, some kind of dire and real consequence. Finally, our whole family was ready to be involved.

I had started to go to meetings for Adult Children of Alcoholics about six months prior to the intervention on my dad. My sister had called me and told me about the meetings. As soon as I started to go, I knew that this was the only place where I was going to get well, the only place where I could recover. But I was there in a rage. I dragged myself to those meetings kicking and screaming. I hated going to them. I just felt rage and terror. Walking through the doors to those rooms, putting down the mask I wore, and knowing that everyone knew who I was and that it didn't matter. There were no more acts, no more masks to wear, no more fronts to maintain, but just walking in the door terrified me, and I could not speak. But I listened.

I never spoke to anyone. I thought that it was going to be like an AA meeting, the kind you see on TV, where people would come up and say hello and go out of their way to make you feel a part of the group. Well, nobody ever did, and I couldn't understand why. It was a long time before I understood that nobody could get near me because of the incredible wall that I had built around myself.

I had been in a lot of therapy. Before coming to the city, I had worked as an art therapist with emotionally disturbed kids, and I loved it. I was good at it. So I knew enough about therapy to know that none of the therapists I had seen were even beginning to touch on what the issue was. Once I picked up the laundry list for adult children of alcoholics, that list of our characteristics, I knew I belonged there, even though I hated everybody in the room and hated everything they said.

The time came for the intervention. One sister and her husband and children came from across the country. My older sister came, of course my mother was there, and me. First we met with the counselor who would take us through the intervention with Dad. We were the fifteenth family that this counselor had worked with, and of the fourteen before, the alcoholic had chosen to go into treatment after the intervention. We were very hopeful. We each wrote out, in a loving way, how my father's drinking had affected each one of us. Then we all sat down together, with the counselor and with Dad and talked to him.

The intervention went beautifully. It couldn't have been done better or more lovingly. My father sat and listened to everything that everyone had to say. He was sober. We were in my parents' home. It was Christmastime. And at the end of the talk, we told him that we had made a reservation for him to go into a hospital for treatment and that if he didn't go, we weren't going to have anything to do with him. "We're not going to cooperate in your suicide anymore. Either you get some help, or we are leaving you."

You know what he said? He said, "Good-bye, see you later."

And we're saying, "Hey, Dad . . . !" And mother starts to tell him that he'll have to leave the house, and he announces that he wasn't leaving, "I'm not going anywhere. I'm not leaving." So here it is Christmastime, and we all packed up our bags and went and stayed with different friends. It was just about the worst time I could ever imagine. We all fell right back into our family roles. I was the scapegoat, the antagonist. My older sister teamed up with my mother, and my younger sister just withdrew from it all. It was awful. We were all ready to kill each other. They wanted to give in. They were afraid he was going to kill himself, shoot himself; that was our big fear. But I kept saying, "Look, he's killing himself anyway. It's just a matter of time, a question of how quickly or slowly he does it. Just hold your ground. Don't give in."

We all went back to our respective homes. Mother continued to stay on with her friends. She was just wonderful; she was incredible. My father would do things like call her up and say, "If you don't come home, I'm going to shoot myself." And she would just say, "You're killing yourself anyway. I'm not doing it. You are." Now mind you, this is after over thirty years of marriage. This is the kind of solidity that Al-Anon had given her. She was like a new person. She just kept saying, "I can't do it. I'm not coming home. If you will go to the hospital, then I'll come home, but not until."

A month after the intervention, my father completely hit bottom. We thought he'd hit bottom before, but now he wouldn't even go to work. His secretary ran his office. He was drunk the entire time. My brother-in-law's mother is a doctor who is very close to all of us. She kept checking on Dad to try to make sure that he was OK. One day she went by, and he was passed out on the floor. She called her son, and the two of them picked him up off the floor and took him down to the emergency room at the hospital, and he stayed. He finally went into detox.

Later she wrote me a letter about that day and told me that when Dad was in the emergency room at the hospital, he had started to cry and told her how bad he felt about me, about how much he'd hurt me, and how much he loved me. That meant a lot to me because at this point I was hitting my own bottom.

When I came back from the intervention, I started to cry and I just couldn't stop. My boyfriend at that time had no idea what to do with me. I had just turned 30. I was not taking care of myself. I wasn't feeding myself; I had money problems. Everything was wrong. He was a wonderful, sweet man, and he was at a loss as to what to do with me. The crying went on for days. Finally, he took me to the emergency room at a hospital. He was scared. I was suicidal, and he knew it.

They gave me Valium at the hospital and set up an appointment for me with the mental health clinic. I felt so helpless. But somehow there was enough left in me to know that I had to go back to the ACA meetings. And I did. I went back and for the first time I opened up. I shared about the intervention, and I was shaking and crying. I was terrified, and I talked about it and how overwhelming everything felt. That meeting turned out to be a life changer for me. The man who was chairing it was very gentle and loving and encouraging. At the end of the meeting, a woman and her daughter came up to me and said, "I was listening to you talk about all this pain that you're in and that you feel like it's never going to end, and I want you to know that there's another way to look at all this. You're going through mourning. You are mourning all the losses that you've had, and you're letting go of the pain, letting it out, and in doing so, you have begun your healing. This is a new beginning." And she was right, so right. Her words just turned everything around for me. I realized that that's what was happening: I was letting go of all this pain that I'd been so afraid to let anyone see that I was in, and now it was going to start to go away. It would end. I didn't know when; I just knew that it would.

I started to go to meetings again and really listen. I didn't speak up, but I heard every word. It took me a long time to share again. I found a very small meeting that had been newly formed, and then I began to share again. As soon as I started to talk, to open up, people started to approach me and talk to me. Within a month someone asked me to be the speaker at a meeting where the topics were sex, food, and money. I talked about money, which is a real bugaboo for me. It was a very emotional thing for me to talk about money. It's really an addictive substance too.

I always have to laugh when I think about a conversation my older sister and I had about this once. I grew up thinking that we were rich because my parents always bought everything they wanted, traveled, had new cars, did things, and my sister grew up thinking we were on the way to the poorhouse. We could hardly believe we grew up in the same family. As a result, she can't let go of a penny, and I can't hold on to one. That's changing now, slowly, as I've gotten aware of all this. The truth was that my father spent every penny he ever earned and was constantly borrowing more. Mother was of the school that when the going gets tough, the tough go shopping. That was her motto, and that's what she did.

So I talked about money at this ACA meeting. I was hardly the only adult child of an alcoholic that had problems in this department. People really responded. I was elected chairperson of that meeting at the next term for three months. That's when I really started to grow by leaps and bounds.

Now another thing started to happen. As a result of this new growth, I was becoming more stable and more emotionally healthy. I went back into an art therapy program. For my internship, I arranged with an alcoholism program to let me start an art therapy group for young children of alcoholics under the age of 10. I designed the whole project myself. There wasn't a single one in existence in the entire city at the time. I ended up becoming the star student of the art therapy program. I was already on a full scholarship. It was very exciting and rewarding; I was doing just what I wanted to do, and people loved it! I started being asked to do some public speaking on the subject.

Although I was very articulate and bright, I was terrified of getting up in public. I finally realized what it was about. I thought that I was going to stand up there and this frightened child inside of me was going to pop out for everyone to see, and my mask would fall off. But the more I talked in meetings, the more meetings I chaired and found out that I didn't die afterwards, the more I began to believe that I could do it. So I began to speak publicly, and now I do it all the time. It was an incredible turnaround. My self-confidence grew, my self-esteem blossomed, and my career began to take off. Everything started to change. After that internship, I got the job I have now, running a program that I designed myself. I love it.

One of the local neighborhood centers for kids had an alcohol program that wasn't working. It's in one of the toughest neighborhoods in the city. They hired me to come in and design a whole new program about children of alcoholics and prevention. So we came up with a presentation that we contract with school systems to present in the classroom.

We talk about alcohol—what it is, what it does, why people drink, making choices, peer pressure, media pressure—the first time we go into the classroom. The next time we go back we present what it's like to live with someone who drinks too much. My partner plays the alcoholic, and I play his whole family, walking in and out of several different roles within this twenty-minute psychodrama, all talking about how his drinking is affecting their lives. We also show the wife and her issues, trying to be a parent with an alcoholic partner. We have his boss talk about how it's affecting his job. Finally, we show a recovering alcoholic woman. These kids believe that there's no such thing as a woman alcoholic. We try to dispel as many myths as possible with them. The woman in recovery that we show is a single parent, because so many of the kids we work with are from single-parent families. But she's in recovery because these kids need to learn that alcoholism, addiction to drugs, chemical dependency in general is a disease that you can recover from. That recovery story is real important. My partner stays in his role as an alcoholic. I come in and out of the different roles, and at the end, the kids challenge him about everything they've seen. We talk about the different roles I played as different members of the family: the lost child who fades into the woodwork; the scapegoat, the kid who's always in trouble; the hero, the one who's achievement-oriented, responsible. Then I tell them that I grew up in an alcoholic family. I identify myself so that they can see a survivor. See, they don't think that they can make it through this situation, a lot of them. We help get rid of the stigma of coming from an alcoholic home.

The program is enormously successful so far, exciting, dynamic. The kids love it, and I love doing it. We found something that works with adolescents, and that's incredible in itself.

I have an enormous amount of creative energy as a result of coming into the ACA program. The humor, honesty, and poignancy of people's stories has inspired me to write a play out of a workshop with actors who all come from alcoholic families. That's what I've been doing outside of work. It's intense! Some of the actors have been involved in AA but never in ACA, so I've been taking them through this process of going back to their childhood and seeing how it's had an effect on their adult lives. We're just beginning to deal with the healing that comes with recovery, and the forgiveness that has to happen, both of ourselves and of the alcoholic.

Back to my own family. My father stayed in a rehabilitation program for six weeks, and he stopped drinking for a while after that, but he never really invested in AA. He went to meetings, of course, but eventually he started drinking again after about six months. Still, we had a wonderful year with him. He and I reached an incredible reconciliation with each other.

In the course of my own recovery, I learned a lot about reaching out. I realized at some point that he had never told me that he loved me. That was devastating to me. All the times he had told me that he hated me, I understood, were just the alcohol talking, not him. He'd actually shown me that he loved me a lot, but still he'd never said it. I understood a lot about the disease by this time and also knew that both his parents had been alcoholics as well. So I started telling him that I loved him. I told him that on the phone. I'd tell him whenever I would see him and we'd say good-bye. He would be embarrassed and he would laugh, but I could tell that there was something in him that was really responding. OK, so far so good. I realized that maybe I would have to ask for what I needed from him.

So, finally, one time I was telling him good-bye, and I told him that I loved him. He laughed a little, and so I asked, "What kind of a response is that?" "Well, what do you want me to say?" he asked, and I just told him, "I want you to say 'I love you.' " And he said, "All right, all right, I love you," and we both laughed. It felt wonderful, and it got to be our routine, that whenever we were saying good-bye and I'd say "I love you," he'd laugh and say it back to me. It was very lovely. We had a year with him, when he was really with us, before he started drinking heavily again.

He died of a massive heart attack, which was directly related to his heavy drinking. That was a year later, on the last day of my parents' vacation. But there had been so much resolution. I was lucky to have that. So many people I know lost their parents before they could have that. He didn't die when we were all still really angry with him and with each other. I'm really grateful for that. I've had a lot of anger to work through with my mother over these years, for letting me as a child take the brunt of my father's anger without her protection, but then there it is again: She was the daughter of an alcoholic. And then both she and her sister married alcoholics. We have four generations of alcoholism in my family, that I know of. She was doing the best she could with what she knew at the time.

I was suicidal when I came into this program. It literally saved my life. That's why it hurts me when I see what can happen to a meeting if people just get stuck in their rage. It's important to identify those feelings and acknowledge them, but they need to see it as something they're doing for themselves, not something somebody did to them. Recovery means saying, "Yes, I do feel this pain, this anger, this sorrow; I acknowledge these feelings," going through them, and moving on, taking steps forward.

I mentioned wearing a mask before. People always told me how self-confident I was, self-assured, and inside I knew that simply wasn't true. That was my mask, my cover. But now, as a result of the recovery process, that person I projected on the outside and the person who lives inside are meshing. I actually am self-confident now; my self-esteem is much higher. Those two people are becoming one person, who I feel good about now. And that's happened incredibly fast.

Some people say that you don't recover from this disease, but I believe that you do. That doesn't mean that there aren't remnants left from the experience of growing up in an alcoholic home, but they're the kind of remnants everyone has—you know, the remnants of life. I do believe you recover from that particular experience and that the point is to evolve to the point where you forgive everyone. I work on incorporating the healing and recovery into something I carry with me all my life. In everything I do, I have a message from the program helping me through my experience. It's become part of me. It was a wonderful experience for me when I finally realized that I liked coming to meetings, loved seeing my friends, but that I didn't *have* to be there. A lot of people came up to me after I said that in a meeting and told me how relieved they were to hear that. It doesn't mean that I don't have lots of other issues to work on, nobody's perfect, but I have a grasp of what happened now that I didn't have before. It's been very illuminating to look at my family through the glasses of ACA, a tremendous relief.

I was lucky, very lucky, to have had a father who allowed us to see his loving side, too. Not everybody has that. Some people just saw a monster, but I got to see my father as sweet and loving, entertaining—oh, he could be funny—all the things he could be when he was sober. The meanness that came out when he drank was because of the disease. It took me years to realize this. I used to think I hated my father when I was a kid, but it wasn't my father I hated; it was the disease of alcoholism—a very separate thing.

2. Ashley L.

When I was 30, I started going to a counselor because my husband and I thought I had a mental problem. We didn't really know what the source of it was. Finally, we came upon a counselor who identified my problem as alcoholism within the first three weeks. Our children were then 4 and 5.

I went into a residential treatment program for twenty-eight days and got sober. Bam, just like that, the pieces started to fall into place. I realized that my drinking really got bad after my mom's death. When I thought about it some more, I realized that I had been drinking alcoholically from the very beginning. I also had no memory from birth through age 11. It was like everything started when I was 11 years old.

Here I am sober, in this treatment center, trying to work on my Fourth and Fifth Steps in Alcoholics Anonymous. That's where you go back and take a look at the "wreckage of the past" and all those feelings that you've been hiding with alcohol and drugs. So I'm going along, and my Fourth Step starts when I'm in junior high. It didn't occur to me that there was anything before that.

How this fits in with being an adult child of an alcoholic was that there were several traumatic experiences that caused that blackout of my memory, and after five months of sobriety, it all began to come back.

God, where to begin. I'm going to tell you the big stuff and just get it out of the way. There I was out of the treatment center, in recovery, going to AA meetings; my husband's going to Al-Anon, and I'm in therapy. All of a sudden, I have these memories coming back. And what I remembered was that I was raped in fifth grade by my best friend's brother. I grew up in this neighborhood, right across the street from here where I live today. So I'm sitting here with five months sobriety, and I realize that when I look out the window of the room I'm sitting in, I can see the garage apartment where I was raped in fifth grade. It's the same room we're sitting in today as I tell you my story.

I must have been 10, I figure, because I flunked school that year. I never told anyone about this until I got sober, and the memories came back. One of the memories was of the period of time immediately following the rape. I remember not going to school for a week because I was sick, and then I remember going back to school and walking down the hall thinking that everyone knows what happened. I remember being terrified of becoming pregnant. Nobody had really talked to me about the facts of life, but that much I had connected. At some point, it must have occurred to me that I wasn't going to get pregnant, and I just put that memory away and everything prior to that.

I've been afraid to even ask my brother and sister about my childhood, because I'm afraid of what they'll tell me. The fear of this forgotten childhood tells me that maybe there's reason to be afraid. I did ask my sister about what she remembered, and she told me that my mother was a nurse and worked every day from the time I was born until I was in the fifth or sixth grade. She worked at a hospital, and maids came in who pretty much raised us. I couldn't believe it. I have no memory of that, not a single one. I asked my sister if she was sure that mother worked. She said yes, every day she would put on a white uniform and leave the house. She came home around three. I believe my sister. I even have pictures of my mother in her nurse's uniform, and yet I just can't remember her that way.

Mother's dead. She died of alcoholism when I was in my early twenties. Five years before she died, the doctors told her that if she would quit drinking, lose weight, and quit smoking, she would live a full, contented life. She couldn't stop. She drank medicinally, every day at five o'clock. She drank to ease her nerves, the pain. She also took Valium. The combination was a sedative for her. She never had the behavior change that some alcoholics have. She never embarrassed us in public or anything like that, but somehow I always felt the need to take care of her.

She was already 40 when I was born. I was not planned but she told me that I was the greatest joy that ever came into her life. We were really close. My family is very, very rigid, not affectionate, except for my mother. My father never hugged me, kissed me, or told me that he loved me, to my knowledge. I was even named after my mother. I find myself having to be careful, because I seem prone to repeat her life. I loved her to death. She was the one stable factor in my life. I knew that I was OK when I was with her.

I think I know why I didn't tell her about the rape at the time. It's taken quite a while to begin to sort all that out. She had a lot of physical problems, in and out of the hospital, and even when I was in college and feeling crazy and suicidal, I would never let her know how bad things were because I didn't want to be a burden to her. I always took care of her, no matter what shape I was in.

I'm the youngest of the four children in our family. My father is an alcoholic, too. The day she died, we were all there, and I was still trying to protect her. Two weeks before she died, just before she went into a coma, she said that before she died, she needed to know that I would take care of Daddy for her. Here I am, the youngest, with my brothers and sisters all married. I just told her to cut it out, she wasn't going to die. But she wouldn't let it drop, and she said it again, "I just need to know that you'll take care of Daddy for me." Finally, I said, "Sure, I'll take care of him for you." Well, that's the last thing in the world I wanted to do, take care of Daddy. I have reason to think that something may have happened with him early in my childhood. In all the pictures of men I have from age 5 that we cut out from magazines, the face and the genitals are cut off. I think it had something to do with whatever happened with my father. I never liked the man.

The day Mom died, the doctor called us all to the hospital and said, "If there's anything you want to say to her, she can hear you, but she won't be able to respond. She has about thirty minutes or so left to live." I was so enmeshed with her, so completely bonded, I didn't know where I ended and where she started. My father and sister and brothers all said good-bye to her and told her they loved her. But when it came my turn, I just stood there and couldn't say anything. I couldn't say good-bye or tell her that I loved her, because I was too busy in my head trying to protect her, take care of her, thinking maybe she'll pull through.

Every time I got drunk after that I'd go out to her grave and stand there and say that I just wanted to die and be with her. She was my ace in the hole, even after she died. Dying and suicide were my ace in the hole. If things got worse, then I could go be with my mom, wherever that was.

One of the greatest impacts of growing up in an alcoholic home was the no-talk rule. You never talked about what was really happening or about your feelings. Now I'm in a therapy group for women who have been sexually abused in some way or are rape or incest victims. I still struggle with not being able to talk about feelings. I often feel that I am imprisoned in my own body. A few weeks ago in our group session, I wanted to scream. When I was 10, I was not able to scream in that rape situation. It wasn't just one guy; there were several boys there. They ranged from junior high to high school. One of them was close to 20. They were all boys from the neighborhood. One of them, I know, was also a child of two alcoholics. He had sexually abused his sister. He was just sick, sick, sick. It was a terrible thing, and I don't want to go into the details.

As I've worked with this material in recovery, I've realized how hard it is for me to ask for what I need or let people know that I need them. My whole life has been based around being in charge, being in control, taking care of everyone else. I remember when I was about 12, we used to go up to our house at the lake. Often fights would erupt with my dad and especially my older brother. Dad would end up going off somewhere drunk. Mom would be drinking and crying. My brother would be mad, so I'd run around trying to find Daddy to be sure he was OK. I'd say to the whole family, "Isn't anybody going to look to see if Daddy's OK?" No response, so I'd jump in our Jeep and go driving around until I found Daddy and made sure he was OK. Now mind you, I never wanted to be with my father. To this day, if you get me in a room with him, I can't explain what happens, except that fear comes over me and a complete feeling of discomfort. I've had to pretty much separate myself from him physically.

I really steered clear of guys growing up. I had them as friends, but that was pretty much it. I now realize that that had to do with the rape. Then I got to know Michael, the man I married eventually. We had a neat relationship, really cared about each other. We did not have premarital sex. But you know, until I got sober I'd never had sex sober. I had to be drinking to have sex. We got married the year that Mom died. She died, we got married, I got pregnant, had a baby, Dad remarried—all within one year.

When I remembered the rape, I went into such a spiral that I isolated myself for three days and did not leave my house. I could not get up to fix a meal, could not function. It felt as though it had just happened. I couldn't go to the grocery store because I felt like if you saw me, somehow you would know that I had been raped. There was such shame! I went to my therapist's office and basically stayed there for an entire day. I had to be in a safe place.

When I started getting out again, at least going to my AA meetings, guys would come up and give me a hug, and I would come out of my skin. I've never liked hugs from guys, and now I knew why. What happened was I ended up going out and drinking again. I just couldn't handle everything. I needed to get away from my house where I could see that garage apartment out my back windows, every day. I needed to get away from where all this had happened and sort out my feelings. I went to a halfway house, and that saved me. We're getting ready to move from this house thank goodness.

A friend of ours committed suicide right before Christmas, so Michael and I went to the funeral. Wouldn't you know it, one of the guys who took part in that day was there. I hadn't seen him in years. He and I and Michael were all the same age. I'd known him up through high school. He comes up to me at the funeral and says, "Hello, Ashley." I said, "Hello, Jack." He said hello to Michael too. Then he looks at me and says, "You look great! You look as good as you did in fifth grade."

I had my women's group that night, it turned out, and I started talking about it straight out. As much as it made me full of rage, his remark about fifth grade also validated what I was going through. When you have memories after a long period of time like I did, you begin to think that it didn't really happen. At least I know that I did. It had been over twenty years since this stuff had happened, and there were times when I didn't want to believe that it was true. But when he said that to me, I knew. I knew it all over again. He's the only one I've seen of the bunch that were there. The rest have all scattered. They were drinking the day that it happened. Who knows how they've ended up.

When I first came home from the treatment center and Michael and I would make love, it would be OK as long as we were just holding each other and caressing. But as soon as it got to the point of intercourse, tears would start streaming down my face. We really loved each other, and we couldn't understand what was wrong. He would ask if he'd done anything wrong, and I'd tell him that maybe I was embarrassed about being fat or that maybe it had something to do with being sober and having sex. My memory of the rape had not yet come back. This was going on during the first four months of my sobriety. Every time we tried to make love those first four months, I would cry. As soon as it was over, I would go into the bathroom. Sometimes I would throw up. I didn't know why or what was going on. So in some way, when I remembered the rape that fifth month, we were relieved. It was a missing page in the story. Now my tears made sense. Now we understood why I was having such a hard time, and it didn't have anything to do with us.

I'd frozen my sexual feelings all my life because of that episode. Suddenly, I understood my weight problem as well. I never knew how to say no verbally, so I said it in another way, by being fat, because if you're fat, the fat will say no. It will keep the guys away. I know that I'm not at a weight that most other people consider fat, but I'm fat enough in my own eyes to feel unattractive. When I start to lose weight, I get scared to death.

On the day that we buried my mom, a minister that I'd known for years came by the house after the funeral and asked me if I'd been out of the house since mom had died. I had not. When I was 16, I'd gotten involved with the Young Life movement, and I'd prayed with this minister for Jesus to come into my life. This minister was the first man in my life that I had trusted, and I'd known the man for seven years. This is right before Michael asked me to marry him. He invited me to come by his house later, saying that he thought I really needed some time just to grieve and cry. He was right about all that. So later a friend of mine and I went over to his house. I drank all through my mother's funeral, and we had more drinks with him at his house that night. He had just been divorced, and in the Christian community at that time, that was a real taboo.

The evening got late, and he told my friend to go on home; he'd give me a ride. We'd been sitting around on the floor just talking informally. He gave me a big hug, something he'd done many times, just like friends, and he said you just need somebody to hold you and let you cry. And I did. The next thing I knew he started to feel me up, and I was shocked. I had been drinking a lot, but that got through. I was a virgin. I said, "No, no, let me go." He said, "I wouldn't hurt you, just trust me. I wouldn't do anything to hurt you." This is a man who drove around the country in a van with his wife and children, going to different churches and schools presenting lectures on how sex ought to be taken out of textbooks.

The next thing I remember is getting out of the car and walking into my house. I had a blackout. That was one of the first ones I had. It was a sign of my alcoholism, but, of course, I didn't know that at the time. I don't really know what happened that night, but what I do remember is that the next morning when I woke up, I remembered thinking that I buried my mom yesterday, and I wonder if I'm pregnant. That was the first thought that went through my head, like it had in the fifth grade. And though I don't have a complete memory of that night, what I know is that I had some reason to be afraid of being pregnant.

The next day Michael asked me to marry him. He didn't know what had happened at the minister's house. I loved Michael, and I would have married him long before all this happened, there's no doubt in my mind. But what went through my mind when he asked me to marry him was that it would get me off the hook. I wouldn't have to take care of Daddy. And if by chance I was pregnant, it would be OK. I carried that around in my mind for years. I've told Michael about all this now; he knows everything, and he hates that man. I later found out that two other friends who were at my wedding were sexually approached by this guy. In a twenty-four-hour period I lost my mom, my belief in God, and my virginity.

Basically I never had any healthy, appropriate physical contact with men. My father never hugged or touched me in an appropriate way. He was always telling me that all guys wanted to do was get in your pants. My whole life I've hated being a woman. The word *feminine* drives me up a wall. I'm having to work on this issue over and over. Somehow being a woman for me connoted being overtaken. If you're a woman and feminine, then you're going to be taken advantage of, used, abused, hurt. So I've always tried to be strong. I was a tomboy; I was tough, rough even. I don't need that today. I want to be a woman, and I want it to be OK with being who I am.

Before I knew about all this sexual abuse that went on, I used to just think that I was defective. I had no sexual feelings. Even though I loved my husband, the feelings didn't come. I thought that I was defective. But now I know that I had suppressed all those feelings and that it was important to my survival. Now that I'm in recovery, that's beginning to change.

Alcohol was the best thing that ever happened to me, because it kept me together long enough to get into recovery. I believe without a shadow of a doubt that my primary disease is co-dependency and that I found alcohol as a way to treat and take care of that. Now that I've gotten into AA and gotten sober, my primary recovery has got to be in dealing with adult children issues, dealing with relationship issues, because if I don't, alcohol will be an option for me to use to deal with my inability to deal with people. Understand? Alcohol saved me from killing myself. The co-dependency started when I was a really young child.

I did an internship last year, working with children who were sexually abused and physically abused. We had a lot of court cases. Someone gave me an article to read on suicidal gestures of preschool children. I'm reading this article, and I'm getting blown away. By the time I finish it, I can't talk. The author had taken every preschool child's death in Los Angeles and gone back and interviewed everyone who knew them: family, friends, baby-sitters, neighbors, nursery school teachers. She was a psychiatrist, and she documented her study. She concluded that you can't determine suicide in preschool children like you can in older kids, because they don't pick up a gun, drive a car, or take pills. What these kids did was run out into the street in front of cars, fall out of the two-story windows, things like that. These kids had been extremely accident-prone. What she found, time and time again, was that there was alcoholism in the home, abuse in the home. These kids would unconsciously put themselves in a position to be hurt. They made unconscious suicidal gestures.

I couldn't figure out why this article hit me so hard. I went to my group that night and talked about that article, and then it began to come together. I have a childhood medical record as long as your arm. I was constantly in and out of the hospital, just like my mother. She didn't know how to be there for me emotionally, but she sure knew how to take care of me physically. You get hurt, you get patched up and hugged. I had stitches here, broken leg, broken hand, more stitches, another broken bone. When I was not quite 2, my brother told me how I just walked into a swing. I have a very long scar on my head, like a horseshoe, where the skin was ripped off. And it all came together. I knew what I had been trying to do when he told me about it, and I burst into tears. I don't know what could have happened at that early an age, but I do know that both my parents were practicing alcoholics at the time I was born. My birth was a tremendous inconvenience, created a lot of stress, and was a burden. For my mother, it was something she had to endure, though her feelings softened over the years. I don't know how I can know so strongly about that situation when I was so little; I just know what I do.

When you come into AA, people will quickly say, "Well, your parents did the best they could with what they had to work with at the time." That's true, but that's only half of it. There's an old-timer in AA who was sober seventeen years before he began to look at the fact that he was an adult child of an alcoholic, and he talks about this stuff. He's sober twenty-five years now and says that sobriety didn't come alive for him until he acknowledged his issues as an adult child of an alcoholic. He maintains, and I agree, yes, our parents did the best they could, but that's just half of it. The other half is how you feel about what they did and the fact that they did a rotten job. Until you come to grips with your feelings about that, you end up feeling pretty bad. You feel like something is wrong with you for having bad feelings about your childhood, instead of realizing that there was something wrong with your childhood in the first place and that you're not to blame. Nobody is. You've got to have both sides. If you only stay pissed off about your childhood, mad at your parents, and try to blame them for your life, you won't get anywhere. That doesn't work. On the other hand, if you never acknowledge your hurt and anger about what did happen, you'll continue to be stuck with frozen hurt and anger.

You've got to come to the place where you accept that they did the best they could, and you've got to acknowledge that that wasn't too terrific for you. Children of alcoholics have trouble feeling self-worth, and until we acknowledge the truth of what happened and how we feel about that, we can't develop our self-esteem, come to know ourselves as worthy human beings.

My parents didn't want a child when I came into the world, and I used to laugh about that when I said it from the podium in an AA meeting. I don't laugh about that anymore. The feeling that characterized my entire life was that of being apologetic. I would say "I'm sorry" for anything and everything. If you spilled hot coffee on me, I'd say, "I'm sorry." If I bumped into a chair, I would apologize automatically, to the chair. I've done that my whole life, apologize for myself. I didn't feel like I had a right to exist, to take up space on this earth, or that I could be of value, and that's all changing through this recovery process. Today it feels so good to have a sense of self-worth, of value, to feel the right to live, to exist.

What I love most about Al-Anon's ACA meetings is that you can be there and be in a terrible place or be in a great place; it's all OK. You can be as pissed as you want to be about what happened, or you can be in touch with some joy. What I've noticed since I started going to meetings is that as I've allowed myself to feel pain and move into some of my negative feelings that I'd been afraid of, then I also began to experience some real joy in my life. The spectrum of feelings that I can experience has expanded immensely.

It's tricky, walking that line between self-pity and just acknowledging the truth of your feelings. I refuse to use that word *self-pity* on myself or with another person, because I believe that the child of an alcoholic has buckets of pain that they've been sitting on for thirty years or more. So if they get in touch with that pain in a meeting and somebody gets judgmental and says, "Oh, you're just feeling sorry for yourself; it's in the past," they'll never get through it, and those feelings will continue to be frozen down inside for years. They have to have some time to acknowledge that pain, and the great thing about the ACA meetings is that people understand that. It's just part of the process you've got to go through to heal.

I was in an ACA meeting a year or so ago when I was really

in a bad place. All this stuff about sex was coming up again, the most painful stuff, and I told everyone that I was so in touch with my pain that I could almost visualize it in my body. It was like a white ball. I could feel it and see it. I just sat there and cried, and then I told them that as bad as I'm hurting, I feel alive. I am feeling again, all my feelings. That's recovery: to let myself have all of the feelings that I have. People came up to me after the meeting and told me how glad they were that I had shared my pain, because that's one thing that adult children, in particular, seem to find hard to share. They will share anger and other feelings, but I think the hardest thing to share is pain. That's what all this behavior is about, keeping ourselves from having to feel the pain we're in. But the reality is that the more I share it, the less painful it all is. Sharing diminishes the pain, helps it subside.

I've worked a lot with young children of alcoholics, and I've been an Alateen sponsor for four years. It is fantastic to get to see these kids, 15 and 16 years old, getting a chance at recovery and having a chance to talk about their parents' alcoholism and what their choices are around that. In feeling the problem, you experience the solution. The answer is in the Twelve Steps all right, I know that, but some people approach them like they are some kind of Band-Aid to slap on, particularly the Fourth Step, where you take a look at your own part.

If you jump into forgiveness without experiencing the anger and grief, then that forgiveness isn't going to be genuine. It takes time, and there are stages you have to go through to get to forgiveness. Forgiveness is the goal, for sure, but it takes some real work to get there.

I've had to walk through a lot of pain and recovery, and it was not about my alcoholism, it turned out. It was about being a child of an alcoholic. Things are not good with my dad and me today. He stopped drinking, but he's a diabetic and had cancer surgery a couple of years ago. The doctor told him in front of the entire family that if he ate sugar anymore, it would kill him. The day he got home from the hospital, my oldest brother and I went over to see him, and he's sitting there eating peach cobbler. My stepmother went out and bought it for him. We just look at him and say, "Daddy, what are you doing?" He explains by saying that they're just celebrating his homecoming. I got hooked into his diabetes, just like I got hooked into his alcoholism. I looked in the freezer and the drawers for candy bars, and there were candy bars all over the house. She'd bought them for him. I repeated what the doctor had told him, about the fact that eating sugar would kill him. I said, "Look, I know what it's like to give something up that's going to kill me, because I was faced with that with alcohol, and I had to do that." As I looked at him, I got connected to that helplessness I felt when my mother died. I told him, "I had to watch Mom die, and I didn't know that I had a choice, but today I do have a choice. If you want to go this way, it's your choice, but I'm not going to watch it." So we talk sometimes on the phone, but I've hardly seen him over the last two years. Recovery has given me choices where I didn't think I had any before.

I go to regular Al-Anon meetings as well as the Al-Anon ACA meetings, because it's such a valuable program and it's structured. I don't have an ACA sponsor as such; I have an Al-Anon sponsor. Turns out she is also an adult child, and we go to ACA meetings together. She's a beautiful woman, Mexican-American. She was sexually abused by her uncle as a young child. We end up sponsoring each other in a lot of respects.

The woman who identified my alcoholism and got me into treatment in the first place was the same therapist I was seeing when I remembered the rape. That would have been a hard thing to share in a meeting at first. I talk about it sometimes, but not very often. Still, the ACA meetings are where I feel like I can really share just about anything. I know that there's tremendous permission to share in AA too, but often people just don't seem as vulnerable in AA meetings as they are in ACA meetings, at least where I live. Of course, that could be saying more about me than about any meetings I go to.

It's taken sobriety for me to get into recovery from being a child of an alcoholic. Al-Anon has a pamphlet that gives a checklist of characteristics of ACAs called "Did You Grow Up with a Problem Drinker?" When I read that list with questions like "Are you afraid of authority figures or angry people? Do you isolate yourself?" and so forth, I knew that I qualified. I knew that all the characteristics I could identify were about growing up in some kind of unusual home. It was a lot like finding out that I was an alcoholic. When I began to ask questions, I got a lot of information that I hadn't had before. My brother told me that my mother had taken Valium up to the day of her death. I thought my dad would go upstairs and go to bed, but my sister-in-law informed me that what he did was pass out every night. Until I began to ask questions and knew what the indicators were, I didn't know what was wrong with our house, just that *something* was. Alcoholism was that "something," and it wasn't just my own. My denial was so strong; I didn't want to see the drinking as it was. The drinking was not as blatant as I've heard it was in other alcoholic homes, not as obvious, but the dynamics were very pronounced.

One thing that I was aware of was that my parents never went anywhere that there wasn't liquor. When we went on a long trip in the car, cross-country, they had a flask. Dad drank and drove. He's a lawyer, and he told me never to drink and drive. He was always a quiet person anyway, and when he drank, he got real depressed. There were times I remember as a child when I was afraid he was going to kill himself. I knew something was terribly wrong. One night he was out in the backyard cooking steaks. He had a knife, and he was drunk, and he'd had a big fight with my brother. I was the one who went out to make sure he wasn't going to use that knife on himself.

I was both the scapegoat and the mascot in my family, if you want to talk about the family system. My brother acted out for a while, but then he had a dramatic religious conversion. He was drinking a fifth of vodka a day, smoking four packs of cigarettes, going through college when he converted, and his life completely changed. He went into the seminary after that.

As a child I had dyslexia, which was undiagnosed. I acted out and played the mascot. I still do it in meetings. If it's a heavy meeting, I'll crack a joke. I was always the life of the party. Alcohol was the only way that I found it OK to have fun. If I was drunk, I could be silly, dance on the table. My sorority loved me because I was the clown.

When I got sober, I did not know how to have fun. I have had to work at having fun. I've been in tons of meetings where we talked about how important it is for our recovery now to experience those things we didn't do as a child. For example, just to go to a park and swing in a swing is hard work for me. It's much easier for me to sit in a therapist's office and cry my eyes out. Pain is so much more familiar.

As the youngest of four children, and the mascot, I was always picked on and laughed at, made fun of. You know, like freshman in college, or pledges to fraternities or sororities. So I just learned to laugh along with them. But that's not what I wanted to do; I wanted to be taken seriously. I didn't like being made fun of. One of the biggest needs I have is that I want to be taken seriously. I don't want to be a joke. I always thought I was a joke. It was a great survival technique to get by, but I'm ready to be rid of it now, and I know it's okay to be serious about my life. It's about time, after laughing my way through the first thirty years. I guess what I'm really talking about is balance. There are some people who've been serious all their lives who need to learn to be funny. I never want to be without a sense of humor; I just want more balance—that's what I'm trying to say.

Some people have been really critical of ACA meetings because of the openness, willingness, and vulnerability of the people in it to tell it like it is. If you've never done that, it can be pretty threatening. But what I found was that when I opened up, I felt like I was sitting in a room full of my brothers and sisters, and everything is OK.

3. Michael P.

My father was an active alcoholic, though we never used that word in our family. I did not perceive that my father was an alcoholic until I was in my mid-20s. What I was most aware of growing up was the constant tension in the household and the atmospheric threat of violence at any moment. When I was in boarding school, I remember watching a television dramatization of *Death of a Salesman*, with Lee J. Cobb. I noticed that I was starting to sink in my chair. I was so embarrassed! I kept hoping that nobody would notice that that play was about my house. I thought, "Oh, my God, how did my father get in there?" I had the same experience in reading and seeing Eugene O'Neill's plays performed. My home was a classic Irish-Catholic drunken, violent scene, though you certainly couldn't tell that from the outside.

My family was a model in the community, that's how it looked from the front. My grandmother was always spoken of in saintly terms, but I was told strange stories about how she would punish my father and his brothers in very humiliating ways: sending them to school at 12, 13, with bows and ribbons in their hair, making them walk around the block with each other in dresses. Mind you, these are young boys, immigrant families, during the depression. That's how *he* was brought up. So it's not surprising that his mode was humiliation, too, but not to the same degree, thank God. He would merely hit us in public, call us out in front of our friends and dress us down.

I am the second child of four. My older brother was the bright star, and I had to work really hard to keep up with him. I did very well. I was an altar boy and an excellent, hardworking student.

Dinner was always impossible. Physical violence could erupt at any moment, particularly between my older brother and my father. Or it could be between my father and mother, right there at the table. Parts of it were healthy arguments over political issues that we really enjoyed and benefited from, but then suddenly it could turn. My father wouldn't just point out issues but would completely denigrate the person who dared to say something contradictory to his point of view. That's what I grew up thinking a discussion was—verbal warfare.

I remember sitting at the dinner table when I was about 12, and for reasons that were completely unclear to me, my father came over and picked up the phone nearby and starting hitting my mother over the head with the receiver. He had been drinking. It was simultaneously shocking and nothing new. It was the first time that I had seen him hit her with something in his hand. Both my older brother and I stood up. My mother said, "You can't do this anymore, these boys aren't going to stand for this. My sons will protect me." Little did she know what was going through my head. I was standing there thinking, "Who are you talking about, woman? I'm not going to fight this wild, insane human being. You and he obviously got into this on your own, and I'm just passing through. I plan on having a meal and leaving. I'm not going to jump into *this* scene." That was my honest feeling. Of course, I didn't say that or do anything.

Tied to that scene is another series of events. I had quite a reaction to all the tension and was filled with conflicted feelings about being a young boy in an alcoholic household. After fights, I would be the one to try to make peace. I would talk to my father and say, "How could you do that? What happened? I don't understand how you got so angry." He would be completely destroyed and humiliated. He would be very sorry and say, "Michael, please just leave and go upstairs. I can't talk about it." Sometimes he would say, "I don't understand it myself, or I don't really know why," but usually it was just, "This is not your place. Get out of here."

That's what it was like at home. To the outside world, my father was a public speaker of such dynamism that he was constantly asked to give speeches at church social functions, political functions, all kinds of events. He was in advertising. He organized political campaigns, managed races for senators and congressmen, wrote speeches for U.S. presidents. This guy was a powerhouse. He was courted and called on by major political figures from all over the country. I'd be on the phone with my friends doing homework, and an operator would come on and say that the White House was on the line and needed to talk to my father, or the governor was calling, or the mayor was on the line. I'd have to give up the line and call my friends back. At Christmas everyone would come to our house, from the street sweeper to the mayor. There would be 500 to 600 people come through in the course of the day. He was a mover and a shaker in his day.

The memory of going with him to the Holy Name Society meetings where he spoke at the different parishes in our town have never left me. I was between 6 and 9 years old. All the men of the parish would come on a Saturday morning after an early mass to the parish hall for communion breakfast, and there would be speakers afterwards. My father would be one of them. The rooms were big, maybe 200 to 300 men, and he would often get a standing ovation. He could move the whole room. Men would be sitting there with tears streaming down their faces, cheering, and I would be wondering, "My God, what did he say? Look at these people." I had this terrific pride in him and how he could move people. What had he done that got this response? This was the same guy who beat me.

As I got older, this image of him as a powerhouse started to fade. By the time I was 16, I began to see him as a raving lunatic, a man who was falling apart, who was deeply troubled, and from whom I could learn nothing about what it is to be a man.

The other side of the violence in our house was my mother's desperate need to deal with her feelings. I've talked to other men who had this experience, too, when it was the father who was the alcoholic: the mother turns to the son, at least my mother did.

Mother and I would be sitting at the kitchen table, and she would begin to pour out her feelings to me, her disappointments, to intimate that there were other men that she could have been with. I would be thinking to myself, "She should not be telling me this," and simultaneously thinking, "This is my mother. She's falling apart; she needs someone to talk to, I'm glad she can talk to me." Then the other voice would come in saying, "She's telling me things about my father I'm not supposed to know." The unspoken statement to me was: "You'll be better than your father, you won't do this. You'll be more kind, you won't do this, you won't be like him."

But the thing that I learned most was to hide my feelings. I was sitting in this incredibly deep, rich, adult feeling place, but none of the feelings were mine, they were all hers. As a young boy I didn't know how to turn around and say "God, Mom, *I* feel so bad." She was already falling apart. Then I was supposed to go outside with the boys and play basketball.

I had this kind of experience again and again with her, where there would be a lot of feelings in the atmosphere to which I was detached, objective, cool, calm, uninvolved. I would be keeping up a front, having all kinds of conflict going on inside of me, ranging from "Get out of here, I'm not supposed to be here, I'm not supposed to hear these things" to thinking "Here I am, and I want to be here," back to "I shouldn't be here." I would tell myself that "It's good of me and it's good for her that I'm here. But it's not good for me that I'm here; it's good for her that I'm here. That's good."

So what I learned is "It's good for me to do something that I don't like. I should not be participating in this, but it's good for somebody else so I should do it." I'm in this world of tremendous feelings, and I learned to look like I'm participating, but I'm not. When there's lots of emotion, lots of chaos, lots of intensity, I keep cool, I keep calm. So I learned to be a truly remarkable person. In any deep feeling crisis, I am right on the money. I'm absolutely clear. When someone says, "Oh, my God, what should we do?" instinctively, I go right to it. Personally, it's a tragedy. I've given up all instinctive feeling and ability to know how I feel about something and what it is that I should do. Instead I learned to check my own feelings and not make a move. I end up staying in situations much longer than I ever should. This has been especially true in relationships.

I realize now that although I saw a lot of physical displays of affection toward my brothers and sisters, I never saw my parents being close and loving with each other, never. They didn't sleep together for almost twenty years. So I didn't trust physical affection. The person who is openly affectionate with me here in a public situation, once the door is closed, might be throwing me across the room. I didn't really trust intimacy. A few times I tried to talk about my problems with my mother, only to find them being talked about at a social occasion by her, like in a cocktail conversation. Intimacy was not to be trusted, that was clear.

Things got so crazy for me that I pleaded to be allowed to

go away to school. There was a race between my older brother and my father of who was going to drink themselves to death the fastest. Another brother had developed a series of psychosomatic symptoms that were so profound that no one could diagnose them, and the doctors had told my parents that he might die. My father was off drinking and becoming increasingly crazy and violent. In the midst of all this, my mother was lecturing to women's groups on Christian family life.

This was crazy-making for me. I was constantly in a double bind. My mother was pointed to as a model for how to live out religious values in family life, yet my experience inside was that we were all in a constant state of crisis and were bleeding all over the sidewalk, so to speak. My mother continued to speak widely on the family, Christian values, and the protection of children during this time. The discrepancy between my experience inside the house and the outer world's perception of my family constantly reinforced the denial of what was really going on.

By the time I was 20, I was married and a father. I got my high school sweetheart pregnant, so we got married. She was the child of an alcoholic, too. I had been headed for law school when this happened. I knew that I had no idea about how to father, so I dropped law and became involved in early childhood education. I spent the next four to five years intensively working with kids, studying child development, getting into children's theater, consulting with day-care centers, Head Start programs, really investing myself in learning how to be with children.

My wife and I were both Irish-Catholics. We both came from active alcoholic households and formed a kind of bond that didn't have a lot to do with love, but with survival. Of course, we didn't understand that at the time. I focused on learning how to be a parent. I didn't know enough to realize that I should learn something about how to be in a relationship.

It was quite clear to me that violence wasn't good, but displays of anger were another thing. Anger was acceptable. I didn't like pushing people around or being pushed around physically, but emotionally pummeling a person to the ground was open territory. I was a hell of a person to live with. If someone disagreed with me, it wasn't just a difference of opinion that we had. I obviously have to be right, and you have to be wrong. It was tied to survival. The other person had to be wrong, because "If I'm wrong about this, what else am I wrong about? My God, I might be wrong about everything." I probably was.

We proceeded to have three children over a period of five years. By the time we were 26 years old, my wife had her tubes tied. She was quite clear she didn't want any more kids. Having had an alcoholic mother, she had been raising kids for ten years. At age 14 she virtually became the mother for her own numerous brothers and sisters. It was a large family and because of her mother's drinking, Jane was left to carry the load and take care of everyone else.

She was determined to be the best, all-present, do-everything, be-everywhere mom as a result. She was *not* going to be her mother, and she, of course, became her mother. She walked right into her mother's shoes and became an alcoholic.

What is amazing to realize as I look back is that I did not see her becoming an alcoholic. During one period of time there were months at a time when Jane would barely leave the bedroom. I'd go off to work, take the kids to school, bring them home, and she was still in bed. We reached a point where we stopped sleeping together. We moved into separate rooms, just like my parents.

She's drinking, and I didn't see any of it. I found out subsequently, when I'd be off at work, she'd be sipping wine, and then when I came home, everything would be cleaned up. I thought she was having a breakdown. I made a thousand excuses for her on all levels: "It's my fault. The fault is that we had kids. The fault is that we got married so young. The fault is that I'm an impossible person to be with." I made her feel terrible. When we had fights, I'd just verbally beat her to a pulp. I never hit her, but emotionally there were unbelievable scenes.

It never occurred to me once that our problems had anything to do with alcohol. I knew about Alcoholics Anonymous. I would go to an AA meeting with friends; we'd celebrate their AA birthdays. I knew all about the program. I had been going to meetings with friends for years, starting when I was 24. I was always listening with the thought of trying to understand my father a little bit better, or my family. I did not see what was happening in my own house, to Jane and me. I did not see myself becoming a co-alcoholic, enabling her drinking. I just didn't see it or what was happening to my kids.

It wasn't until after we got divorced that I realized that she was having a drinking problem. She would show up at school meetings with liquor on her breath and look like hell. One parents' meeting, in particular, she was staggering around.

I started going to Al-Anon meetings and began to hear a lot of things that I could identify with. I began to see something about my part as a co-alcoholic. I started to understand the whole "enabling," "people-pleasing" role that I'd carved out for myself from long, long ago, way before our marriage. From listening to other people, it became increasingly clear that there was a familial transmission of this disease from generation to generation to generation. This was the most striking jolt in Al-Anon meetings initially.

I remember a wave of sadness of realizing how many of Jane's and my issues were not really between us but were because of the alcoholism in our families that we'd grown up with. How many years had we sat in AA meetings with our friends and just couldn't hear or see how alcoholism applied to us? Ignorance and denial. The denial gets passed on from one generation from another. Denial is the code, that's what allows it to continue. I was able to trace alcoholism back to my grandparents' generation, see it in various aunts and uncles. One was a compulsive gambler; others married alcoholics; another was schizophrenic and committed suicide. It's just part of my lineage. Completely unacknowledged, completely unspoken.

I had been in Al-Anon off and on for a few months and had listened to enough that I stopped going to meetings and thought, "OK, I got some insights now." I found myself as one of the few men in the room. I heard a lot of women talking about their husbands and their boyfriends. At a certain point it was just hard for me to continue to identify, though I learned an enormous amount.

The most important thing I learned from that initial period was that it was a family disease, passed on from one generation to the next. I thought that if I didn't want to give it to my children—even though I'm not chemically dependent myself—that I had better start doing some serious work right now. The second important thing I learned after listening to woman after woman say "My father was an alcoholic. Then I married an alcoholic, got divorced, married a junkie, and got divorced. Now my boyfriend is alcoholic, and I just left him" was that all of a sudden I saw that this thing is so much bigger than anything I have ever thought of before. Suddenly the First Step became real: "Admitted that we were powerless over alcohol and that our lives had become unmanageable."

I began to take in the level of the forces at play in my life and to realize that I have been totally surrounded by an environment of chemical abuse. It also became obvious that I have participated in this unconsciously, and so there is no way in the world that I'm going to find myself out of this maze by myself. I had a very profound insight at that point when I saw how, my God, I have been surrounded by nothing but this conditioned reality so therefore, by definition, I have no tools to get out of here. I don't know anything else but this.

I had some time in which I had come to accept completely my role as a part of an alcoholic family and that I had participated as a co-alcoholic in my marriage. Then someone suggested to me that I go to a meeting for Adult Children of Alcoholics and told me about the program. I walked out of that first meeting realizing that not only was I an adult child of an alcoholic, my ex-wife was, too.

I left that meeting with a profoundly bittersweet feeling. Had the both of us been in that meeting, who knows what might have happened? Had we both been able to understand how completely we were conditioned by this disease, how thoroughly, how there had been no way out for us, could things have turned out differently? I'll never know.

At the time of our separation and divorce, it was clear that we both really wanted to make it work and that we had no idea how to do it. Oh, the sadness of it. No therapist had the tools to help us. We had gone to a family therapist, but we just kept coming up against a no-win situation. None of us, including the therapist, had a clue about what we were really up against.

There was a great relief when I found the ACA meetings, a place where I can hear, listen, talk, and learn. And there was also this bittersweet sense of "how sad." Where was this ten years ago, five years ago? Where was I five years ago?

I found that ACA meeting because I went back to Al-Anon realizing that my ex-wife was further down the road of alcoholism than I had allowed myself to see. She'd become involved with a big-time drug dealer. I had to get my kids out of her house. We had joint custody, a week with me and a week with her. I started listening in a different way to what my children were saying about what it was like for them over at her house.

My denial was so strong that it wasn't until some family friends finally took me aside and said, "Hey, do you realize how bad the situation is at Jane's house?" that I finally clicked in and thought, "Oh, right, my kids are being destroyed. Do something."

Jane's situation was getting increasingly seedy and down. I took the kids full time at that point, and the children and I went into family therapy together. Only then did I begin to see how crazy things had become with Jane. I went into therapy on my own as well as attending ACA meetings and got the kids into Alateen.

Once I began to understand the whole phenomenon of ACA, I knew I needed help for my kids as well. I insisted that they go to eight Alateen meetings to give it a try. They went to the eight meetings and didn't want to go back. That's OK; they gave it a try. But what came out of that was their awareness that "Hey, Dad's not lying. Mom is really sick. This is not going to go away."

The first two weeks of being back with me full time, therapy, Alateen, and all the talks we were doing were really hard on my youngest child; he was 7. Every single night he would be in hysterics on the floor, crying, screaming, saying, "Why are you saying this? It's not true. Why are you saying this about my mother? She's not an alcoholic. It didn't happen. You're all lying." Then his sister would remind him of something else that they had all witnessed, like their mother passing out, and once again he would scream and cry and say, "No, it's not true, it didn't happen, you're lying!" What a time!

I kept going to the ACA meetings for nearly a couple of years, but I didn't work the full program. I didn't get a sponsor, and I didn't go beyond the first three Steps, and I'm really feeling the need to go back and do more work. My recovery got to a certain point and a lot of things got clarified, but it's gotten clear to me now that I really need to work the Steps.

I remarried not long ago, a wonderful woman who has two children. No chemical dependency, right—I'd learned that lesson. See, I'm doing better. But what I've stepped into is a situation where her daughter's biological father was molesting the child on visitations. I found myself in another family system in which the basic elements of abusive behavior were all there.

I started going to a parent's support group and began to understand the issues of child abuse, and what became clear was that the elements of child abuse are only a little different from those of alcohol abuse. Sure, there are differences, but there are more similarities than differences. In hearing people's stories in the support group, there were all the elements that were so familiar in the Al-Anon and ACA stories that I'd heard: the denial of reality, the low self-esteem of the abuser, who invariably turns out to have been abused as a child. I had begun to understand the family system in which I existed. Now I suddenly got a glimpse of the societal system in which the issues of substance abuse, physical abuse, sexual abuse, and emotional abuse all have such similarities. It all gets passed down in families through collusion, denial, and co-dependent behavior. Abuse is abuse, whether chemical or physical.

I started back into ACA with renewed awareness. This is profound, spiritual work. It's bigger than anything I can do alone or without accepting that this is a life-changing process. Learning how I got to where I am and how desperately essential it is for me to learn to get beyond this myself and for my children makes for the most compelling reason to return to the program over and over again. I want to make sure that I have done everything that I can to break this pattern in my family, for here, for now.

It is a true gift to have these programs for a way to go. The anonymity and the spiritual direction provided by the Steps provide a great opening to move in and out of. The program offers me a glimpse of the quality of life I want. I see people who stay with program more and those who do less, and I can see the differences in their recovery, their happiness, their ability to handle problems. Teachings are offered in such an embodied way in the program. In fact, to me the Steps represent a way back into an embodied Western spiritual path that's long been lost in the tradition I grew up in.

There's been a lack of a knowing person, a teacher, a spiritual friend who could say, "Here's where you are and here's where you could go next." What the program offers me is a way of looking at all these day-to-day issues and problems in a way that is surrounded by a higher power—spiritual direction amidst a fellowship of fellow travelers. I'm looking for a sponsor in the program, not because any church says that because this person has a collar or he or she is an authority, but because I recognize that this person has development and growth that I want. It's an experience-based reality. Nothing dogmatic or intellectual about it. Suggestions: "Here's what worked for me, maybe it could work for you. You choose to do it or not." How do I know what works? Because it worked for me, not because the pope said it, or because that's what I was taught in school. Everyone is the teacher. What is shared is experience, strength, and hope. The program has the practicality of "if it works, use it; if it doesn't, don't." It gives me an eminently wholesome and caring experience.

4. Sam S.

My whole early experience was of feeling totally different, awkward, and unlike other people. By age 9 I had concluded that I probably wasn't a human being. I decided that there was something wrong with me that made me fundamentally different from the other people in the world. I never talked about these feelings with anyone.

I was born on the East Coast. My father is from what was a relatively prestigious family in that they owned a local business that had been there forever. He was never comfortable with the notoriety and status in the community. As far back as I can remember, he made an effort to keep our family away from the other people who had money and power and said "we're different."

He ended up being a gadfly in the community. He would sit on the community boards and criticize what "the wealthy folks" were doing. He would create a ruckus in the church because of what "the wealthy folks" were doing. As his alcoholism got worse, his paranoia grew. I grew up living on the wrong side of the tracks in a very large house with a lot of money, though we never had much evidence of money. We didn't have nice clothes, and we were kept separate from the other students in the wealthy school we were sent to. Eventually I was taken out because I was really unhappy there and put into a country school, where I also didn't fit in because I still had some money and some prestige from the family.

I was the family hero in the alcoholic family system: the child who is always responsible, a high achiever, who excels, and whose achievements help the family feel good about themselves. The only hitch is that I didn't feel good about myself. There was a tremendous discrepancy between my insides and my outsides. As far back as I can remember, I was performing. I was getting excellent grades in school and enjoyed being my grandmother's star grandson and pleasing my parents. In truth, I lorded my good grades at school over other people, beat up my little brother, and was a bully. I was arrogant. I knew that something was wrong. Inside I felt inadequate, left out, alone, abandoned. At the same time, I was aware that other people saw me as this very successful kid who was on top of everything. I developed a dual perception of myself. Somewhere around this time, when I was 9 to 10 years old, my father's alcoholism started. I can see that now as I look back, but then, of course, I had no idea that he was an alcoholic. I never really knew that as I was growing up.

Today my father is recovering in AA. My mother's recovering in Al-Anon. My sister's recovering in Al-Anon. My brother's recovering in AA and Al-Anon. And I am in Al-Anon. One sister has not joined the program, the only member of the family not in recovery. I've been in Al-Anon for six years and in the Adult Children of Alcoholics program for four years.

Back to what it was like growing up. Things just began to go bad. My father changed from a happy-go-lucky, play golf on Sunday, have occasional beer party with the boys kind of guy, to somebody who became increasingly religious, increasingly incensed with the immorality of the community around him, the dishonesty of the bankers, and with most of the people in town. As this happened, he began to move more and more into a position of the lonely crusader, and as he did that, things got worse at home. There were frequently two-hour lectures at the dinner table on the immorality of the city that we were forced to sit through.

This was not a family where people laughed or felt comfortable or where anyone could joke around. The tension just increased, and we became more and more isolated from each other. I don't remember any closeness with any of my three siblings, much less anybody else in the world.

I started to experience myself as someone who had a serious problem in adolescence, when people started to date and have friends. I became acutely aware of how lonely I was and how different I felt. I had no idea what to do about that, and consequently I really didn't make any friends in high school. I was incredibly isolated.

At home my father had begun to believe that people were out to get him. We had private detectives guarding the home from time to time. I spent one summer writing a book that he had dictated to my mother and I was forced to edit. It was all about the sins of the city we lived in and what a Sodom and Gomorrah the place was. I became angrier and angrier at my father. I hated him, but I was completely frozen. I never confronted him. I never acted out in any way like the children in these families that we call the "scapegoat." I never got in trouble at school, never went out and got drunk, never stole the car, got anyone pregnant, or ran away from home. I just sat there at home, hating my father, listening to the endless lectures and waiting. I was powerless to choose anything else. I felt like I didn't have any other options. I was 16 years old. I had no idea that alcohol had anything to do with what was happening.

My father drank through this whole time but was never perceptibly drunk. I have no memory of his drinking. I know what he didn't do: He did not get arrested, he did not have work difficulties. To the contrary, his company was very successful and he was making a lot of money. He was a very successful businessman. Still had friends. Never got drunk. Never had medical problems. Was never sick a day in his life.

He experienced no consequences of his drinking, except that the family got crazier and crazier. We had no idea what was wrong. We did not discuss what was wrong. We just lived in it. Later on, just to give you an idea about his ability to function while under the influence of alcohol, when I got to psychology school at the age of 21, I had to find somebody to test because I was learning how to administer intelligence tests. He agreed to be a subject for me. So I gave him an intelligence test. He took it with a cigarette in one hand and a full glass of bourbon in the other. This was at 10:00 at night after he had had about ten drinks. He scored 133 on the IQ test. There was no perceptible problem with his functioning. He just functioned very well. So it never occurred to any of us that the drinking was at the bottom of his behavior.

Our whole life was an illusion. We looked like the all-American family. We had an upper middle-class income. We had people who came over to the house. They weren't friends, but they looked like friends. I was on the swimming team. My sister was a cheerleader, but if anybody had taken the time to look at any of us, none of us had any intimate relationships or ever talked to anybody about how we felt. We were all doing what we imagined was appropriate.

As we got further along as a family in the progression of the disease, we had more and more difficulty maintaining the illusion of normalcy. But through my high school years, early in the disease, everything still looked fine. There were a few bizarre episodes, like my having to edit that book for my father and his hiring private detectives from time to time, but outside of that, life looked "normal."

My mother was certainly aware that something was wrong. But my mother is a very kind, loving, devoted, and loyal person and never would consider criticizing my father or talking with him, or about him to us or to anyone else. So she kept her perceptions to herself just as I kept my perceptions to myself. My two sisters would routinely break into tears at the dining room table, but we never talked about why they did that every third night. A standard theme for my father's lecture was his belief that the president of the largest bank in town was involved in funding businesses illegally and then calling in their loans when he knew they couldn't repay. That way, according to my father, he could repossess the business and break the man, making him destitute for the rest of his life and either taking his business into his own personal fortune or into the bank's fortunes. So he would go on and on about this for two hours at the dinner table, and if my sister didn't eat her peas or my other sister got bored or dropped a fork on the floor, God forbid, he would stop in the middle of his story and yell at them for being clumsy or incompetent. "What did you do that for? Aren't you listening to me?" he would demand, and then they would break into tears and go running off from the table. He would yell at them some more and make them come back to sit down and listen to the rest of his story. Everyone had to give him their complete, undivided attention. Since he is 6'5" tall and weighs 200 pounds, we listened. He is a very large, powerful man.

I went away to college. I would have liked to have gone to a very large, academically easy school where I could make some friends and become a normal person, but all I had going for me was my brains, so I ended up at a top Ivy League university in the East. I got there totally unequipped to cope.

I had no friends, no self-confidence, no ability to cope with any situation; but at least I was going to a top-notch school. I didn't realize how much I depended on my parents for my whole world. Even though I hated my father, I didn't know anything else. I had a real rough time that first year, almost flunked out. I never made any kind of friends. I just stuck with the people who were assigned to me as roommates. I put a tremendous amount of effort into meeting girls, because I had no idea how to talk to another man. I knew that you're supposed to make some connection with girls at that age, and it was a way to get some closeness. But I was terrified of getting close to anyone, and I didn't do very well with it. Nonetheless, I ended up graduating cum laude and was captain of the fencing team. I also managed to meet and begin dating a girl who ended up being my first wife.

For all intents and purposes, I was doing quite well, but the internal experience of being damaged or feeling in some way inhuman or unable to cope just kept getting worse. My anxiety level was really getting high by the time I was finishing up at the university. I tried drinking; I thought that might help. I had some good drunks. I wrecked a motorcycle and had some blackouts. But I just didn't have the ability to become an alcoholic. After I had a bad episode, I just did not want to drink after that for a while.

After I finished college and had to make a decision about what to do, I was terrified of going into the real world, so I just stayed in school. I decided to go to graduate school in clinical psychology to try to cure myself. That was the only way I could figure out how to become a normal person. I thought that I could find out from books what was wrong with me, that I could fix myself. I moved to New York. It was good for me. There was a wonderful kind of freedom because of all the strange people who live there. And I liked my classmates a great deal. Many of them were Jewish and I marveled at their very emotional and responsive way of being in the world. That gave me a new kind of freedom as well.

In graduate school we had to learn how to do psychological testing, as I mentioned before. But before we could test anyone else, we were given a battery of tests ourselves so that we would know what it felt like to be tested. Two years after I had gone through the testing, the woman who had given me the tests stopped me in the hallway and told me that she had found my test records while going through an old notebook of hers. She asked me if I would be interested in seeing them. I was very interested, because I knew how to interpret the tests at that point. I was working at Bellevue Hospital in New York, a central admitting ward for the craziest people in New York. I was testing folks right off the streets and getting some pretty bizarre records. To my surprise, when I looked at my own record, it was in no way distinguishable from the psychotic people coming off the streets that I had been giving the test to. It was the record of a very, very disturbed person. The Rorschach test in particular was interesting. The Rorschach is the test done with inkblots, and it's a good measure of internal feeling states that people may not be aware of at the time. There is one indicator on the Rorschach that has a lot to do with anxiety, free-floating anxiety. That indicator appeared on my results more than anybody I had ever tested. I was shocked. It really raised the question in my mind of what I was doing testing other people. The results of my tests indicated a tremendous inability to cope and extreme anxiety, the kind of anxiety that psychiatrists were routinely putting other people on medications for. I knew I was in bad shape.

The Rorschach is generally divided into those responses that have to do with introspection and identity. You looked at my Rorschach and you would say this person has no identity. They have no awareness of who they are; they have no beliefs, no values, no convictions of their own. All that showed up on my test was responses to others or responses to the world around me.

Though at the time I didn't understand the results, I knew now that they reflected a pretty good description of the adult child of an alcoholic. We are chameleons. Put us in a situation, give us fifteen minutes to watch the players, and we can adapt, we can con our way in there and act appropriate. We will always feel outside of it, but we can present ourselves however we need to present ourselves in order to exist. I walked around a lot thinking I have no idea what I really believe. I always used to admire those people who knew that if a bus driver short changed them, they would just stand up and say, "Goddamn it, don't do that to me." They had convictions and feelings and they knew who they were, and I don't know how they did that. Because I didn't have any convictions, I didn't have any rights,

I didn't have any beliefs, and so I would go along with whatever you told me you wanted.

As part of my graduate work, they said if you wanted to work with anybody as a therapist, you had to go through what was called Training Analysis yourself. I was in Training Analysis for three years. We talked endlessly about my father and about my problems and what was wrong with me, and we never once touched on my father's drinking. The man I found to work with was very aware that I was not there for the training. He knew that I was there because I was really disturbed, and I knew that he knew, and he knew that I knew. We just didn't tell anybody. We kept that our secret. The only problem was that he didn't know what a child of an alcoholic looked like, so he never knew what was wrong with me. There was not much I could tell him myself. I had gotten far enough with psychology to tell him that my father was a paranoid schizophrenic. If you looked his symptoms up in a psychology book, that's what you would call it in terms of nomenclature. Nonetheless, I got a lot out of therapy. It was the first time that I had talked to anybody.

I was 22 years old, and until that time, I had never told another living human being that I was frightened, that I felt inadequate, that I was alone, that I had difficulty being with women, that I couldn't make friends. I just never said those things. It wasn't "manly" on top of it all. I had been living this kind of lie of "I'm just wonderful, and I'm fine, and you don't need to help me. I'm OK, I don't need anyone." The isolation that accompanies this disease is profound. And I thought I was going to help other people.

Two years into graduate school, I got married. I married another child of an alcoholic. She was from a very wealthy New England family. About every two months, her mom would not answer the phone. So we would get in our car, and we would drive up to her elegant country estate where she would be all drunked up, lying in her bed with vomit all over her, having urinated all over herself and shit in the hallway. We would load her in the car and drive her out to a drunk farm. They didn't have real treatment centers then like they do now. They just had places where you could go for ten days and go to some AA meetings and then you would go home again. We would go pick her up and bring her back to her house again, and she would be all right for a while. It was like a social visit almost. We would never talk about what was going on. We would pick her up like we were picking her up from vacation and take her home and say, "Well, take care of yourself," and then we'd leave. We never asked her if she wanted to quit drinking or simply said, "What the hell is the matter with you?" We never told her that we wouldn't come back. Nothing. Even as my wife and I were going home in the car, we never talked about what was happening. Now remember, I'm a graduate student in psychology, and my wife had a master's degree from Radcliffe. I never said, "God, what the hell is the matter with your mother? Do you think we ought to get her some other kind of help? Is there something else we can do to help with this situation?" I never said anything, and she never said anything. We just accepted that her mother was a drunk and every two months we had to go pick her up and dump her in a drunk farm. That was just the way you lived.

Eventually her mother remarried, someone she had met at the drying-out farm, another wealthy drunk who couldn't stay sober. He didn't stay around very long. They were only married for about two years. Not long afterwards, she was smoking in bed one night, drunk, burned the house down, and died in the fire. Died of her alcoholism, I should say.

While we were going through all this with her mother, we had the attractive apartment in Greenwich Village and the right friends, and we were happily married. She was working and I was in graduate school. Then one day at the end of my therapy, I went out on one date with a girl that I went to school with, and went home and asked my wife for a divorce. I did this without any thought, without working the idea through or discussing it with my therapist or anyone else, much less my wife. We hadn't even had an argument to that point. My wife was devastated. Her father had left her mother and her greatest fear in her whole life was of my leaving her. She wanted to be sure that she would never, ever get divorced, like what had happened to her mother and father. I felt horribly guilty, like I was a bad person, but I also felt like I was going to go crazy if I didn't get out of the marriage. We were not good together, despite all the appearances of a happy marriage. I wanted to be a normal person, to live a life where I wasn't dependent on my parents, or my wife or school to protect me. It was difficult for me. I didn't cope well with the world I was in.

I had gotten past the master's degree level in my Ph.D. program and was doing counselling in a clinic in New York. I was also on a college faculty doing some teaching. It was during this time that I had begun to have a recurrent dream, the only one I've ever had in my life. I would dream of being outside somewhere naked, no clothes, and knowing I had to get back to my apartment to get some clothes. I would sneak into an elevator, and the elevator would stop at the next floor, and twelve people would get on. There I would be standing naked. The way I would cope with it in the dream was to pretend like nothing was wrong. In the dream I would tell myself that I can make it through a few more floors, and if I just get out of here, I'll be fine. Then I would wake up with a horrible sense of anxiety, embarrassment, and horror. That was the kind of life I lived, pretending on the outside that everything was fine, but inside having the terrible feeling of being totally exposed all the time.

Everybody thought I was fine, wonderful, doing splendidly, coping well. I was at the top of my class. I was beginning to make some money. But I didn't feel fine.

I quit being a psychologist. Quit New York. After the divorce, I tried to go be a normal person. I went to the West Coast with a girl and worked as a waiter in a gambling casino. It was good for me. It was the closest at that point that I had gotten to feeling normal, to feeling like I didn't have to pretend to be a psychologist who had all the answers. I didn't tell people that I'd graduated from Princeton. I didn't have to act like I was part of the New England high life. I was just one more waiter in the casino that nobody knows. I was making $200 a week, and I had the girl that I lived with, and I skied. That was it. It was a very good experience for me. It was a major achievement that I was able to do it without being overwhelmed with anxiety. I ended up getting married to that girl, and she is still my wife today. She is not the child of an alcoholic. She is Jewish. She doesn't know anything about alcoholism. She's a wonderfully normal person. I had finally found one.

Then an important event happened. My father called me while we were still out West. I had grown further and further away from him during this time. I was getting more and more angry with him and feeling hatred toward him. I hadn't even seen him for a few years at the time when he called. He called crying, saying that his business had burned to the ground, and that if I didn't come back and bail him and the business out, the family would lose all the money we ever had. My mother would be left a penniless widow and he needed me, which was something he had never said. I hung up on him. That's how I felt about him. But my good Jewish fiancée started with, "How can you do that to your father?" She couldn't imagine treating her father that way. By the second call, he was raining tears and even worse off. Between the two of them, I ended up agreeing to go back. She gave up her job, I gave up my job, and off we flew to the East Coast where we took over running his business for six months. That was her real first experience with him, and at this point he was drunk almost all the time. And the astonishing thing is that we didn't realize it.

The building that the business had been in was burned to the ground. Our home was still there. My mother had left him. He was sleeping in a hotel, using that for his office. All the files were smoke-filled and burned, and there we were trying to sort out the mess. Mother had gone to my sister's to stay. Not really left him for good, but just couldn't stand it anymore.

On an average day, he would be there when we got in at 8:00 in the morning. At 9:00, he would go into the closet for some coffee, and he would come out with this clear liquid in his coffee cup and wander around drinking his "coffee." He would have about four or five of those clear coffees, and he'd get pretty strange. We would go out for lunch, and he would drink four Scotches with a glass of milk because he was sure the glass of milk would keep the Scotches from affecting him. He'd pinch waitresses on the bottom, talk at the top of his lungs about the conspiracy in town to do in his company, and how no-good the goddamn police chief was. He would just go on and on about whatever topic was on his mind, and I would sit there embarrassed to death, wanting to crawl under the table.

We would get him back to work, and if he lasted that long, he would call up the chief of police and announce that there was a plot. Occasionally, he'd called the newspaper to say, "I want to have an interview and tell you about the conspiracy of the bankers in this community." Then he would pass out. We would call the newspaper back and explain that he didn't really want to have an interview that day. Then we would conduct the day's business and the next day it would start all over again. It was crazy.

My fiancée was sane enough to say, "What are we doing in this situation? This is horrible!" But I never really focused on the drinking as the problem. I still had this idea that he was a paranoid schizophrenic because I was a psychologist, that he was a seriously psychotic man, who just happened to drink a lot. It did not occur to me that the two things were connected, his bizarre behavior and his drinking.

We stayed for six months until his drinking moderated enough so that he could function. We got the business rebuilt, moved it into a new building, and I got out of there. I was at least sane enough to do that.

I started to look for work and there was an opening at an alcoholism treatment center for group therapist. I needed work. We wanted to get married. I walked in for the interview, and ten minutes after I was there I realized how comfortable I felt, what a neat place it was, and the interview hadn't even started.

Everybody was laughing and hugging and yelling at each other, talking about how they felt—all the things that didn't happen in my family. It just looked like a great place to work. It was in an old hotel that had sixty-five recovering alcoholics in it. Turns out it was one of the oldest and best treatment centers in the United States. Ironically, it was only about ten miles from the town where I grew up.

I interviewed with these people, and every one of them interviewed me. I had ten interviews. I sat in on a staff meeting. I really wanted to work there. They told me that I didn't know anything about alcoholism and that I would have to go through the patient's recovery program for twenty-eight days as a patient. I agreed. It was amazing; I loved it! It just felt wonderful. I could relate to those people, the recovering alcoholics. They spoke my language. I got help from the group, I got help from my counselor, and I could never figure out why I fit in so well when I'm not an alcoholic.

I never did feel comfortable working with crazy people: the psychotics and neurotics of the world. They always seemed so strange to me. But those recovering alcoholics felt like my people. And I still didn't know my father was an alcoholic. Still didn't make that connection. I worked there on the counseling staff for about four years while my father got worse. My mother joined Al-Anon.

I didn't have a program at this point. I didn't think I had anything wrong with me anymore, so I didn't need a program like the people there in recovery. I had been through three years of analysis, I had twenty-eight days of treatment behind me. I had a wonderful wife, I was the counselor. I finally had a good job.

I knew about the Twelve Steps and had gone through the first five steps during the twenty-eight days of treatment. But because I was not an alcoholic and did not yet understand that I was the child of an alcoholic, I didn't see any reason to go any further than I went in those twenty-eight days. How strong denial can be is pretty astonishing. I was still blind about my own family. That's pretty typical though.

I had been there for four years when my father called me and said, "If I had a drinking problem, would you know someone who I could talk to, who might help?" I was amazed.

My brother had joined Alcoholics Anonymous two years before that. He's been sober for many, many years now. He had taken off hitchhiking back and forth across the United States about fifteen times, taking acid and drinking beer when he couldn't get acid. He was really a mess, and we had all decided that he was crazy. Somewhere in there, he joined AA and got sober and turned out not to be crazy at all. My father had been watching him get sober for the last two years. Periodically, he'd make remarks like, "Boy, if I ever had a problem with drinking, it sure is good to know where to go, because Jack's really doing all right."

When he called me and asked for help, I got one of the folks who worked at the treatment center to go talk to him. He took him to his first AA meeting, and then they put him in detox. Withdrawal from alcohol can be dangerous. After he dried out, he became active in AA and has been sober ever since. That was almost ten years ago.

When he went into AA, I began to tell myself and other people that he was an alcoholic. I had been unable to know that until then. I just never thought about it. If anyone had ever stopped me in a hallway and said, "Do you think your father is an alcoholic?", I would have said, "Yes, of course he is." But no one ever asked me, and so I never thought about it. I didn't want to think about my father. My way of being in denial is indirect. It's not like the kind where you get presented with a fact and then just sit there denying it. I just don't think about things that are uncomfortable. They just don't come up. It was uncomfortable to think about my father so I just didn't think about him or his drinking. Whether or not he was an alcoholic just never came up.

The denial continued. Now that I knew that he was an alcoholic, I still didn't go to Al-Anon. And there I was working as an alcoholism counselor where I would sit with families on a daily basis and say to the wife, for example, "Now you understand that your husband is in here for treatment for the disease of alcoholism. That doesn't mean that you don't need to do some recovery work too. You're sick as well; you have been seriously affected by this disease. You need to go to Al-Anon. It's for the friends and relatives of alcoholics. It's not enough for him to go to AA, you need something for yourself as well. I'll set you up with an Al-Anon contact. There are the meetings in your area. Please make sure you go to these meetings."

If anybody had ever asked me why I didn't go, I wouldn't have had an answer. Then I went to a training workshop in Minnesota, and everybody there was in Al-Anon except me. I was embarrassed, so I decided to go. That first meeting was really powerful. It was not a special meeting in particular, but there I was, the only man in a room with nineteen women. Here I was the professional with all my education, my counseling experience, and so forth, and these women were just talking about themselves and their spiritual life, about their feelings, and I realized that these people are about one hundred times better off than I am. I can see that I am a mess, that I am depressed most of the time, and that I'm terribly anxious again. I had started to pick at my marriage even though the marriage was a very good marriage. I had started to think that maybe I should change wives, maybe I should change jobs, maybe I should move. I never had a reason for any of these feelings, but I was just more and more dissatisfied with who I was and where

I was. I started looking around and realizing that these people had what I needed. So that got me started in Al-Anon, driving thirty miles a night to get to a meeting. I didn't want to go to the meetings where all the patients I was working attended.

When I started the program, nobody talked about sponsors, nobody talked about working the steps. It was more just a fellowship thing for me. I just needed to be with people, and I was very frightened to talk about myself. I was very self-conscious. The people were really good to me. They accepted me as I was and let me come out of myself very slowly. I was in Al-Anon about two years when somebody decided to start an adult children's group.

I was starting to get something out of Al-Anon, really starting to feel better, and it took at least two years of meetings. It took me about a year to begin to talk easily in meetings. It took me three years before I got from the First to the Second Step. It was a long time before I could even begin to trust that there was something in the world that was good. My fear of the world, my fear of people, my fear of everything, particularly God, was so great that I had to be in Al-Anon for two years before I could consider that maybe there is higher power. Maybe there is something to this whole program.

When the meeting for Adult Children of Alcoholics started, we had four people. Within eight weeks there were over thirty-five members. There was a tremendous rush, an unspoken need that was suddenly addressed when all these people from Al-Anon and AA sat down together to talk about experiences they'd never brought up in AA or in Al-Anon.

Then we moved, and I wasn't active in Al-Anon or ACA for some time. I couldn't find a meeting I was comfortable in. I still had trouble reaching out to people, so I floundered. I kept going to meetings where they didn't reach out to the newcomer, and that was hard. Finally we moved across the country to a city where there were ACA meetings going on all over the place, and Al-Anon as well. The meetings were tremendously vibrant. People really got you involved, so I started back into both programs.

Within the last four years the Adult Children of Alcoholics has begun to change as far as I can tell. In the beginning, it was a broad mixture of everybody who was working a Twelve-Step program, whether AA or Al-Anon, who also needed to look at what we called adult children's issues. When we moved cross-country, I found a lot of people in meetings who didn't go to another Twelve-Step group. ACA was their only group. They seemed sicker. They were people with tremendously painful stories that were locked into their pain and unable to get out of it. They were very sincere and attempted to work the program, but they were lost and unwilling to go to a regular Al-Anon meeting and unwilling to go to AA, which some of them clearly needed to do. I found myself gravitating toward the regular Al-Anon meetings. For the first time, I was able to hear that I needed a sponsor. It still took me months to ask someone to sponsor me, but I did.

We moved a couple more times until we finally settled down in our present home. Fortunately, there are some terrific meetings here. I did another Fourth Step at the encouragement of my sponsor, and a Fifth Step again. I began to make amends to people, beginning to do things you're supposed to do to "work" the program after being in it for five years. There was part of me that was unable or unwilling to sink my teeth into the program. Part of that is Al-Anon itself. Al-Anon didn't give me the message the way AA gives you the message. In AA people are a lot more outspoken. If you don't have a sponsor and you've been in the program for a while, people will tell you to get one. They'll tell you to get to work on your Fourth Step. It's a different side of the disease. They don't do that in Al-Anon. In AA your life is at stake. In Al-Anon, your life may be at stake but it's more subtle, not so obvious physically.

Now I've found a tremendously good Al-Anon group that reads the Twelve Traditions every meeting, has a Traditions meeting every month, works the steps, tells people to get sponsors, and I have really done very well there. It's done very well for me. I have a new sponsor. I still tend to be a workaholic. I am very successful at what I do, so it's easy for me to get strokes there. It's much harder for me to make friends. It's much harder for me to be by myself and just do nothing. Part of my addition is an addiction to activity. I think I was in Al-Anon four years before I understood what they meant by serenity. Sitting and being quiet is tremendously difficult for me. I am only just starting to get some of that. I have been praying and meditating every day for six years, and I think this year is the only year I have really started to experience some peace and some real belief in a God. I feel like the sixth year in the program is the first year I have really had any level of comfort. And I have worked pretty hard to get to that point. I think that I've had a long way to go. I've seen a lot of others get lost, quit, not follow through on the issues. It's a temptation; progress in this program can be very slow.

A certain amount of time just has to pass. There are no shortcuts to the process of recovery. Nobody gets better overnight. To summarize: I got into therapy when I was 20, had three years of analysis, followed by twenty-eight days of treatment, three family weeks, six years of Al-Anon, and ten years of working in the field. The work itself has been therapeutic because you are sharing experiences with other people who are recovering. That represents a lot of work, and I really think I've only been moderately comfortable in the last year. And I've got a long way to go. I don't think I'm particularly unusual; I'm just being realistic.

I thought I understood all the issues in recovery from the alcoholic family system in the first three months. When I was asked to share at a meeting, I shared what I could and then I'd explain it all to you. I'm sure there were people there who wished that I would shut up and grow up, but it was the best I could do at that point. Some of the worst offenders are people like myself who have degrees in psychology or are MSWs or marriage and family counselors.

It was easy in the beginning to confuse an understanding of the structure with getting well. Those are two entirely different things. You have to come to the understanding and willingness to know that this process takes a lot of time. I thought because I understood the structure of the program and could give you an answer, that meant that I was getting well.

I went into psychology because I wanted to help people. At the time, I had no idea how I wanted to help other people because I was too sick to begin to know what to do about myself. I was co-dependent, completely focused on everyone else's behavior but my own. Many people are drawn to the helping professions for those same sick reasons, in all innocence. Recently I did a presentation to a group of people in the War on Rape program. It was to the counselors who were working with rape victims. I started talking about adult child issues and what happens in the alcoholic family, and twenty minutes into the lecture, everyone in the room was in tears. They had just fallen apart, saying things like, "I didn't know I was a child of an alcoholic," or "You are talking about my family, my God, it was horrible. I need to tell you what happened." I've had that happen with nurses, all sorts of people. The whole room falls apart. It happens to anybody who routinely does presentations to any group of helpers. By the end of the presentation, half the room will be in tears if they haven't dealt with these issues. We know there are a tremendous number of ACAs in the helping professions. They have no awareness at all of the fact they are adult children or how that affects them and continues to run their life, affecting their careers, their relationships, everything.

I am an example of somebody who got addicted to their role in the family. I am totally addicted to being a hero because that's how I learned to feel good. I have to work on this all the time. When I was absolutely alone as a child and frightened to death, there was one thing that I could do that made me feel better and that was to produce something that my parents recognized as good. Then I got a pat on the head, was praised and rewarded, and that has stuck with me. If I am not working my Al-Anon program and getting to meetings, and I start to feel frightened or insecure and shy, I will be pulled toward performance. Part of me will want to do that, and it's a very unhealthy way to deal with the world. You push people away and show off, whether it's to get good grades or please your supervisor at work. In any case, you end up alienating the people around you in order to be number one, the top dog. It feels good in the short run, but it never lasts.

Being in Al-Anon meetings that are focused specifically on adult children is powerful. When I'm in the regular Al-Anon meetings, I have to make a translation of everything because they are mostly wives of alcoholics and somewhat older than me. Not too many men, whereas in the ACA meetings there are men my own age with the same kind of experiences I had.

When I'm with people who are talking about their feelings, it makes me blossom because that's something I lived without my whole life. I go to at least one Al-Anon meeting a week, and I sponsor an Alateen group one night a week. The progress I've made has been slow and painstaking, like I've told you, but I'm glad I did it this way. I don't know where I would have been without the Al-Anon program and the Steps. I'm glad it's taken me six years to get to this point. I finally feel at home.

5. Marion P.

Marion is Gloria's younger sister (see story following). I interviewed the two sisters together and additional comments from Marion are included toward the end of Gloria's story.

I was raised by two alcoholic parents. My father died when I was 18 from acute alcoholism. He got sober only one time that I can remember. He was in AA for a week and I can remember how happy I was that Dad was sober! It was the very first time I remember him being that way and I was thrilled. I was 13. It didn't last. We went on a family vacation, and I knew on the way that Dad was going to drink. I could just feel the buildup happening. Then when he did drink, I knew that he was gone—that's it. It was really bad. I was crushed. He never got sober again.

Mom started to get sober when I was 11, and it took her a while. When I was 13, she finally got sober and stayed sober. She's been sober twenty-one years now. I'm 34 years old, the second of four children.

There was conflict all the time at home. Dad would just yell and scream at Mom. There was never any physical violence, but there was this terrible yelling. I would lie in my bed, night after night, not being able to sleep because Dad was screaming at Mom, taunting her, making fun of her—"Can't you even play cards, Molly?"—being really loud. Somehow I understood that it was the alcohol even as a kid, and I knew that if they didn't drink, the fighting wouldn't be going on. I promised myself I would never, ever drink.

One of my earliest memories is of coming home from school and sometimes finding my mom passed out on the couch. I took care of Mom and protected her from Dad. Since I started looking at the fact that I'm an adult child of alcoholics, I've gone back into the family photo albums. In the pictures I'm always with Mom protecting her from Dad. The rest of the kids are always together. The separation is obvious. I remember that feeling of needing to protect my mother very strongly. I loved my father very much, too, it's just that I always knew that he was sick.

Dad had the kind of presence that would fill a room. He was very magnetic. Mom and Dad were both very outgoing people. People looked up to my parents. We were voted "Family of the Year." Mom was always head of one thing or another, and Dad would be running for state office. They were politically prominent and very well liked. There was always some kind of activity going on over at our house. Dad was active in sports; he was a successful businessman; they had four beautiful children—they had it all. That's how it looked on the outside. Nobody ever thought there could be anything wrong with our family.

I was always getting into trouble. People just thought, "Poor Bill and Molly," for having to put up with me. I'm the second child, and I was the scapegoat. I was getting picked up for shoplifting, called into every principal's office in every school I ever attended. I was in their offices more than I was in the classroom. Everybody always said, "You're so good-looking, and you have so much going for you, why are you so bad?" I didn't know. I didn't have a clue. I just thought I was a bad person. This went on from the time I started grade school. Right from the get-go. I can remember stealing when I was 6 years old and not knowing why I did it. I didn't need to do it.

When I was older, I remember Dad coming and picking me up at the police station. The chief of police knew my family quite well, so they wouldn't book me. They just called my parents to come get me. This was the big cover-up. So Dad comes to get me, and he's half in the bag. I could always tell. He's got his Clorets in his pocket and he comes and just looks at me. I was sitting there petrified. I still had some of the stuff that I'd stolen on me—they hadn't found it all. I was scared to death they were going to find the rest of the junk. Dad was huge (6'3", 240 pounds), and he comes in and starts saying, "Why did you do this? Don't I give you everything you want?" To myself I thought, "Yes, everything but what I need." I needed him and when he drank, he just wasn't there, and I knew that. I was 12 then.

Then Mom comes in and she's crying and upset. So that time they sent me to a psychiatrist. I would go to my appointment, and all I did was cry. I don't remember getting a word out. I just cried for an hour straight. After the third time I went, the psychiatrist talked to my mom and dad instead. My mother has told me since that what happened was that the psychiatrist really got on my dad's case and just said, "Your daughter's fine. You two are the ones that have a problem." That wasn't too well received.

When I was younger, my mom took me to some kind of meeting at my grade school where they talked about alcoholism in the family. I don't know how old I was. We were pretty young kids. I just remember the man who talked to us; he said things that made me feel wonderful, gave me some hope. I left the meeting and went right up to my mom with the good news: "He says that the reason I'm always getting in trouble so much has to do with your drinking." She was not ready to hear that! She became hysterically angry and said, "That's bullshit. It's not that, it's you!" That's before she got into AA.

But I had heard hope there, hope that I wasn't a hopelessly screwed-up kid, that what was going on with me had something to do with my family. The family interaction that was going on was really awful. Whenever I got into trouble, it was always thrown back in my face how much money Dad was making and what important people they were in town. "How can you say things aren't OK?" they'd ask.

All four of my grandparents were alcoholics. It's on both sides of my family. My father's mother died when he was born, and evidently she had a problem with alcohol. His father had a drinking problem and quit, found religion; I don't know how old Dad was when that happened. My mother's mother was a periodic alcoholic until she died. It was kind of a joke on holidays how Gramma would have her stash in the bedroom. She would just get more and more tipsy as the evening went on, and nobody would ever confront her.

The wild thing is that my mother never knew her real father. But just two months ago, my mother's niece found my mom's father—just looked him up in a phone book. The end result of that was that he called my mom. As they were talking, Mom told him that she was a recovering alcoholic, and the amazing thing was that he said that he was too, and it turns out that he has the same amount of sobriety as my mother, the same exact time, twenty-one years right down to the month. They both got sober at the same time. Isn't that too much?

We were always told some story about him that never made much sense. My maternal grandmother lived in the Midwest with her husband and they had one son, my mom's older brother. When Gramma was pregnant with my mom, she came out to the Coast to be with her family who had moved two years earlier. She came out without her husband, my grandfather. The story goes that when he came out on the train, my grandmother's father and uncle met him with a shotgun and told him not to bother to get off. We were never told why. My mom said that in her entire life, her mother might have talked to her about her real father for about ten minutes. Grandma remarried. My stepgrandpa, who was always Grandpa to me, was a violent alcoholic.

When I was pregnant with my first child, I went to the doctor, and there was a family history form I was supposed to fill out on the back of the card. I put grandfather, deceased—alcoholism; grandmother—alcoholic; mother—alcoholic; father—alcoholic. There was this list of about ten people, all alcoholics, some deceased, some recovering, some not recovering. I went home after my checkup, and within a couple of hours the doctor called and said, "Did you understand this form?" I said yes. She was concerned when she saw all the alcoholism in our family, and I had neglected to put down that my husband and I, the baby's parents, were in recovery, that we were no longer practicing alcoholics. Our family is just riddled with alcoholism. I'm real interested in the stuff that's coming out now; you hear a lot of people talking about one alcoholic parent, but we're talking two alcoholic parents, four alcoholic grandparents. My husband's mother and father were both alcoholics. So what kind of predisposition do my children have to alcoholism?

There was something I remember about being in grade school: Whenever my mom came to school, I was ashamed. It was strange, because all the other mothers would come in their polyester pants and just be normal, no makeup, maybe even a vinyl purse. But here comes my mom just decked out to the max, mink collars, pillbox hats, makeup, just been to the beauty parlor, and I would be mortified. I thought, "Can't you just be normal?" I can still remember her walking in and thinking,

"Oh gosh, she's here." I thought maybe she'd get drunk and not show up. It was always that way. I can still remember it.

I was very active in grade school in school plays and school activities, but nobody from my family ever showed up. I had the lead part in the school musical when I was in the sixth grade; it was really a big deal. I was thrilled! I can remember performing in the play and thinking that my whole family was out there watching me. Then after the play there was a coffee and cake party. I went backstage to change and come out, and discovered that there was nobody from my family there. I was crushed. I went home really upset thinking, "Why didn't anybody come?" But I didn't say a word. We don't talk about the fact that nobody showed up. Mom just acted like nothing happened. Finally I said, "Well, what did you do today?" Turns out that Dad had been hospitalized again for alcoholism. Nobody came to my graduation either; I don't know why. So I knew that something was real different about our family, and I distinctly remember *not* talking about it to other people.

When I was in eighth grade, I was in the "Evening Frolics." To my surprise, my dad, who had never participated in anything as far as the girls went, came to pick my girlfriend and me up. I was in junior high, about 13. The place was closing down and Dad still wasn't there. My friend and I are sitting out on the front steps. I'm so used to this kind of waiting by then, that I'd just wait and wait forever, until somebody shows up to get me. Finally Dad shows up and he's smashed and I'm thinking, "Oh, God." My best friend who is with me pretty much knows the situation, but we have never talked about it. I just didn't bring people home for a long time because Mom might be passed out or Dad was drunk or they were fighting, or something weird was going on. So Dad comes to pick us up, and I'm surprised that it's Dad for some reason; I don't know why Dad's picking me up. We get in the car; it's probably a fifteen-minute drive home, and the whole way home, he's saying, "Goddamn it, doesn't anybody else have parents? Why am I the goddamned taxi driver?" I'm just sitting in the backseat stone-cold pissed, and I don't say a word all the way home. He just goes on and on. Finally we get home, and my girlfriend looks at me and she says, "I have never seen my dad drunk." I didn't believe her. I did not believe that that was possible. I thought, "You're lying." I thought everybody's parents were like my parents. I still thought for years afterwards that she was lying, but now I know she was telling the truth—she had never seen her dad intoxicated. That was the only way I saw my dad.

It was about that time that I started drinking myself. We stole some port wine from somebody's house and went to a gas station bathroom and drank it. I can remember loving it from the very beginning. It took away the pain. It filled the hole I had inside me, made me feel that I could be anything I wanted to be, do anything I wanted to do, be the life of the party. Alcohol took away all the shame and guilt and remorse that I felt. I drank on weekends from then on, Friday or Saturday nights. I was still juvenile delinquent material, stealing and acting out. But then my dad was still drinking, but my mom was sober. Nobody knew I was drinking and smoking cigarettes. Mom and Dad were getting a divorce, and so everyone was focused on their situation. We kids were pretty much on our own. We each went our individual ways. We weren't like a pack; we didn't stick together. We all had our safe homes that we went to, our safe friends that we would talk to.

There was never a teacher or a probation officer, anybody, who ever said to me, "Hey, what's going on at home? Something bothering you?" It was always poor Molly and Bill with this child who's a delinquent. "What are we going to about Marion?" I was on probation for years for stealing. I still have a lot of shame about that; it was pretty bad. I was ripping off anybody, going into homes where I knew nobody was there and just ripping off the house. I don't know why. I didn't need anything. Screaming for love. So Mom got sober, and Dad and Mom separated, and he started living in an old hotel downtown. He was getting really bad, wino material. I wanted to take care of him so badly. I felt sorry for him. Mom got all the kids and the house—everything, it looked like to me—and what about Dad? I wanted to go live with him in the hotel and take care of him, pick up the wine bottles. Whenever I would go see him, it made me very sad. After a while he remarried, a real co-alcoholic. She was pretty sick herself, but she took care of him until he died. He died when he was 45.

Forty-five seems really young to me now, but at the time, he seemed ancient to me. I was with him the week before he died.

I went to be with him for two weeks. He had blood vessels popped all over his face, his stomach looked nine months pregnant. He was really sick. He was drunk all the time, that sad kind of drunk, just a drinking-to-stay-alive kind of drunk. I can remember praying to God to just let him die when I left. Two nights before I left, we were looking through a scrapbook of his from the days when he was very prominent and when he was a sports star. He started crying. I didn't know what to do. I wanted to fix it, I wanted to get him sober, I wanted to do it for him, but I couldn't. He just sat there and wept. I was 18 then and drinking myself. I didn't know why he couldn't get sober, because it was obvious that the pain that he was living in was worse than dying. I said, "God, if you can't get him sober, then let him die. This is awful." He died.

It's like I hit a wall with grief. I can't cry any more tears, but I still love him so much. I guess the thing that makes me sad is he never got to meet his grandkids, never got to know his children. He never got to find out what neat people we all are. The pain that alcoholism causes in families is devastating.

After the funeral there was a big party where all his cronies got drunk. I'm 18 years old and I'm standing there saying to myself, "Don't you see what happened?" I knew. All his sports friends, his business associates, over three hundred people were there. They had rented a hotel ballroom. You would have thought it was a wedding. They didn't see all the pain that the alcohol caused. All they saw was this gregarious, wonderful person who drank. He was their crony, and they were looking at him from a totally different perspective. A lot of those men have since gotten into trouble with their own alcoholism, so absolutely they were not going to look at Dad's death as having anything to do with his drinking. "He worked too hard," they'd say. "Bill moved in the fast lane. He experienced in a short period of time what most people won't experience in a lifetime." What did he get to experience? He got to experience being a sports star, selling a million dollars worth of products, and becoming an alcoholic, but he never got to know his own family. He never got to experience love.

Growing up in an alcoholic home, I never learned how to express feelings, never even knew when I was having feelings. But now I'm working on those issues and learning how to become intimate. I feel really lucky to be in recovery. I can get angry at Mom to this day about her alcoholism and what happened and wasn't this awful, but there's a much bigger part of me that's so thankful that she got sober and she found AA, and consequently, that I got to AA when I got to AA. Now I have the opportunity to even go a step beyond in learning about my feelings and pass that on to my kids, so that this disease doesn't keep going from generation to generation to generation. At least I hope I can play a part in stopping it in my family.

Like so many ACAs, I married a child of an alcoholic as well. He's still out there doing drugs and alcohol, though he was more of a drug addict than an alcoholic. The big thing we had in common was drinking and taking drugs, and that's how we went around the world. That was our whole marriage; it lasted two years. He was dropping acid daily, and I was wondering why we weren't having this intimate relationship.

When I was still at home at 18 years old, I would read the *Grapevine*, the Alcoholics Anonymous newsletter, and just cry and cry. I could relate so much to what they were talking about. I felt so sorry for "those poor people" and was unable to see the alcoholism in my own life. After Mom got sober, we always had lots of AA literature around the house. I especially remember reading the twenty questions about drinking when I was 18 and passing the test for being an alcoholic with flying colors. They say that if you answer any three of the twenty questions yes, that there's a good chance that you're an alcoholic. I think I answered all of them yes except for the one that asks if you've killed anybody. I remember thinking that AA must really be hard up to make up a list of questions that are so easy that anybody can be an alcoholic. I thought, "Well, if I'm an alcoholic, anybody can be one." I really believed that. That was how I denied my own developing alcoholism.

After she got sober, Mom's answer to everybody's problems was to tell them to go to an AA meeting: "You're an alcoholic." I said, "Mom, *everybody* can't be an alcoholic," but the truth was that everybody that *we* knew was.

Then things started happening pretty fast for me. I was blacking out all the time, at 18 years old, blacking out almost every time I drank. The first time I drank, I blacked out, and I thought at first that that happened to everybody. Then I started asking people if they could remember last night, and they said yes. Well, I couldn't remember what I did. I would end up in weird places with weird people and not know how I got there. I couldn't relate to myself as an alcoholic because I didn't get like Mom. I didn't pass out. I didn't have to drink all day and I didn't have to drink every day, but that's only because I did a lot of speed and cocaine. I could stay awake.

At the end, I was doing drugs twenty-four hours a day, all day long, and denying I was an alcoholic because I wasn't drinking all day. I was taking ten hits of speed in the morning to get up and a couple of Quaaludes at night to get to sleep. I remember a TV commercial about alcoholism that showed a mother lying on the couch with a bottle of vodka on the coffee table. There were bottles of prescription pills and an ashtray full of cigarette butts, smoke hanging in the air. I was shocked. "That's my mother" I thought, but the trick was, it was me. I couldn't see that yet. I could only see Mom. I couldn't see what was happening to me.

I started to see that I drank differently than the other people I was with because of the blackouts. People started not wanting to be with me when I drank. I was very alcoholic from the start. Finally my first husband left. I didn't come home one night, and when I walked in the next morning, he said "OK, good-bye." He packed his suitcase and he was gone. I was devastated.

I called Mom and said, "Mom, I'm crazy, I'm insane, and I want help. I want you to do something, but don't take me to one of those goddamn AA meetings." I said, "I need you to come, I need help, but just please don't take me to AA." I had just turned 23. It was January. So she came up. She didn't know at that time if I was alcoholic or not. I never drank around my mother, never ever, because I knew if I did, she'd have my number. She used to say, "Well, if any one of you kids are going to become alcoholic, it's going to be you." "Not me," I'd say. After she got sober, she went to work in the field of alcoholism and she knew a lot about the disease. But I set out to prove her wrong. "You can't drink, but I can," I would tell her. Well, she came up like I asked, and before I knew it, she had me at an AA meeting. Everybody was twice as old as me. There were some women there, not too many. It was in some basement. But I went and I felt wonderful after the meeting. I don't remember anything anybody said. I just remember having this immense hope and knowing that this is it, this is my problem—alcohol. I felt like I fit in some place for the first time, I belonged. My husband came back home, and we were going to work things out. I decided that I was fine and that I was never going to drink again. I didn't think I needed to go to AA meetings. The next morning, there was an AA Big Book on my doorstep and a Twelve-by-Twelve and a Twenty-Four-Hour book, and I stayed sober. I don't know how long I stayed sober, I think about three months on my own. I was still going to all the keggers, all the parties, still doing all the stuff I did before, just not drinking or going to AA meetings. I did cocaine and a few other drugs, but alcohol was my drug of choice. I liked alcohol. I never liked marijuana, so that was no big deal. A friend of my husband's came into town and said, "Let's go out," and after three months of not drinking, I ordered a drink at dinner. I don't know why. There was no support for *not* drinking. I remember being in a bar in the middle of the night, slipping into a blackout and watching myself go into it. I can still remember it, and just going, "Oh God, here we go." The next morning both of them said to me, "See, you're not an alcoholic. You did fine." I said, "You didn't feel what I felt inside." Maybe I behaved all right, but I remembered one bar where I was sneaking and ordering doubles, because they weren't drinking fast enough for me. I felt this awful guilt and remorse, and that was what really got me to want to stay sober, just terrible remorse the morning after.

I called Mom again. She was leaving for an AA world convention and she said, "Come on, you're going." She just put me on the plane. I had a purse full of pills because I knew I couldn't drink around Mom. I remember taking two on the airplane; I don't even know what they were. When we got there, we were in a huge city with thousands of other recovering alcoholics. Mom walked right into the young people's dance, right up to the people that she wanted me to meet. She just turned me over to them. I stayed with them for the entire time I was there, and I've been sober ever since. That was well over ten years ago. So I never went back to my husband. I got a divorce and hung in with AA.

When I was three years sober, I remarried. He's also a recovering alcoholic and has a Ph.D. He's very different from me.

I had three criteria for my second husband: He had to be in AA, he had to believe in God, and he had to have a job. He was the director for a center that I went to work for. He believed in God, and he had the same amount of sobriety that I had. We met and six weeks later we got married. He was ten years older than me.

He started telling me that I had a problem with communication not too long into the relationship, that he wasn't getting enough from me. My response was basically, "Fuck you. You want intimacy, go find it. This is all you're going to get." That was my response. "You don't like me the way I am? Good-bye." So immediately, things started getting difficult. But being a typical ACA, I just rode the waves. I didn't cause any friction, didn't cause any problems, didn't rock the boat. We just started going our separate ways.

Then all hell broke loose after nine years of my sobriety. I was fired from a job I had for eleven years and my husband walked out on me, all within the same week. We have kids that we both absolutely adore. I was devastated. I probably hadn't been to an AA meeting in six months. I started going back to AA. I had hit rock bottom emotionally. So I packed up the kids and moved back home and was going to start over. As soon as I started getting my feet on the ground, Rob came back into the picture and wanted to work things out. At first I said no. I just didn't want to try again. He started going to therapy, and then his therapist called me and said, "I'd like to see you. I understand that you and Rob are separated. I think I could help make things easier. I don't have anything invested in you two getting back together. I just think that I could be helpful." I saw him that day and I absolutely loved him from the very first minute. He was neat, warm, communicated wonderfully, and confronted me at the right times. I left feeling great. About a month into that, I decided, well, maybe Rob and I should try to make things work. It didn't work after all, and now we're separated for good.

Going to the therapist helped me see that my husband was right—I was incapable of being intimate. I had walls that were miles thick from all the issues from my childhood that I had never dealt with. I didn't realize that. Nine years into my sobriety, I didn't realize that what people were getting from me was just the surface. Underneath, I always felt like if I really shared myself, they wouldn't like me. I always felt there was something really bad about me. I could go to AA and give these wonderful speeches and talk about how wonderful life was and I believed it, but what I didn't realize was that the level of feelings that I was speaking from was about one-inch thick.

Having gone to therapy and started to work on some of these issues, it's like a whole other world has opened up for me. My family notices the differences, my friends notice the difference. I'm going, "Well, how am I any different now than I was two years ago?" because I don't see the change, but people are talking about it. I'm starting to share feelings.

When I first started going to therapy, I discovered that I was really mad at Mom. It was like somebody washed my glasses. You know you don't see what you aren't seeing until you see it. I got catapulted into another dimension. My husband couldn't get enough from me, and I didn't know that. That was all there was at that time. But now it's changing. My self-esteem was about a quarter-inch high and I had no ego whatsoever. So for the last one-and-a-half years, I've been working on self-acceptance, letting myself be all right just the way I am. My defenses were so strong because I thought if you got to know me, you wouldn't like me. If you really saw who I was, you would see what an awful person I was. So I just gave you what I could give and what I thought you wanted.

I've turned my Mom on to ACA. She is hesitant about it still, but she's starting to listen. She knows that she's an adult child of an alcoholic too. My sponsor in AA is also an ACA. She's the one that turned me on to some of the workshops I've done in ACA that have been so powerful. She's active in ACA, Al-Anon, and AA. I go to probably five AA meetings a week and about one ACA meeting a week, and I continue to go to therapy once a week. I go to lots of conferences. Now that I've been sober ten-and-a-half years, I'm interested in nutrition and exercise and how that affects my sobriety today. When I first got sober, I did not believe that I was hypoglycemic. There was all this talk about alcoholism and hypoglycemia going around, and today I know that I am. I have sugar and I'm gone—it's just like being intoxicated. I like being around people who are positive and want to continue growing and are willing to take risks.

When I started ACA meetings, I was still going to AA meetings at eight years sober, judging everyone like mad, being so negative and not even realizing it, thinking everyone was that way. What I realize is I'm not that way today, and the reason is that I'm not so judgmental about me. That's because of ACA. I can remember the day I was sitting in an AA meeting and people were walking in and I was thinking positive thoughts, for a change, and not negative thoughts, because I was feeling positive about me. It was like my God, what a difference. I remember sharing that day. I am learning to like other people because I'm learning to like me.

I guess the thing I'm most excited about is having feelings. I know there's a long way to go for me. I know that because of just the little bit that I've done. Just being able to feel and acknowledge the fears is wonderful progress for me. One of the main things that happens to me when I get in an uncomfortable situation is that I freeze. My mind goes blank, my body freezes. I may look good, but I am frozen. A day later, I'll think of something I should have said or a response or something I could have done. What my therapist says is that as I become more comfortable and able to simply acknowledge what I'm feeling when I'm feeling it, I'll be able to respond at the appropriate time. That hasn't happened much yet. At least now with my family, I am able to say, "Boy, when you say that, it hurts my feelings." How different that is than always being angry, than saying, "Well, the hell with you!" That was my reaction to everything and everybody, and that's changing today.

6. Gloria D.

Gloria is Marion's older sister. I interviewed the two sisters together and additional comments from Marion are included toward the end.

As the oldest child in the family, I have a very different perspective than the other kids. I had more years with our parents before their drinking got out of control. I'm 38 now and there were four years in between my birth and Marion's. There was another child born two years after me who died right after birth. I don't have any recollection of that at all. I don't even remember seeing my mother pregnant until my brother came along nine years after me.

The memories that I do have are funny. I remember being in a stroller going golfing with my father and having a bag of cookies. He was still in college. He had been in World War II, was going to college on the GI Bill, and my mother was working. I was the mascot of the campus. Everyone knew me and took care of me. I went to a lot of games to watch my dad play. He coached for a while as well. We lived in a small town.

My first recollection of being uncomfortable with alcohol was before age 5, at the first house that my parents bought. I can remember my mom and dad going out to dinner and leaving us with Grandma. It didn't take long for me to realize what was going on. I remember standing at the window, looking out, and thinking to myself, "Oh God, my Grandma's drunk again." By the time they came home, Grandma was snockered. I can even remember the dress she had on. It was blue and brown, horizontal stripes with a waist and three-quarter-length sleeves. I remember thinking that I hate it when my grandma drinks because she's not the same person. I don't remember my mom and dad being drunk at that time, though I'm sure they were. Mother was probably 26 or so at the time.

I was the family hero. While they were growing up, all my brothers and sisters had to listen to "Why can't you be like

Gloria?" I made straight A's and was very active in school. On the inside I felt that if anybody knew what was really going on here, they would kick us out of town. When I was in grade school, I remember wanting my mother to come to school for various activities and at the same time not wanting her to come because I wasn't sure what was going to happen. There was a facade that was put up for the community, but when it came down to showing up for us, my parents just weren't there. I don't ever remember my dad coming to anything. I always remember him leaving on Saturday and Sunday mornings with his golf clubs and wondering what was going to happen when he came home at night. Basically, his golfing was an excuse for him to go to the club and sit there all afternoon and play cards and drink. I think my mom felt like she'd like to be at the club partying with him but she was home with us.

The grade school years weren't too bad, I don't believe. I was never home. I had some wonderful friends. As I look back on it, I think that someone was watching out for me. There was a little girl across the alley from us that used to come and visit her grandparents in the summer and I spent a lot of time at her house. I have always been one to sit back and watch and take things in by osmosis. I remember doing that at her house. That's how I'd figure out how I'm supposed to behave or what I should do. I still do that. There was a lot of the stuff I just didn't know. I learned how to clean a house from the woman who was my mom's best friend. She was compulsive about cleaning. Unfortunately, she's still a practicing alcoholic. She used to hire me to come and help her when I was a kid. I've been around a lot of alcoholism, but I've never really acknowledge how it affected me.

When mom got sober and got through those first few months and early years, I thought that everybody would be OK. Her getting sober would fix our family. For years I never knew that anybody else had any problems. Even after Mom got sober, until Marion and another sister were in AA, I bet we didn't talk about anything, anything that went on in our family, let alone to each other at the time. We didn't talk about any of what happened in our family until three or four years ago. Our brother is still not real comfortable with discussing any of the past. He figures that it's gone and that's that.

When I was still at home, I always felt in conflict because I felt like I needed to be there for my younger sisters and brother, but I was just a kid too. I didn't want to be saddled with cooking and cleaning and taking care of all these little kids.

The school counselors knew what was going on in our family by the time I was in high school. My counselor knew my dad. They played golf together, and he knew that my dad was a drunk. When I went in to talk to him about going to college, his only question was, "How are you going to pay for this?" I knew what he was saying. He was saying, "Your dad's a drunk. How are you going to do this?" And I thought to myself, "You crumb, you're supposed to be here helping me," but I was too afraid to ask him for help. I didn't want him to know the truth, even though I knew that he knew. He was too close; it would have been easier for me to go to a stranger. We couldn't do anything in that town without everybody knowing. It was a small town and my family was very prominent. We'd break the eggshell and everybody would know. It would be just like having this runny egg yolk running all over the sidewalk, and our whole family's facade would be destroyed. I couldn't do it. This was back in the sixties. I don't think this counselor was actually trained then. He was a teacher who they pulled in to be a counselor. He really didn't know what he was doing. Not only did I not know how to ask for help, he didn't know what to do in the first place.

I remember my mom being more sick than drunk. She always had a lot of health problems. Of course when Valium came out, the response was, "God, these are great for Molly and her nervous condition. This will help her cope. We'll just give her these pills and she'll just be great. Poor Molly, she just can't keep up with Bill." That was the attitude.

When she was in her mid-30s, mom had stomach surgery and she almost died. She had lots of female problems, and I know now that probably a lot of her medical problems were directly caused by her use and abuse of alcohol and/or drugs. At that time no one realized that. To give her the level of sedation she needed for the stomach surgery, they had to sedate her so heavily that the doctor thought he might kill her. Well, that's because she was an addict, but nobody understood that. They just thought she had this really high tolerance. She was so out of it on all the medication that she kept pulling the tubes out of her nose, and at that time they were glass, not soft plastic. It was just awful and I remember. I was about 11 or 12. I remember not being able to go to the hospital after that to see her and feeling terribly guilty. I was physically not able to go see her.

Two or three years before she got sober, there was another episode that stands out in my mind. It was in the morning, before school. She was on some kind of medication that somehow I had the sense to dole out to her. She had had some kind of woman's problem. I didn't know what it was; I just knew I had to be careful with this medicine they gave her. I walked into her room and there she was, lying in a pool of blood on the bed, and there was smoke everywhere coming up out of the bed. She'd been smoking and set her bed on fire.

I put out the fire, changed her bed, changed her, cleaned up the blood, and went to school, like nothing had happened. We never talked about it. That was just par for the course, that's just what you did. You just took care of it and you didn't talk about it. I was in grade school then, probably in the seventh grade. A lot of my coping mechanism is simply not being able to remember a lot of things. They're just not in my memory bank. I have a real hard time with mornings now in my own house as an adult. I don't like people talking to me.

We had an aunt who came to live with us when she was in college. I just loved it when she was there, because there was this other person who was there for us and it wasn't so scary. I really looked up to her. She was cute; she was a cheerleader at college, a neat person.

I didn't realize how much fear I had growing up. It was unacknowledged at the time, but when I think about my aunt being there, I realize it. I'd go off with my friends to their place for the weekend, or I'd go off to camp for a week, or to the library with my friends, or just go to the neighbor's house. We had families all around us with kids my age. Kids didn't come to our house; I always went to their house. At younger ages, I can remember my mom trying to be a Blue Bird leader—my mom and her greatest drinking buddy, another mother. It was pretty difficult for them. Somehow I was able to separate my mom and dad both from their boozing personalities and their normal personalities, if there is such a thing. I always knew that if they wouldn't drink, that things would be OK. I liked being around them a lot better when they weren't drinking. And I remember times when my mom purposely would not drink. My mother never got drunk at Christmas, ever, because my dad always did. To this day when I hear "Silent Night," I just die inside. That song brings back so many painful memories. A couple of years ago I heard a song by John Denver, "Daddy Don't Get Drunk at Christmas," and I'll never listen to it again. I still can't listen to the theme song from *The Days of Wine and Roses* because that song and the movie were popular when my parents got divorced.

My parents forgot to tell me they were getting divorced. I read it in the paper. I was off with some of my friends when they sat down with the rest of the family to tell them, but they forgot I wasn't there. Dad put up a fight about the divorce. He was going to take us, he said, and they each were going to take us away from the other. In looking back now I think that I had more problems with that divorce than I did with their use of alcohol. Maybe I'm just trying not to see the alcoholism, but the divorce was really hard for me. I was in junior high.

Getting back to Christmas, what I remember so clearly was all the waiting. Everybody is all dressed up and waiting and waiting. In my mother's family we always did everything Christmas Eve, but in my dad's family they didn't, so somehow there was a compromise worked out and it always involved this interminable waiting. There was a big facade of happy-go-lucky feelings put out on my mother's part about Christmas; "Aren't you lucky? You've got millions of presents." But I remember now that there was a family that lived down the street with five kids, four daughters and a son, almost exactly the same as our ages. I knew that their dad made more money than my dad, although they were perhaps comparable. They never got as many presents as we did, and I never could figure that out. I always felt sorry for them, but maybe their parents weren't trying to make up to them for something else that was wrong.

The Christmas that I had the hardest time with was after my parents got divorced. It was the first year I was away from home at college and when I came back, they had sold the house. That was painful for me. It felt like my whole life history had just been flushed down the toilet. Selling the house was never discussed, never talked about with us. They just sold it and left.

Mom moved into a three-bedroom apartment, which sounds roomy but when you have four kids and they're all teenagers, it felt small. I slept on a hide-a-bed and felt very displaced.

Dad came over Christmas Day. It was so difficult for me to see my dad and mom together because I knew they both still loved each other. The power of their relationship was incredible, but we knew that unless my dad would stop drinking, there was no way my mom could be with him. She couldn't survive with him because she would drink too. I felt so sorry for him, my own dad, because here it was Christmas and he was all alone. We tried to make it a happy occasion, but he excused himself and we knew he was in the bathroom crying. I don't think he stayed for the meal; he just came to see us kids. He was so sick. This was almost twenty years ago now. We didn't know where to take him—who had heard of intervention? I think the problem he had with AA was that he was such a perfectionist that he couldn't believe that alcohol was going to lick him. Everything he ever did, he was the best at, tops. And he was the best alcoholic I ever knew. He died at 45, still working, still making a living, when his pancreas just exploded.

Part of the way I dealt with all the chaos and pain in my family was to eat. I was never super overweight, just heavy, and I'm already a tall person. I was taller than all the boys in the high school. The weight problem for me has been a self-esteem issue. Not too long ago I reached a point where I decided that I was tired of being tubby. The baggage is leaving, the weight is dropping off. The more I deal with my feelings, the less excess weight I have to carry around with me.

When my father died, I was so busy running around taking care of everybody else that I never shed a tear the whole day. I was especially worried about my baby brother. He was only 10. I thought he'd never make it.

Dad died before I had my kids, so he never met his grandchildren. That's why a lot of this adult children of alcoholics stuff is hard for me—it's painful. I'm just at the stage now where I'm ready to look at it, where I feel secure enough in my own life that I know I'm not going to fall off the face of the earth if I allow my feelings to surface. I'm finding that once I can acknowledge them, I can let them go. I need to do it, I know. I can see how my past is affecting me right now. My oldest child is 12 years old, and I catch myself freezing up and not wanting to deal with things because I feel real uncomfortable. So I don't do anything. It's very hard for me to deal with the topics of sexuality and abuse that I need to talk to my girls about. Anything that's uncomfortable for me, I just take a left, detour, go down another path.

Talk about stuffing feelings down inside—I was so sad and upset when Dad died that the doctor gave us all tranquilizers. The idea was to help us get through the ordeal, but it also meant that I didn't experience my feelings about his death. All his friends were drunk; we never saw them again. We had all looked up to these men and thought they were really good friends of Dad's, but I've never seen any of those men again, never received a phone call, a Christmas card, nothing. All those men that he worked for and with and was in civic affairs with, I never saw them again.

Four months after he died, I was in bed sleeping when all of a sudden I just sat bolt upright and started crying my eyes out and I didn't know why. It was grief; it was all those feelings that I'd stuffed way down inside about Dad's death. They just broke out. It took me a while to figure this out because at first I hadn't a clue as to what was happening. I had tried to put the grief in my pocket and go on. That's how I had always dealt with my feelings, but I guess I never had anything quite so devastating to contend with before.

I know that my parents' alcoholism affected me. I've seen it coming, and I've done a lot of acknowledging in the last couple of years, but there are some things that I still need to work on. I have a few problems with relationships myself. Although I've been married for a long time, it's come back around again. There was a time in our marriage when things were difficult, but I made a vow that I would never make my children go through what I went through over my parent's divorce. My husband was raised in a very religious family, where his feelings were stuffed down too. The answer to any uncomfortable feelings or situation was that "God will take care of it." So it's not been easy for him to open up either, but over the years we've worked through a lot and feel real comfortable with each other. We have both grown in the process. He's a wonderful father to our daughters and they're very close. I don't think I could ever take that away from my girls, because I know what I missed when my dad was gone.

Ever since Marion started going to the Adult Children of Alcoholics meetings, I've been reading and listening to what she's had to say about it. I haven't started going to meetings yet myself, but that's next. I'm almost ready, I can tell. Just beginning to think about alcoholism as a family disease and the fact that we were all affected, as my parents were by their parents, has helped me realize some things about myself.

I missed a big part of my childhood. I was a 40-year-old teenager. I was dealing with things as a teenager that many people don't have to deal with their whole life. I feel like I'm very mature in a lot of ways as a result, but I've skipped a whole chunk of my life. People talk about joy and frivolity, playfulness, and I don't feel too comfortable about any of that yet. Staying in control of things is very important to me. I think that I'm afraid that if I step out of line, I might fall off the face of the earth, something disastrous will happen. Marion and I recently took a trip and we both showed up at the car with our maps, all marked with our route drawn in little red lines so that we knew exactly where we were going. Maintaining control is extremely important to both of us. We have to know what's coming up next. We're not rigid about it. We're able to go with the flow, but we have to work at it.

All my friends know that my mother's been in AA for over twenty years. They know something about what I went through in the past, and yet they think of me as being easygoing, casual. It just knocks the hell out of me when they say that, because that's not the way I feel at all. I feel shaky right now, just talking about all this. I feel frenzied a lot of the time. I have too much going on in my life. Intellectually, I know that it's going to be all right, but I don't even know what *it* is sometimes. A lot of times it takes me a day to figure out what emotion I'm actually feeling, and half the time it's not anger, it's fear. I've just recently been able to get in touch with the fact that I'm afraid. I can see that in certain situations, somebody's tone of voice, somebody's smell can set off all sorts of feelings. Smell, that was one that knocked me for a loop. Mom used to use a certain kind of baby lotion, an old-fashioned brand that people don't use anymore. Somebody had it on one day and it brought back all kinds of memories and feelings about when the kids were babies. Mom was always sick when she had babies because she would hem-orrhage and have to be in the hospital for some time. My grandmother would come and there would be all kinds of people around, but it was as though Marion and I were put behind a glass wall. Everybody was running around taking care of the new baby and my mother, and they forgot about us. Nobody ever talked about feelings, never ever, ever.

It's pretty remarkable when you think of all the years that my mother spent sober and all the years that we've been with her through that process, that it's only been since my sisters started in the AA and ACA programs that we talked about any of this. Marion and I didn't even have a relationship until about a year and a half ago, when she started into therapy and the ACA groups after her marriage fell apart. Then when something would happen, like at Thanksgiving, she started talking about how she felt and it started a chain reaction. Everybody would respond in their different ways and a whole new avenue of communication opened up.

Someone pointed out that the roles shift in the alcoholic family. A family is in process for better or for worse and roles shift within the family. I was the family hero and Marion was the scapegoat. But I don't think of myself as the family hero anymore. I think that Marion has taken over that role. I don't know what I am anymore, some combination I sense, that I haven't yet identified.

In the last year Marion and I started to talk about some very intimate things that had happened to us both that we'd never talked about before. She's 34 and I'm 38. We grew up in the same home and had many of the same things happen to us, but we never talked about it. We discovered that we may have both been sexually abused by the same man. Neither one of us knew that about the other. I just dumped it on her one day, and she said, "Oh, that happened to me too." I had no idea, none, for all these years. I thought that I was the only one that this had happened to. It turns out there may have been other people abused by this man as well. I'm being so tentative about all this because I still have such a hard time talking about it. I think that I would have to get hypnotized to find out what really happened. I don't know exactly what happened. I don't remember the specifics, and I know that I don't choose to remember it at this point. Maybe I don't need to. I know that there's something in there about that feeling though. That's why I have a hard time sometimes stepping off into something I don't know about, because I know it's there, but yet I don't know what it is. I'm really careful not to listen to anything about sexual abuse. I cannot watch movies with rape, incest. I can't read about it in the paper; it's just too hard. I'm not saying that's unhealthy in itself, it's just that I have such a strong reaction.

MARION: I was sexually abused and it was just another thing that you don't talk about in an alcoholic home. Years down the road I found out what happened to me. The memory has been real clear for me. There were three occasions and I remember them very clearly. I understand how you can block that kind of a memory, but it's real OK for me if you put that in this book. You can say that there's a possibility that my sister was sexually abused by the same person.

The first time anything happened I was under 5 years old, probably 4. Then there was another episode when I was about 5, and then it happened again when I was 13. I don't remember anything in between, so I think those are the only times, but I'm not sure.

I tried to talk about it with my best friend one time. I was in maybe the seventh grade. I told her that when I was little, a man did these really awful things to me and that it made me feel dirty. She said that it was my fault if any man did things like that to me. After that, I chose to never talk about it again.

I knew it wasn't my fault, but after her remarks I thought that somehow it was. I still feel like I did something to make that happen. How do you do that at 4 years old? I was sexually abused. It was really awful! It was devastating, and it was a man I absolutely loved, someone close to our family whom I trusted. This was a man who paid attention to us, read books to us, and now I understood that he was priming us for the abuse, whether he did so consciously or not. Here was a man who I looked up to, one of the few adults that paid any attention to me at all, and he turns around and sexually abuses me. No wonder I had a little trouble with intimacy. No wonder I couldn't trust men. Now that I am beginning to understand all this and get out my feelings about it, it can begin to change, but not much could happen with all those feelings buried under the surface.

GLORIA: I have a real hard time with all this stuff. Even when somebody tells a dirty joke, I just feel like I've got to leave the room. I just have never found them funny. I never talk about sex to anybody.

MARION: When we grew up, nobody discussed sex. I didn't even know Mom and Dad had sex. When I started my period, I went to Gloria because I didn't know what it was. I walked into her room and said "Gloria, the toilet is full of blood," and she said, "Get out the equipment." I got out what I thought I needed and away I went, and didn't say a word to anybody. I didn't even know if I had it on right . . . "I think the thing that's interesting about sexual abuse that I've learned since I started dealing with my own is that I thought I was the only one he did it to, that I was the only one that was promiscuous enough to attract it. I know I could hardly have been promiscuous at 4, but this isn't rational stuff we're talking about. What I found out is that men who sexually abuse children do it to a lot of people. If they've done it to one person, chances are it will happen again and again and again until they get caught, because it's an illness, just like alcoholism. The denial of a sexual offender is worse than an alcoholic. You can catch them in the act of abusing someone and they will deny it.

GLORIA: If Marion hadn't gone on her pilgrimage or whatever you want to call her therapeutic journey, I don't know where we'd be. What's happened in our family is similar to what happens in an intervention. One person cracks that egg, it opens it up, and it changes all the relationships in the whole family. Just having one person get sober, one person go into recovery does not necessarily mean that everybody is happy. It doesn't happen that way. The whole family needs to be in recovery.

Years went by before I quit testing my mother's soda pop,

before I trusted her to go away and come home on time. There was so much unpredictability in our growing up. Our parents would go away to a convention, and we wouldn't know where they were. They would be in New York City, and the next thing, who knows where. It was years into my mother's sobriety before I felt comfortable even at that level, with her just physically not drinking. Then when I started going to meetings with my mom and she'd be a guest speaker, she would always acknowledge us and talk about the fact that her children suffered. It was a release in a way for me to hear her say that. So that was about as much as I could take at that time, just knowing that she knew that we all had problems, and that they were acknowledged, but we thought that was it. We thought that took care of it, but it didn't. Our ability to handle feelings and emotions with our children, husbands, co-workers, friends was very undeveloped.

MARION: How I've chosen men for relationships in the past is a good example of how we tend to unconsciously keep repeating the same behavior that we developed in our family of origin. After I divorced my first husband, I said that I'm going to pick the total opposite of this guy. I thought I had done that, and it turned out that my second marriage was identical to my first marriage. It didn't look that way on the surface at all. My second husband was ten years older, he had an education, he was sober, he looked completely the opposite of my first husband. But what was amazing was that the fights we had were identical, the things we argued about were identical, and that's when I started to realize it's not them, it's *me*. There's something that I'm doing here that I'm not aware of. What turned out was both of them were totally unavailable emotionally. They were both adult children of alcoholics, as well as both alcoholics— one recovering, one not recovering.

What I was doing was still trying to get Daddy to love me. I was trying to find Dad and trying to make Dad say, "I love you." The problem is that no husband is going to be able to be Dad for me, so I had to go to therapy and find that out and start dealing with my ACA issues. I have to learn how to parent myself, to ask for what I need, to be able to go to someone I trust and say I need a hug, for example, or I just need to have you listen and be with me. And if they can do that, great, and if not, I'm learning that I can do that for myself. No one human being's going to be there all the time.

I know that ACA issues had a lot to do with losing my job as well as the failure of my marriages. Lack of self-esteem, problems with authority figures, these and other characteristics can make work life pretty hard. Claudia Black's book, *It'll Never Happen To Me*, really triggered my understanding. She says that whether it's relationships, school, or work, we will be drawn to react to these situations just like we reacted to our situation at home. If you don't think much of yourself and somewhere deep inside you believe that you don't deserve to be treated well, you won't be. You will let that be the pattern in school and work as well as in relationships. It's familiar and so often we're completely unaware of these underlying feelings and beliefs about ourselves. Until you have some self-esteem, you're not going to say, "Hey, I'm not going to take this anymore. Find somebody else." One of the things that Claudia's book talks about is how often ACAs will take a job where they will not be treated well.

GLORIA: Every job I've ever had has been exactly like that. I always had jobs that were helping jobs. It started out as a clerk-typist with the court system, so I knew a lot about that. I always ended up being under the thumb of some authoritarian figure—always men, mostly lawyers or judges.

I've worked for some real miserable characters. The last one I had was a real corker, and I think that's the one that really made me open my eyes and start to think about all this. I've always been the superachiever who had done well, gotten praise, praise, praise, although underneath I was always feeling you're full of baloney. The last boss really kicked me right in the gut. I worked my tail for them, did a really good job. I got them through a big move, and then I was laid off. Money was the excuse; then they turned around and purchased $35,000 worth of artwork to put in their new office. That was a blow for me. But it's also been a key for me. I've had to deal with all my feelings of rejection and loss and grief that were triggered by this that really have more to do with my parents than my job. Now I'm starting to think that this job loss was essential. It's served as a trigger as a catapult to really get me moving forward. Recovery is a never-ending story.

7. Molly M.

Molly M. is Marion's and Gloria's mother.

My grandparents had ten children, of which my mother was the youngest. It was a very musical family; my mother was a marvelous pianist. She could have done anything with her music, but she ran off and married my father. She was the rebel of the family. She drank and smoked, which I imagine made her "fallen woman" in her day. She was 21 when I was born. She was spoiled rotten.

She had a wonderful talent for music. She was an artist. She worked hard and excelled in everything she ever did. She was smart, an excellent student in school, and a writer as well. Unfortunately, she became an alcoholic and married two of them. My natural father, whom I never met until a few months ago, was an alcoholic, and my stepfather, whom she married when I was 13, was an alcoholic. I became an alcoholic too, though I've been sober now in AA for over twenty-one years. I'm 59 years old.

I was raised in my grandparents' home with my mother, brother, and grandparents from the time I was born. My grandfather was a successful member of the community, and my grandmother was a saint. I had wonderful models in them and I'm grateful for that. My brother and I feel that we were fortunate to have our grandparents in our formative years, given our parents' alcoholism.

When we lived together at my grandparents' house, Mom was just sort of there. She was more like a sister to me, I guess, though I do remember her disciplining my brother and me. He was a year older than me. She'd separated from our father when my brother was only a year old, and she was pregnant with me. I never really knew what happened. It was never talked about and we didn't ask. You didn't ask those kinds of questions. It would be like prying and we were taught not to do that.

At the time we lived at my grandparents', I didn't know

about her drinking, though now that I'm older and have the benefit of hindsight, I can look back and know when she had been drinking and when she was hung over. She played in dance bands a lot, so she would go out until late at night and then next morning she'd be different. That's all I understood as a child. Now I know what the difference was—it was a hangover. She played classical music or popular music. If she heard it, she could play it. She played in church. She played everywhere and anywhere she could. Music was her life.

When I was nine, my grandfather had a stroke. My mother and another aunt took turns staying up all night so that they could keep my grandfather at home. He was not in his right mind. It was a very tough time for the whole family. But we had a very close-knit family, and you took care of your own. You didn't stick people in hospitals and nursing homes like today. So I was sent to live with another aunt and uncle out of town. They were childless and had wanted to adopt me when I was born, but the family had decided that it was better that my brother and I be raised together at the time. But with grandfather as sick as he was, they couldn't manage us as well. My aunt and uncle were very good to me, but I was incredibly lonely. I only got to go home at Christmas. We would phone Mother at Thanksgiving and all we'd do is stand there and cry on the phone. My aunt was just as bad as I was.

Mother came to visit us on Washington's birthday. I'll never forget it. I had been gone almost two years by then. It still makes me cry to talk about it. Mother walked me halfway to school and then turned around, and I went on alone. When she got back to the house that day, she said, "That's it, she's coming home with me," and I never had to leave her again. Even with her alcoholism, she was a wonderful person to me. I hated her and I loved her. Every emotion there is, I've gone through with her. She was so different from her sisters, wanting to be a performer in those days. She was very self-sufficient, independent, but she never got to live out that dream fifty years ago.

My mother remarried and we moved from my grandparents' home. My stepfather was an alcoholic. I was 13 years old. Mother and my stepfather had two children of their own after that.

I remember the smell of alcohol mostly. I remember the first time I ever saw her drunk. It was after we moved out of my grandparents' house. We went to a family potluck dinner and dance. We were taken home by our neighbors, my brother and I, and I guess we must have had my baby sister with us. Pretty soon, my stepfather came home, and he was carrying my mother into the house. I saw that she was drunk and I could smell it. The smell is the thing I remember, that awful smell. He said, "She hasn't had anything to drink for a long time." End of story, period, the inference being that you could expect this kind of thing to happen and that it's OK. That's the first time that I ever remember seeing her drunk. She was passed out; he had to carry her. I don't remember anything more about that incident, but that seemed to be the beginning, at least as I remember it. From then on, every time they went out, they would drink. He would be mouthy, and they would argue and argue and argue and yell and holler and keep us awake or wake us up, and we always knew it was going to happen. I'd grab my baby brother and sister and take them in bed with me. My brother and I hated it. We'd never been exposed to this kind of thing before at our grandparents' house. We hated our step-father mainly and thought that he was causing it. We were just kids. He was the new guy on the block, and so as far as we were concerned, it was all his fault. He became the enemy. He must have sensed our feelings, because he became really cold with my brother and me, more me than my brother, for some reason. He would not talk to us for days on end. He never hurt us, never spanked us, or laid a hand on us, but I think some-times that mental cruelty might be worse. Sometimes I wished that he would just hit us, but he wouldn't. He just wouldn't speak. It put my mother in a terrible position. This went on all through the years until my brother and I left home. I despised him and so did my brother. He was not good to us in those days. Momma would come up to my room when she'd been drinking, and he would ridicule her saying, "That's right, you go on and go to your little old Molly." It seemed that he didn't know how to handle things after his children were born. He somehow expected Mother to just forget my brother and me. Her priority was supposed to be his kids. It was very strange to me because my sister was like my own baby. I'd take her to school with me, everywhere; she and my little brother were never any different to me than my older brother. We were all brothers and sisters as far as I was concerned.

I never felt like I had to take care of my mother though,

except when she drank, then I kind of would. I never even thought about that before. I would certainly take care of the other people, especially my little brother and sister. I can remember times after I had left home and I would find them. Mom and my stepdad were drinking in a bar someplace and would leave the kids in a car. I couldn't believe my mother would do that, and I'd go get the kids. I wouldn't put up with that. I was just out of high school then. My little sister was about 6 and my brother was about 5. I always took care of them. They always came to me. Even after I was married, they came to stay with me in the summers.

It's ironic how things got better with my stepfather and me. Getting sober, I'm sure, had something to do with it, but I wound up closer to him than his own children. I was the one who was with him when he died. I was the one who took care of him. I was the one he wanted around. He told me this himself. After my brother and I had left home, things got different and he treated us like his own children. It had been a difficult situation for him, I'm sure. My mother's family were all good achievers. I think he felt inferior to that. My mother may have added to that because she was so talented. He was a musician too, but nowhere near as accomplished as she was.

I married not long after I finished high school. The man I married was voted the most likely to succeed, was on the honor roll, was the athlete of the year. He was to become an alcoholic as well.

I started drinking when we met during World War II. I went right to work for a doctor out of high school. I didn't want to go to college. He was just getting out of the navy and he got scholarships to go back to school. We were married in the fall. We didn't drink that much at first. We didn't have a lot of money, and drinking was not a big priority. There were a lot of young married people in school in those days too, we were all on the GI Bill. We lived in housing units at college and that was exciting. Then everybody started having families, us included, and I had Gloria and a little boy who died not long after. It seems like there has always been something big going on in our family, and it feels normal, even though I'm not sure it is. I've had a lot of stress tests given to me because people thought I should be down-and-out with all that happened, but it doesn't affect me that way. When you're from an alcoholic home, I think sometimes we look for excitement to keep the pot brewing, keep things in a hyper state because that's what we're used to: chaos, drama, excitement. I think that's pretty common, although today I know the difference between positive excitement and negative excitement.

Our family grew. Bill went into business after we got through school. He continued to excel in everything he did; both of us did. We were always sought after. We looked good on the outside. We were even voted the outstanding young couple in the state and awarded trophies. We were a fine American family until alcohol began to destroy us from the inside. It's like an apple that rots from the inside. We were pillars of the community; active in church, clubs, politics, the chamber of commerce, Jaycees; respected in business; active in both local and state politics. I remember telling myself, "Well, he works so hard." That was my excuse when he would get drunk, "He works hard and he plays hard." We had four beautiful kids, a huge home, company over all the time. Our friends brought their kids. There was a lot of cooking and playing bridge. We were the champion bridge players, too, and we drank. It kept getting progressively worse, as alcoholism always will. Periodically, my mother would come and she'd get drunk. Then I'd be mad as hell. I didn't get drunk on the holidays. I watched myself. I'd wait until the kids were in bed, then I'd get drunk.

During the last couple of years of my drinking, I was drunk all the time. I was trying to keep everything together, trying to make everything like it was for me when I was a little girl at my grandparents' house, trying so desperately to make it that way for my kids. I would be thinking about my grandparents all the time. "Why can't I get it together like they did?" I never knew it was the first drink that caused my downfall. I always thought that I'd just have three or four at the most and then quit. Alcoholism doesn't work that way. It's never predictable. The alcoholism began to take its toll on me more than on my husband at first. It does progress more rapidly in women, we know that now. They were taking me around to psychiatrists. Tranquilizers were just becoming used more widely, and the doctors thought that that's what I desperately needed. I ended up an addict as well as an alcoholic.

I began to do crazy things. I'd get my kids up in the middle of the night to get them ready for school. I didn't know if it was morning or night. I'd go on trips, come to in airports, and wouldn't know how I got there. I wouldn't have any clue as to what city I was in, let alone what I was doing. It was terrifying. I would be alone and I would just take off. I had that awful feeling that no one loved me. I felt completely alone, emotionally washed up, and I didn't understand what was happening to me. Whatever it was that I was hunting for was never there. The only thing I wanted to do was be a decent mother, and I couldn't do that anymore and I knew it.

I just thought I was crazy. Meanwhile, the disease was progressing in my husband in a different way. We were always going to make things better. We'd have wonderful philosophical talks, while we're drinking, of course, and we could never pull it off. The marriage began deteriorating, as well as my health. I had ulcers and had to have three-quarters of my stomach removed.

My mother was always there when I got bad. She'd be there picking up the pieces for me. I think it was her way of saying she was sorry for what I'd been through with her. We never discussed any of this and she never put me down, was never critical. She was always the one who was there. When I got to the point where I wouldn't want to see my friends, she'd come and take care of me and I'd be her little girl again.

I finally got some help from friends who put me in a hospital that was experimenting with LSD and mescaline as a cure for alcoholism. They tried all sorts of drugs, and I had them all. But the reason I'm sober is I was told to go to AA. There was some value in the drugs they gave me. That time was unquestionably my lowest ebb, physically and mentally my worst. I don't know how my body took what it took. There had to be a spiritual reason for me to survive. I got addicted to the methadrine (speed) that they were using there in the hospital as part of "the cure," probably the worst stuff to come off of that I'd ever experienced.

Then I got to AA. When I went to AA, I was the only woman there and by far the youngest person there. This was over twenty-one years ago. But I knew the minute I walked in, that I was where I had been trying to go all my life. There it was. I knew they had the answers. I knew nothing and I knew every-thing, all at the same time. I felt full for the first time in my life without being drunk. I felt like I had what I would call now a real spiritual awakening. I knew I was home. The people were so good to me. They got me through every day without a drink while I was still living with a practicing alcoholic, and that's not easy to do. I didn't lose the compulsion to drink. I had that every day for a long time, for a couple of years, but it dimin-ished. Everywhere we'd go, my kids would sip my drink to be sure that it wasn't alcohol. I knew what they were doing and they knew I knew. It was four years into sobriety before they finally trusted me and stopped doing that. I can remember the day.

When I got to AA, I was still seeing a psychiatrist. My marriage was shot. I had never had to support myself, I had no way to earn a living, and I had four children. I knew that I couldn't count on an alcoholic husband, even though he had a large income. But recovery kept making me stronger, spiritually stronger. People in AA kept telling me that I had to learn to stand on my own two feet; I didn't understand what they were talking about. I'd never been responsible in my life and didn't have a clue how to be now. My recovery accelerated my hus-band's alcoholism tremendously. He stopped drinking at home because I wouldn't drink with him anymore. He started going out to drink.

He went to AA for a month and loved it, but he still wanted to drink. When he said, "I know that I'm an alcoholic but I want to drink," I had made my decision. I was over a year sober. I filed for a divorce. Then the choice was mine. It wasn't his anymore; it was mine. I always hoped that he would get help. He stayed in AA for almost five weeks, loved reading anything he could about it, and yet that ego and the false pride wouldn't let him break through into recovery. He'd been raised with a very chauvinistic attitude: A man is a man and it was weakness to get help for yourself to stop drinking. He main-tained the attitude of "I can do it myself" and he did, all the way to his grave after his pancreas exploded. Most of his cronies are dead now, too, or on their way. They drank like he did. At his funeral, one of his friends was drunk and turned to me saying, "You realize this is all your fault, don't you?" The kids were there. It was incredible. Though we knew it wasn't true, it hurt.

I went on and made a career for myself. I have some self-esteem today. I know I can do pretty much what I want to do and do it well. I never had that before. I never felt worthy. I always felt less than, even though that wasn't the way it was. When I was a child living in my grandparents' house, I was always front and center. Everybody loved me, but I never felt worthy of it. Never. When I met my father a few months ago, it was like putting the final piece in the puzzle. That's what it felt like. I've finally come full circle after all these years.

It's uncanny how we met my father. He's a recovering alcoholic too, with the same amount of sobriety in AA that I have, twenty-one years plus, right down to the same month. And here I never knew anything about this man my entire life.

One of our cousins whom I've never met began to look up his genealogy and wrote to all the people with the same surname in the country. My brother, who still had the family name, received one of his letter. The families corresponded and, as a result, found out that our real father was alive and well and living just a few states away. My niece got out the phone book and looked him up—there he was. She called him and asked if they might be related. My father asked who her father was (my brother) and when she told him, he said, "Yes, he's my son that I've never seen." At that, she hung up the phone and got on a plane and went to visit him. She fell in love with him immediately. He's her grandfather. My brother and I decided to go down to meet him a month later. That way we had a chance to adjust a little to the idea.

All my life I've wondered what he looked like, what kind of a person he was, and yet we never talked about him. We were told that he was a nice man but he was immature, and that was it. All my life I've rattled around wondering. I got very curious about him about the time I was graduating from high school. I wrote to him, but I don't think I ever mailed the letter.

Meeting him was quite an experience! How my brother could come out of this whole thing mostly intact amazes me. I was always called the emotional one. I remember that phrase as I was growing up—"Oh, she's so emotional"—as though that could explain everything. I would cry if my mother went to the grocery store. I hated saying "goodbye," and I do to this day, even to people I don't know. Sometimes I'll still cry. I don't know what that means or if it explains anything, but that's me. I do feel things strongly. Meeting my father certainly brought out all my emotions. I had never lived with the man, known him, spent any time with him, never known anything about him, and there we were, so much alike. Neither one of us can talk without moving our hands. I saw so clearly so many of my own characteristics, in our facial expressions, the way we walk. Walking into that room was like having time run forward and seeing my brother twenty years from now. I'd never seen anything like it. They are like twins. My brother just gasped. We all did. That's what I mean about coming full circle. There was a great sense of completion in that meeting.

Looking back at my family of origin and what happened there helps me see why I've made the choices and decisions I've made. I now understand that this especially applies in the area of relationships. Inevitably, I'll pick out people who I think need me for various reasons. I used to think I was making sacrifices, but actually a lot of what I called "a sacrifice" was really a way for me to fill a terrible need to be needed and wanted and approved of. That's normal, wanting approval, but maybe I have an excess amount of that. I don't know what "normal" is. Do you? What is normal? Whatever it is gets intensified in an alcoholic home. I've been in Al-Anon for some time now as well as AA. I've been listening to my sister and my daughter Marion and reading the material on ACA. It all begins to fall into place, I see, particularly since that meeting with my father and realizing that I, too, am an ACA.

I just got back from a trip to the Soviet Union with thirty AA people from all over the United States. It all began with one woman who had a vision of taking AA to the Soviet Union. It took over two years to put the trip together and receive the necessary permissions. The Minister of Health arranged for us to visit different treatment centers where they're using a variety of approaches, such as hypnotism, aversion therapy, and so forth. They really see the need to do something about the horrendous alcohol problem they have, but they don't understand alcoholism. Meeting a woman alcoholic there was like seeing myself twenty-five years ago—searching, knowing that I needed help, and just getting sicker and sicker. I was going to church and trying to find it there, trying to find it everywhere, but you can't find it. That's what's going on over there.

On our trip the miracle of AA happened in meetings in both Moscow and Kiev. There probably were 250 to 300 people in Kiev as well as the 30 of us. We just conducted a regular meeting of Alcoholics Anonymous. It had nothing to do with politics, only alcoholism. That's part of the Twelfth Step of our program, "carrying the message to the alcoholic who still suffers." We all spoke a little bit with the help of a translator there. We had an 18-year-old boy with us who told his story. He spoke the longest, about ten minutes or so. We opened with the serenity prayer and talked about how the program of AA works. At the end we all held hands and said the serenity prayer, and I don't think there was a dry eye in the house. It was just beautiful. They had learned American songs in honor of our visit and brought guitars, and we all sang. Afterwards we were swarmed by people, asking us questions, touching us. In Kiev, there was a small meeting that I chaired. An important scientist was there, and he kept saying, "Well, what is it? How does this thing work?" He could see the power in our AA group of people, but he couldn't tell what it was. Very few of us knew each other before we went, but it's the way it is in AA. He couldn't figure us out. We had been warned that talking about a higher power or a concept of God might be unacceptable in the Soviet Union. But this man kept after us, so finally I said to my friend sitting next to me, "This has got nothing to do with politics or religion. This is one alcoholic talking to another, I'm going to tell him." So I talked about the Third Step and the concept of a higher power, whatever that might be for someone. Recovery is really about putting your life on a spiritual basis, and they understood that. Everything opened up after we got over being afraid to talk about a power greater than ourselves.

People in the Soviet Union are just as spiritual as anybody else. That country is anything but godless. But they haven't yet understood that recovery is a spiritual matter. Alcoholics are banished from the society if they don't respond to the treatment they get. Their whole outlook on alcoholism is so archaic. I just hope we can continue to teach them more about what alcoholism really is. They seem to understand that it's a disease, but they continue to hold on to the mistaken notion that if there was no alcohol around, no one would have it. We know that's not true. That just creates a black market for booze. They also think that people can stop on their own, of their own free will. They don't understand the compulsion and the realities of a physical addiction.

We broke into smaller groups to create more meetings, then we'd get together in the morning to share our experiences. Most of the people told us that they have no drug problems, yet at one of our hotels, four young people found out we were in the city and came to our hotel. They were drug addicts. The girl was on heroin. She had tracks up and down her arms. It's there.

One young man I met was an adult child of an alcoholic too. He couldn't stop talking about his father, who was the alcoholic in his family. The young man didn't know where his father was. He'd been sent into exile because he was a "bad" man. I felt sorry for him. I'm grateful that we've come as far as we have in understanding that alcoholism is a family disease.

A Conversation with Robert Bly on Leaving the Father's House

RACHEL V: Robert, I know you've been speaking at men's conferences and that you've begun to talk about your own experience as an adult child of an alcoholic. What are you thinking about that now?

RORBERT BLY: I'll tell you a story. The storyteller, Michael Meade, tells a wonderful African story, which goes this way:

Once upon a time a hunter went out hunting with his son. During in the morning he killed a wood rat and gave it to his son. He said, "Please take care of this rat and keep it." But the son said to himself, "This rat is nothing; we'll get something bigger," so he threw the rat in the bush. But that day nothing else turned up. So when it got to be dusk, the father said to the boy, "Give me that rat and I'll cook it, and at least we'll have something to eat." The boy said, "I threw the rat into the bush." The father became furious, took an ax, hit the boy, left the boy lying on the ground, and walked away. The boy lay there unconscious until night, then he woke up and walked back to the village. Everyone in the village was asleep, and he went to his father's and mother's hut. He took his clothes. He then left the village and began to walk through the forest on a long path in the dark, wearing only his shirt. He arrived eventually at another village. The chief in that village was awake, but everyone else was asleep. The boy entered the chief's house and the chief said, "How is it with you?" The boy said, "I went out hunting this morning with my father, and he killed a wood rat and gave it to me to keep. But I thought it was of no consequence, and I threw it into the bush. At dusk my father asked me for the rat to cook. I said, 'I threw the rat in the bush.' My father got angry, took an ax and hit me, and I fell down. After dark I got up and walked to the village, where everyone was asleep, entered my mother's and father's house and took my clothes. Then I walked along the path in the dark and came here. That is how it is with me.''

The King said, ''Can you keep a secret?'' The boy said, ''What secret?'' The King said, ''I had a son and he went into battle and was killed. I want to have you as my son, and I want you to keep that secret. Can you keep that secret?'' The boy said, ''Yes, I can keep that secret.'' So then the chief began pounding on his drum very loudly and his wife woke up. She said, ''O Lion King, why are you beating on your drum in the middle of the night?'' He said, ''Because my son has come back, the one who was captured in battle.'' So the mother then raised the cry all over the village and everybody woke up and got out their drums and were glad, because the son had come back. Everyone thought this was wonderful except a few of the ministers, who said, ''Indeed. Indeed.'' That's how the story goes. The ministers set up various tests for the son to see if he is the son or not. With the help of a spy and the father, he passes those tests and he's considered to be the King's son. All goes well, and maybe a year or two passes. Then one day his father appears in the village and says, ''I want my son back.'' Well, you can see that will be a dilemma. The story goes on from there, but I want to concentrate on the early part of it.

One could say that the rat is the father's occupation, and most of us threw our father's rat away. When people hear the story, they feel angry at the father for giving the ax blow and leaving. Then as one goes into the story, one realizes that the son gave the first blow. When you give a blow, you will receive one back. That's not right or wrong; it's just the way it is. The blow the son receives back could be called the wound. It's a wound connected with initiation; we know that initiation always involves a wound. Then as one goes further into the story, it becomes clear that if the boy had not received the wound, he would have never left his mother's and father's house, nor met the King. To me the great image in this story is the long road from the parent's house to the other village, which is a long walk and takes place in the dark. One can brood a lot about that walk in the dark, what it felt like when we left our father's and mother's house, what the walk was like, and whether we were ready to be the son of a king.

To return to your question: As the son of an alcoholic, my danger is to go over and over the wound that my father gave me; and if I do that, I basically don't get *on the road*. Every alcoholic's child seems to begin by denying there is any pain at all. That stage is called denial, I guess, and I know that stage well. My first book was called *Silence in the Snowy Fields;* I see no pain in that title at all. As children, my brother and I were asked to keep a secret, and the secret we were asked to keep was that it was not a happy house. So if the King said to me, "Can you keep a secret?", I could say yes. However, it was someone else's secret, and I wasn't in the King's village. A time comes in middle age when the denial system begins to break down. That happened to me eight years or so ago. Five years ago I began to work with men and participate in week-long conferences with men. I noticed that I spoke then for the first time in public about my father as an alcoholic and the pain of that. All that is complaining about the wound. I think it's wise to complain about the wound—just stay there for a while. I never let people deter me from that.

Yet I remember a remark that James Hillman made. We invited him to our conference at Mendocino. The men participating told some horrendous and moving stories about wounds given them by their mothers and fathers. Some of the men were telling these stories for the first time to other men. The stories were often touching, and we were touched to realize how much grief the men had in common. The talk was marvelous. Later Hillman expressed the other side of the truth when he remarked to me, "When are we going to get past this whining about our fathers?"

RACHEL V: Do you think it is just whining about our fathers, or could you extend that to whining about our parents?

ROBERT BLY: It's easy to extend it. He may have used the word *parents*. His remark concentrates on the danger. It's a delicate matter, I mean avoiding denial and yet not getting stuck in self-pity. I think it's important to be able to lay out the kind of wounds one has received and how it felt lying there in the dark. The worst part of it was that the boy's father hit him and just walked away. Of course, that's exactly how the son feels. That your father just walked away. That's how the daughter feels. Sometimes the mother hits you, sometimes the father.

Every child of an alcoholic receives the knowledge that the bottle is more important to the parent than he or she is. That's the same feeling we pick up in the story. The parent walks away and leaves you lying there on the road in the forest. I think it's important to lie there near that wound for a while. But when one listens to certain men talk about their wound—and women too, I'm sure—it's clear that they haven't yet gathered up their clothes to leave the house. We can retain anger for the father or the mother for twenty to thirty years. It remains perfectly fresh.

RACHEL V: Freud talks about the unconscious having no time, so that if these things are not brought to some kind of awareness, they still have power over us.

ROBERT BLY: That's true, but they *can* be brought to awareness. I don't even know if I like the term *unconscious* anymore.

Interesting things develop when people listening to the story try to decide if they would choose the new King or the old father, later, when they have to choose. Some men declare themselves highly suspicious of the King. They feel that the King is manipulative, untruthful, self-seeking, and deceitful. It seems that one can take the road in the dark but not truly *arrive* unless one has some trust of the King in the second village. If one distrusts the King, one will go back to the mother's and father's house. I would guess that many men and women walk the path from the parent's house through the forest to the King's village more than once. Their attempt to attach to the King fails because they transfer their anger at the father to the King or perhaps transfer their anger at corrupt politicians to the King.

To speak plainly, if your father was an alcoholic and gave you a wound, you're liable to believe that all male figures will give you a wound. That means that you cannot move truly into the King's house. You will keep going back to pick up your clothes left behind. There's something in us that wants to remain in our father's and mother's house, blaming them for our own behavior. As you said to me earlier, children of alcoholics can fall into the trap of explaining everything that has ever happened to them by referring to what happened in their parents' house. The story suggests that a child of an alcoholic may have trouble trusting "the King." Maybe it doesn't suggest that but provides the images through which we can see that possibility. I think it's a likely possibility, and interesting.

RACHEL V: No, Robert, I said that I have difficulty when I hear people making their problems in life a direct result of their parents' alcoholism. For me it's more complicated than that, not that that's not an appealing way to explain my difficulties. It gets me off the hook, but I suspect that it's an easy way out. My own experience suggests that life is more complicated—there's no *one* cause—and that somewhere in the mix, I've got the responsibility, no matter what cards in the deck I was handed.

So I like your interpretation of the story. It helps delineate our part—not trusting the King and the confusion we have about who the King is. There's a big difference between understanding and responsibility. I think I need to come to some understanding of what happened, like you say, stay near the wound, say what happened, but then I am responsible for the healing, no one else. We are all wounded and so were our parents. That's part of life, not something unique to alcoholic families.

ROBERT BLY: The whole matter of the ax blow evokes a lot of memories. Michael Meade asked the listeners yesterday, "Where did the boy receive the blow?" The story does not say. About half of the men said, "the head." Some identified the left side of the head; some the right; one man said, "right down the center of the skull." A few felt the blow on the back of their head, about eight felt it in the stomach, some on the shoulders, two or three on the legs, one in the groin. Those men felt the blow fall the second that the father lowers the ax. A few men were not sure and hadn't really *felt the blow*. It became apparent that these men in a way were worse off than those who did. The process of healing seems to involve feeling the blow deeply first. It's important, repeating myself, to feel what it's like to be left in the forest, what it's like to pick up your clothes, what it's like to make that long walk in the dark, what it's like to tell your story clearly to the King.

RACHEL V: It's important to notice that the boy is left alone in the forest. He has to go back alone to the parents' house, and he makes the journey to the King's village alone. This is one of those passages that no one can make for us or with us, I think.

From your comments it sounds like some of us don't even know that we were wounded.

ROBERT BLY: If the son had never felt the wound deeply, then his surprise would not be so great when the King asks him if he'd like to be his son. The son might not be willing to keep the secret either. Some men don't feel the wound. Such men would drop out of the story at this point. The big surprise to me each time I go over the story is the realization of how many men—and women—end up remaining in the father's house, because they can't imagine who the King is. The danger in the United States is the materialization of consciousness, so we don't see any world beyond the physical world. A dog is a dog and all houses are houses, and all fathers are fathers, and there are no Kings. If someone immaterial like a King appears, we don't trust him.

RACHEL V: That's exactly what I see as a danger in the ACA movement. We identify the fact that we're an adult child of an alcoholic for the first time and suddenly that explains everything wrong with one's life. I don't think it's quite that way. I have to remember not to take this concept too literally. I think the "child" is also symbolic, just as the King is in the story. It represents something larger that is trying to happen, the soul needing transformation. It symbolizes the mythical divine child as well. There are many layers and levels of meaning here. It's not just the literal child of our own personal histories.

ROBERT BLY: When we follow the boy and come to the King in the second village, we come to the other world, which is a world inside or outside, or beyond or below or however we want to think about it. The story says beautifully that we can never become the King's son unless we are willing to tell our story clearly: "First we went hunting, then I threw away the rat, then my father asked me for it, then I said, 'I threw it into the bush,' then he hit me with an ax, knocked me down, and left me alone in the forest. I woke up after dark and went back to my parent's house while they were asleep and got my clothes and walked for a long time in the dark, then I came here." Oh, that's so beautiful! Note that no blame in his telling attaches to himself or to his father. He simply tells what happened. There's clear stating of the story; clear stating is a beautiful thing. Another thing I love is the recognition that the teller has to be able to keep a secret if the story is to move forward. From Jung's point of view, the secret would be that we have two fathers; one's in our own house, and there's another father. We might add that there's one mother in our own house, and there's another mother.

I know the danger of this materialized consciousness very well. When I talk of my father's alcoholism, I can easily fall into the "one father position": He was my father, and he did this and he did that, and because of all that, now I am suspicious of men. That's why it's difficult for me to be intimate with anyone.

RACHEL V: The statement that follows is, "Therefore you must understand and leave me alone. You'd be this way too, if you'd been hurt like me."

ROBERT BLY: That's right. I feel a real danger of that self-pity, especially in the non-symbolic culture of the United States. What we see on TV are houses and rivers and forests with no symbolic content. If you can believe that an underarm deodorant will make you more attractive to women or to men, you will believe anything. If you believe a cold medicine contains a new magic ingredient, you will believe anything. With the sort of culture we have, it's amazing we aren't all stuck in mother's and father's house forever. It's astounding that anyone gets on the road at all. And, of course, if we do arrive at the King's house, there's still a problem, as I've repeatedly said, in trusting him. Throughout the literature of fairy stories, one runs into the father and the King or the first King and the second King. The first King will somehow kick one out of the castle and eventually one finds the second King in another castle. The difficulty in the stories lies in coming within range of the second King and making a good contact with him.

I'll read some lines to you that I wrote last week while sitting next to my father who was in the hospital.

MY FATHER AT 85

His large ears hear
everything.
He looks up,
and a hermit
wakes and sleeps
in the hut underneath
his gaunt cheeks.
His blue eyes
alert,
disappointed
and suspicious
ask me
for some maternal excitement
I cannot give.
He is a small bird
waiting to
be fed,
mostly beak,
an eagle, or a vulture
or the Pharoah's
servant
just before death.
My arm
on the bed
rests there
relaxed
with new love.
All I know
of the Troubadours
I bring
to this bed.
I do not
want or need
to be shamed
by him
any longer.

The general of shame
has discharged him,
and left him
in this small
provincial Egyptian town.
If I do not
wish
to shame him,
then why
not love him?
His long
hands, large, veined,
capable, can
still retain
or hold what he wants.
But is that
what he desired?
Some powerful
engine of desire
is inside him.
He never phrased
what he desired,
and I
am his son.

How often I have sat beside him and how seldom I've felt free enough to write!

RACHEL V: This time you did.

ROBERT BLY: I did, but I'm 59. That's how easy it is to stay long "in the father's house." The African story suggests that leaving the parents' house is more important than shame. I heard James Hillman say one day, "If you are still thinking about the moment your father or mother damaged you when you were 8, it is the thought that is damaging you now."

I have mainly spoken of sons and fathers here, because those are the characters provided by this story. But I believe that the griefs, the walks, the secrets, and the choices the boy faces belong to the experience of daughters and fathers as well, and daughters and mothers. Rachel, I could hear you already making those adjustments. Thank you for this conversation.

Robert Bly is a well-known poet, storyteller, and minstrel who lectures and gives poetry readings throughout the country. He has integrated Jungian and mystical perspectives in this poetry. Among his many published books are *The Light Around the Body*, *The Kabir Book*, *News of the Universe*, *The Man in the Black Coat Turns*, *Loving a Woman in Two Worlds*, *Selected Poems*, and most recently, *The Winged Life: Selected Prose and Poetry of Thoreau* (Sierra Club).

8. Sara J.

Both my parents were alcoholics. My dad left when Mother was in the hospital having me. I was the first child. She was already an alcoholic at the time she had me.

Early on, I became her protector. She told me often that I was her only reason to live. I didn't have much of a childhood because I spent most of it taking care of her. By the time I was 4 years old, she was having blackouts, and I would think she was dead. I would push her and shake her, pull her hair—anything to try to get her to come back. I was terrified of losing her.

I can remember so clearly the space on the hardwood floors between the dining room and living room rugs. I found her there passed out one day. I can still smell the beer she'd been drinking and the vomit she was lying in. I remember shaking her and pouring cold water on her and calling out to her. I was frantic. Finally, she came to, and she started crying. She felt so bad. She kept saying that she was sorry, "I'll never do this again." She felt so guilty. But it happened, again and again. That was not the last time.

When I was a little older and had started school, I would come home sometimes and find myself locked out of the house. She would be at the corner bar. I knew where to find her, but I felt so ashamed that I never wanted to go up there and get her. I would just wait on the back porch. The worst part of it for me was that sometimes I would end up peeing in my pants because I couldn't get into the house. Then I'd be cold and ashamed of myself as well. I felt terribly embarrassed, and then I had even more reason not to go up to the bar and get her. I smelled awful and felt "icky." Eventually, she'd wind up coming home. Either somebody would drop her off or she would get a ride in a cab.

A lot of times there was no dinner. Sometimes we had dinner at eight or nine. When I remembered this, I realized that it's no surprise that I later developed a problem with food. I have a fixation about not being able to wait for food.

There was a neighbor who would look in on me once in a while, but I never connected with her. Shame was such a big part of my life. I never wanted to go over to the neighbor's house. That was my part of the denial. I covered up for my mother. I never said, "Hey, I'm hungry, or I'm cold, or I'm scared." I didn't want anybody to know. I would just sit there alone on that back porch, waiting, waiting. I was too ashamed. When she did get home, she'd stumble through a meal and would kind of sober up in the process, and then we'd eat. That was kind of a routine for a while, at least between the time I was 6 and 8. Then she remarried. She later told me that the only reason she married him was to give me a father. Well, he and I absolutely hated each other. He was mean and he beat me. He was an alcoholic, too, a naval officer. They would go on drunken binges together. He beat her as well.

He and I would always fight about food. I couldn't get up from the table until I'd eaten everything. So I sat there for hours. Every once in a while, I'd get nasty about it and show a little spit and fire and get angry. Then he'd really hit me hard. It would start out like a spanking, but it went out of control.

He hit my mother a lot as well. She had black eyes and bloody noses often. He would beat her to the point where she was a physical mess. I never *saw* him beat her up; I'd just see the results. Finally, she got rid of him.

With my next stepfather, I saw the beatings happen. They binged together, and I saw him beat her as well. This second stepfather later turned out to be our salvation, but initially things were worse than ever. During this time, I took over a lot of the household responsibilities. I did all the shopping, because she had become agoraphobic. She refused to leave the house, was terrified of going outside, so anything she needed I was sent out for. This went on progressively from about the time I was 8 until I was maybe 12.

Sometimes she would sober up for a while. There were periods in between episodes when she was all right. I loved her, and she was all I had for such a long time. I was 15 before she had any other children. The bottom line was that she loved me too, and somehow she got that across. I didn't hate her. As a child, all I knew was that I just wanted to make things better for her. I kept trying to fix everything. Somehow I thought that if I just kept the house clean, if I just could just . . . , then she would get better.

We had a big, two-story house that took about ten hours to clean. I did it every Saturday. I remember one day in particular when my grandparents, my mother's parents, came to see us. They lived way out in the country with no telephone, so when they came in to town, it was unannounced. They didn't visit very often. I wouldn't see them for a long time, and then they would just show up at our door. My mother didn't like that. She didn't like it when anybody showed up at the door if she'd been drinking, much less her own parents.

They came up to the door and knocked. Mother had been drinking, so instead of going to the door, she grabbed me and pulled me into a closet with her to hide. They didn't go away. They just stood outside, pounding on the door for about ten minutes. Then they went around the back to try another door and, sure enough, that one wasn't locked. We just lay low in the closet while they went through the house, calling for us. I felt so strange, so much like a sneak. I know they knew something was wrong, just intuitively, but they never found us. There I was in the dark closet with my mother, not able to come out and see my own grandparents. The fact that I stayed there in the closet with my mother is *my* part of the disease. If I'd been in my right mind, I wouldn't have gone in there with her in the first place. But you know, when you're a kid, you don't know any better. I knew it was strange. I knew I didn't like it, but I didn't really know what to do at that point.

I fronted for her a lot like that, helping her pretend, lie, deny. We did this a lot whenever people came to the door, just hid in the closet, like nobody was there. Denial, pretending, it was just a way of life. A lot of times I couldn't go play with my friends because I had to take care of her. I helped her cover up her drinking, helped her hide from people. I became her accomplice.

School was the saving grace for me. That was where I made contact with other people, had a sense of community, got acknowledgment, recognition. I got straight A's. School was everything to me. I hated summers because it was all that drinking and hiding and sneaking around. I loved the school so much that when I was sick, I would fake it and pretend like I

was well so that I could go to school. I was very bright. I'd go
to school with a 103° fever if I could get away with it.

Eventually I caught on, and I learned to cover so that I could
get what I wanted, and I didn't want to be at home. She was
trapped and tried to trap me at home, so I started planning my
escapes to get out, all sorts of reasons why I had to be at
school. I had a aunt and uncle that took me places, too. My
uncle was a surrogate father for me.

Mother married my second stepfather when I was 11, and
by the time I was 13, she had been told by the doctor that if she
didn't stop drinking, she was going to die and soon. That didn't
stop her. What happened, and I just found this out from my
stepfather last year, was that he took her to a drying-out hospital at midnight one night while she was drunk and just
dropped her off. When she woke up the next day, she was
madder than a hornet and in a rage for days. She was there for
two weeks.

That was the end of her drinking, and his. This story came
out because I asked my stepdad how in the world he got her to
agree to go to that drying-out hospital. Mother was sitting there
too, and they both burst out laughing.

"Agree?" he said, and then he told me the real story. She
came out two weeks later and simply has never taken a drink
since. Ever. Cold turkey. No AA. Sheer will and strength, and
his complete support. They changed all their friends, changed
their whole life around, and just made a clean, fresh start. It
was very powerful for all of us. They really leaned on each
other. He said that he wasn't as far gone as she was when he
took her to the hospital. He decided to quit while she was in
the hospital there. That marked a passage. Neither one of them
ever drank again.

Three years later, my little sister was born. She was completely an accident. My mother had already begun menopause.
She was a menopause baby, and that surprised both of them. It
gave them a new lease on life, having a baby together.

Right now my sister is in therapy dealing with the issues
from her childhood. Though she was born fifteen years later
and mother no longer drank, she still had a lot of difficulties.
After mother stopped drinking, she became a hypochondriac. I
think it was because she didn't go into a recovery program. She

was still agoraphobic. She had one disease after another. She had her uterus taken out, her gall bladder taken out, her appendix—everything you could think of. Still, she never picked up another drink again.

After that, we made a big move. My stepfather seemed to feel that he had sacrificed a lot in order to take care of her and help her in her recovery. Suddenly, he felt like it was his turn, and that meant moving across the country. So we left the place where I'd grown up and started over. I was in high school at the time, and that was hard.

My sister was born during all this. My stepfather and I began to battle. Mother was upset about leaving all her family behind. We were all at odds. He couldn't find work. I immediately put on twenty pounds and felt terrible about myself. But I had school, and I continued to do well. That was my place to shine still.

I went on to college and continued to do well. By my junior year I had won a lot of honors and awards, been elected student body secretary for the following year, and was hitting my stride when I fell in love and got pregnant. We had just started experimenting sexually. He was my first lover. He told me that he was sterile. He had already asked me to marry him once and I had said no, but when I found out I was pregnant I said yes.

I was getting successful, and then I threw it all away. I couldn't enjoy my success, couldn't have anything, and I didn't know why. There was something familiar about all this, but I couldn't understand it at the time. Unconsciously, I was repeating an old pattern. Not having a sense of my own self, I couldn't keep anything for myself. My stepfather was so upset that he threatened to kill my husband. We left the area. I left school, the honors, my family, friends—everything I'd worked for—and walked away pregnant.

We moved to a new town and started over. My husband worked eighty hours a week. He was a workaholic. I had my son. My husband was not an alcoholic, though he drank heavily, as I did too at that time. I blacked out a few times, and that's when I decided to stop drinking, and I did. I still carried on with an addiction to food, and then later I progressed into a real problem with marijuana. I smoked a lot.

My husband I were married for almost twelve years. I had a

daughter too. He had an incredible temper and would fly into rages. The whole cycle of battering that I had seen with my mother and hated so much, I found myself locked into with my own husband. And it just got worse. The last time that it happened, I was almost killed. He had become financially successful, and we had a big house with a marble entryway. He grabbed me by the hair, had me down on the floor, and was ramming my head against the marble, over and over again. He was completely out of control, in a blind rage. He didn't know what he was doing when he was like that. He would get incredibly strong during these rages. He wasn't triggered by alcohol; he had not been drinking. I can remember thinking while my head was being battered against that marble, "This is the last time. This is the last time I'm taking this. This is the end." The children saw the whole episode. I tried to fight back, but I was no match for his strength. That was a turning point. I knew that I had to get out of the marriage, and I did. The children were 11 and 13.

He told me that I was going to have to be the one to leave, and I took it, I believed him. I hadn't the faintest idea of how to stand up for myself, of how to fight for my children. I left my home, my children. I didn't know that I had any other options.

We lived in a very small town in the Midwest. He told me that there wasn't room for both of us, so I moved to the nearest town possible and drove over to visit the children. They moved again, to another town, so I moved again, to be two blocks away from them. I was always on the outside, visiting. It never occurred to me that I could change the situation. A terrible rift happened with my daughter at that time. She blamed the divorce on me. She and I had a period of about seven years when she didn't want to have anything to do with me. It was a very painful time. I'd walk by their house at night and look in the window and see them, and not know where to begin to make anything different. I would just go home and sit alone and cry.

Finally, I moved away. They were older. I had been living in a rural area and moved down to the city. I had a 1955 Ford. Believe it or not, it was that car that brought me to my bottom. That car broke down about once every three weeks. I was always struggling with not having what I needed, even for bare survival.

I couldn't count on getting from here to there. I never had the money to fix it because I was terrible with money. I could earn it, but I couldn't hold on to it. I gave everything away. Once again, it was that unconscious belief at work, telling me that I couldn't have anything for myself. So here I was, with this car constantly breaking down, having to drive through really bad neighborhoods in the city to get to work, and always terrified. That's when I began to make the connection. Something finally started to get through to me. At first, I told myself this story about how I was in this situation because I was used to living in the country. All of us in our rural community had had old broken-down cars, and that's how the country folks lived. But then several of us from this rural community had moved to the city, and suddenly they all had new cars that worked. Every single one of them, but me. I still had my old one that always broke down. It kept me in a constant state of crisis.

It began to occur to me that there must be something *I* was doing to make things keep coming out this way. It was a gradual awakening. I had a friend that I worked with who was in the AA program, and we used to talk about alcoholism and recovery. I started talking about the alcoholism in my family. Then I saw an article about Adult Children of Alcoholics. Next thing I knew, I was calling a woman who ran a therapy group for Adult Children of Alcoholics. I asked her if I was a candidate, and she said that she would send me some information. When I sat down to read the material she sent me, I was shocked—there I was in print. The description of Adult Children of Alcoholics read like it was written about me. I felt like I couldn't breathe, like I was caught. There was a tremendous relief though in seeing what my struggle was really about and having it in front of me in print.

I had been in denial all my life about so many things. I read how often people who grow up in alcoholic homes never had a childhood, and that was me. I had never recognized how the alcoholism in the family affected me. Yet it was pretty clear that I didn't know how to operate as an adult. I had a very childish approach to everything, living only from day to day. I couldn't hold on to anything, couldn't pull my life together to get a car, credit, or anything I needed for myself. "Not having" was the theme. I thought I was very spiritual. The truth was I was in denial. I lied to myself about it. I just didn't know how to have anything.

As I read more about ACAs, I saw the pattern of being abandoned in my own childhood and realized that, unconsciously, I had turned around and abandoned my own children. I was repeating the pattern.

Though I didn't know this at the time, I had terrific problems in trusting men. The original abandonment was by my father, and then there were the betrayals by my stepfathers. Throw in my bad experience with marriage, and the truth was that I didn't trust men at all, and I was completely in denial about that. I went into the ACA therapy group and begin to look at all this and began to understand my part.

I discovered that in relationships I would pick men who were younger than I was, so I had control of the situation. Maintaining control was a big issue for me and is for many adult children of alcoholics. I wasn't able to be with a man who was my equal, because if I couldn't maintain control, that meant loss. If a man saw that I was vulnerable, that meant I would be abandoned. I didn't know that this was the way I felt about things. None of this was conscious on my part, which is precisely why it was so powerful and ran me like it did. I wasn't aware of these equations. So I always picked men I could manage, and it never worked. Nothing would last.

I was addicted to having a relationship where I was in control; I was addicted to "having" somebody but not being in a relationship. Those are two different things. I wanted somebody there so that I wouldn't have to face my own emptiness, look at my own inner core. That's what I had to look at when I went into ACA therapy.

As I worked with my therapist, I went through layer after layer of emotion, went through the rage at losing my father, rage at all the losses with men, the betrayals, the break, with my children. I went through all sorts of hurt and sadness and finally became willing to just hang in with myself, my own loneliness and my own humanity. I finally became willing to just *be* and not have to always be reaching out for something or someone to take my feelings away.

It was hard to let all those feelings come up, especially about my dad. In fact, it was terrifying. He died at 44, on skid row.

He had been a wealthy man when he and Mother started out, but in the end he lost everything. I have a lot of memories of my mother telling me he was coming to visit, and then he wouldn't come. I would sit in the picture window overlooking the street to wait for him. He had a sea-green Buick convertible. How I would wait for that car!

One time he did come, and we went off in that car, that sea-green convertible. I was so happy! He drove me downtown to where he lived, and it was a dive, a tavern, a bar on skid row. He took me inside to introduce me to his cronies. They were all lined up at the bar, and they were already drunk. It was still broad daylight, only noon or so. They were kind of nodding over beers, and there he was walking in proudly with me on his arm saying, "This is my little girl. Isn't she a doll?" He lived upstairs in a room right up above the bar, so he didn't have to go far for his booze. That's my last memory of him. I was 7 years old.

I did a lot of things over the years that were helpful, good, and important. Don't get me wrong. To look at me, you would have never known how I felt inside. I didn't either for that matter, not fully. What's different now in this recovery process is that I'm finally dealing with the core issues, so that everything else I've done is finally falling into place, making sense in a way it never has before. Bearing fruit. That would be a good way to put it.

After my marriage fell apart, I went back to school. I studied psychology. I was always trying to figure things out, so I became a therapist. It was perfect for me. I could always keep the focus on other people on their problems, their feelings, not my own. I was brilliant at ferreting out what was going on with somebody else. I did a lot of therapy as well, but nothing really touched the core of my dilemma until I began to look at the fact that I was an ACA.

I was part of a spiritual community for years. I became a vegetarian, practiced meditation and yoga, taught yoga, became an outdoor leader, took groups off into the wilderness, started my own company, did a lot of good things that were helpful. Yet my life continued to be such a struggle. It just didn't make sense to me after all that good work. The problem really showed when several of us from the rural spiritual community moved

to the city. Everyone else was able to make changes, be successful, move on in their careers, have good relationships. I was the
only one who was lost and floundering. The old, broken-down
'55 Ford was a metaphor that made that very clear.

My problems with relationships and money seemed insur-
mountable until I began working with the ACA material. Once
I began to see what was underneath a lot of my behavior, what
I was really up against and how much denial I had been in
about my childhood, I began to make progress. I had a lot of
unconscious beliefs about myself that really ran me ragged. I
had always seen myself in the role of rescuer, caretaker, someone who was there to take care of others and support them.
That's what I did with my mother. And that was important and
intelligent coping behavior, given the situation I was in as a
child. But as an adult, that behavior really worked against me.
It never occurred to me that I could or should have anything for
myself. That's where having gotten involved in a spiritual community was really tricky. It reinforced all those ideas of selfless-
ness and poverty, but I was doing it for all the wrong reasons,
out of denial, not out of choice.

I had never let myself look at or admit how painful it was to
be separated from my children. Never acknowledged how lost I
was, how much I was floundering at the time. I was grief-
stricken, and I denied it. I had a very intellectual explanation
about my kids not being with me and being with their father
instead. I would just gloss over what happened. And it still
hurts. My body aches just talking aout it, but I need to face my
part in what happened. I have to take responsibility. It wasn't
that they just chose to live with their father; I was playing out
my own abandonment, and I never fought for them. I had no
idea what I was doing. It's only now that I can see all this, and
it's only been through ACA. Until just now, I never even described the breach with my children in this way. I thought of it
as something they did to me, didn't see that I had any part in
what happened. It's not easy to admit these things or come to
terms with all this. It feels like I committed a crime by not
fighting for them. I wanted to have them with me, but I didn't
know how as soon as their father opposed me.

I invested so much of my life in being good, in being kind
and loving, and giving everybody what they wanted that I never

learned what it was that I wanted, much less how to ask for it or get it.

I've had to find the rage in me over this, and that's part of the ACA recovery process. What I had lived with was fear and terror, and the fear covered my rage and closed off my voice. I never demanded my rights as a mother, as a woman, as a person. Underneath all my fear was this huge rage flying around inside of me. I had everything ripped away from me—my father, my mother, my children, and my self-respect. There was nothing left of Sara but an empty shell walking around crying. I was furious with everyone, and most of all with myself. After I realized that I was angry, then I had to work on forgiveness, first of all of myself.

I've had to reconstruct myself, to discover what I want, and know that it is part of my right as a human being to want something. That doesn't mean that I'll get it, I know that, but just that it's OK for me to want something for myself, like my relationship with my children.

I have been close to my son but estranged from my daughter for years. But just recently she told me that she doesn't know who I am and that she really wants to know. She wants to know my side, what I went through all those years. She wants to rebuild our relationship. And she's invited me to come visit, to come stay with her for a week. This will be the first time in over twelve years that we've spent more than just a day together. I'm excited, nervous, full of all kinds of feelings, and it's going to be fine, I know. I'm so moved, so glad that she wants to know me. There's a way in which I need for her to know what I went through. For years, she thought that I left her dad because I was on a women's lib kick. She had completely blocked out the battering, denied it. That's what she needed to do to survive her part. Now she understands. We're both ready, I know, or she wouldn't have asked me to come. There's a recovery process that's going on, and it's vital to both of us. I've never told her how it was for me as a child, and I'm going to, when the time is right.

My son has been a godsend, and we've stayed close through it all. When he was just an infant, maybe 9 months old, I was bathing him and walked out of the room for a moment, just long enough for him to reach up to the hot water faucet, turn it on, and scald himself. He had a terrible burn on his face after that and grew up with other kids taunting him. I spent years with self-recrimination and self-hatred about that happening. He's had plastic surgery now and looks fantastic. He's a very handsome man, and he's turned out to be an incredibly compassionate person through this. He's now studying to be a doctor. He would always say, even as a child, "Mom, it's not your fault. It was an accident, Mom. You did everything you could." What a gift that relationship has been to me.

Turning a life around takes time, and I'm still in therapy once a week. The therapist I work with uses a lot of Marion Woodman's material, which she is slowly taking me through. We call it a descent. Very systematically, we're working through these issues in my life. Last year we worked on money, and I am happy to report, I have a new car, credit, and a good income now. This year it's health and relationships. I still have a lot of issues around food and can get very compulsive about it, so I'm working with that too.

Part of what's fascinating about all of this to me is that as I read about and work through my own issues as an Adult Child of an Alcoholic, more and more ACAs seek me out as a therapist. I know what my limits are. I can't take anyone beyond where I've gone myself, but I can bring someone up to what I've already dealt with, so I'm getting to work on all this from both sides, both in my own therapy and as a therapist myself.

I'm no longer in group therapy, just individual therapy, so now I'm interested in finding some of the Al-Anon ACA meetings here to become a part of.

For the first time in forty-six years, I have a grip on what makes me tick. I can see what my problems are, and I can reach out for help and support now. I'm no longer isolated. The isolation I used to experience was one of the worst problems that I was dealing with. There are systems in place for me to reach out to when I find myself sinking. It's so freeing to finally be able to talk about these things.

Religion, spirituality, none of that alone could get me through. But spirituality linked with the knowledge of what I've come from is an unbeatable combination for recovery. The spiritual realm is what my life is dedicated to; it's the strongest part. That's why I love the outdoors so much. I feel the spirit there is rich.

When I was a child struggling with my mother, I started going to church by myself at age 6. That's one of my early memories. I would walk seven blocks by myself to go. I remember how uplifting it was when I looked up at the stained-glass window. My mother wouldn't go with me, but she let me go on my own. I broke away from organized religion when I was a teenager.

I came back to a spiritual path when I started doing yoga many years ago, but no spiritual practice could get to the bottom of my difficulties for me. Now the spiritual path is an essential element in my recovery. The help of other women has been crucial as well. I think there's some very special healing my daughter and I will experience yet. It's a beautiful process that we've begun.

9. Bill J.

I was born in the South in the late thirties. My father was a minister, and my mother was a school teacher. From the outside we looked like a typical black minister's family. It's still hard for me to identify my father as an alcoholic. It was hard for him to see that I was an alcoholic as well. I never drank much around my family, and my family didn't keep alcohol in the house because it was considered sinful to drink. We were good people. My father would do his drinking and running around in another town; that was one of the reasons it was hard for me to see. He was brutal toward my mother, that I saw, but I didn't connect it to alcohol.

When I was about 9, my younger brother and sister and I all slept in the same bedroom with my parents. My parents slept in one bed, and the three of us shared a bed to one side of them. This particular night my parents started out kidding, but that soon turned to an argument. My father hit my mother, and I jumped out of bed. The room was pitch dark, and my father yelled, "Where are you going?" I said, "I'm going to call the police!" And he said, "Why?" I just froze. I don't have recall after that. I can't remember what happened, just that I was aware that there was nobody outside that house who could do anything to help me.

My mother's father was an alcoholic too, though I never got to know him. He was dead before I came along. The center of my life as a child was my mother's family. Half her brothers were alcoholics and half were ministers. I remember one of the ones who was a minister saying when I was a kid that he wouldn't put alcohol in his toilet. He was estranged from his brothers who drank. It was a family that loved one another, but there was a boundary, and that boundary was alcohol.

That uncle was a very successful minister, one of the best preachers around. He was also very rigid. I grew up aware of this division in my family between the rigid, successful nondrinkers and the other uncles who drank and took care of themselves but who were not as successful. I preferred the ones who drank and told stories. They were fun. I didn't like my father's family particularly.

When I was about 5, my parents sent me to live with my grandmother so that I could start first grade. She lived in another town, same state, but different town. I'm not too sure about the chronology of all this, but I came back home after two or three years with my grandmother. That's been a touchy subject. When I was 11, in the seventh grade, they sent me back to live with my grandmother again. She was there alone. All of her sons had left home to join the army during World War II. I was the oldest nephew in the South, and so I was sent to live with her. I stayed that time until I finished high school. She was still teaching school at the time; it was just to be company for her.

When I look back now, I realize how much of my purpose in life was centered around, in this case, my grandmother and when I was at home, my mother, protecting her from my father. I didn't learn much about what it was to be a black man, much that was useful at least. My world ended up being fantasy. I loved to read, science fiction especially. On top of going back and forth between my house and my grandmother's, we moved a lot so I went to different schools in a lot of different places. I learned early to detach from my feelings. To this day, I don't think I've ever had what I would call a close friend.

I was afraid of my father all my life. He was a black man with a different attitude. He would fight anybody that crossed him. He didn't perceive danger the way other people around him did. He threatened to kill a man who'd come out to repossess his car for nonpayment. That was in the early 1940s. The man was white. That was not the way things usually worked in the South in those days, a black man threatening a white and getting away with it. At home we would laugh about this kind of thing, but I felt uncomfortable.

My mother was always putting my father down. She didn't really want us to be against him; she just wanted us to be on her side. So it was my mother and the three kids on one side, and my father on the other side. He was having his fun on the outside. He was also very ambitious and worked hard. Churches didn't pay very much in the beginning, so he managed a cleaners.

He wasn't a very good business manager, so that he didn't last. He finally did get off alcohol. He was a Mason, and I think that had a lot to do with it.

For being a black man, I've never taken in black culture as such, and it's an odd experience. I've been so isolated that I made a culture of one person. During the time when I was growing up, there was so much self-hatred amongst blacks that I didn't want to be a part of them. Black people were condescending to their own kind, and it was primarily along the color line. There were little idioms in those days like "If you are white, you're all right." I couldn't go along with it. So I was cut off from blacks as well as whites. My culture and my world was my family. It was big enough.

At Christmas we got together at my grandmother's. There would be lots of aunts and uncles, plus all their spouses and other children as well. Though I felt isolated from the world outside, my family did not. My parents managed to convey the feeling that they knew almost everyone in the state, both black and white. They would tell us stories about these connections to the outside world, but we weren't permitted to participate in it. They didn't say that they were protecting us, but they were. There was a boundary to stay inside of there, and that boundary had to do with who was black and who was white.

In high school it was evident that you stayed within the black boundary. No one had to tell you. It was just all around you; everybody knew it. I will never forget a conversation I had with my mother once when I was home on leave from the army. My mother was telling me what I had been like as a 2-year-old. I got very excited about this lively 2-year-old that she was describing because I didn't see myself that way at all. I thought of myself as almost an inanimate object. I can look at other people who are really alive, but I've never had their spontaneity. I'm aware of that. I asked her what happened to that liveliness and, in so many words, what she told me was that "we had to break you so that you could survive." It was so painful to hear that. We have never talked about it since. It was uncomfortable for her to tell me that and for me to hear it. We both understood and went on to the next topic.

The truth is that I am deeply embarrassed that I don't have any concern for anything. My therapist says that's changing, but

I have had such ambivalence about life. I saw people having wants and desires, but somehow I associated that with anger. If my mother wanted anything, my father got angry. If my brother or sister wanted anything, there would be an argument. I have never been able to deal with anger. If someone started to argue with me, I would just give them everything they wanted and just cut off my life some more. I was always frightened when my father expressed displeasure about something. Somehow I got locked into that forever it seems. That's one of the things I see now and am changing.

I would get terrified when my father was going to give us a whipping. My brother was just the opposite, and he went at him, which frightened me even more because then I though he was going to get us both killed. That fear has gone on for me, the fear of pain, and I am now learning that I can get through pain—it isn't going to kill me—thanks to AA and ACA. Those years with my grandmother seem idyllic by comparison. She had a big house; it was comfortable, pleasant. There was a flower garden. I studied piano for a while. It was peaceful.

Since my parents were always fighting, my mother took refuge in the fact that she was a teacher and she was going to make me smart. So by the time I went to first grade, I was up with the second and third graders. Black schools were terrible to begin with in those days, and a lot of kids in first grade never learned to read. I went in knowing it all. My mother used to show me off, call me into the room to stand up and recite my lessons for company. I became a performer, I got focused on how can I please this person. And that trait has stayed with me still. In school I never had a desire to learn anything unless it was going to please someone. The teacher had to really focus on me, and then I would please her. If she focused on the other kids, forget it.

I had two worlds and what was significant in one had no meaning in the other. Some of my friends in grade school would pull me aside and try to teach me how to "shoot the dozens." A lot of blacks did this. They'd stand on the corner making these rhymes. They'd say here's what you do: Say, "I fuck your momma," which was repugnant to me, and I would say it anyway, and they'd say, "I fucked yo' momma on a bale of hay. You can smell the pussy a mile away." Some of these guys just stood around on the corner drinking sodas, "shootin' the dozens" any evening. You couldn't do anything with that, oh you could become the hero of the group, but you couldn't take that anywhere off the street. I wanted to talk about what I read, and my friends wanted to make these rhymes.

When I went to college in the fifties, I understood for the first time that I was relatively poor. I went to a black college on the East Coast that got the cream of the crop of black students from that part of the country. A lot of them had a much better academic background than I did, and they were better off financially. That all just served to make me feel more like an outsider. I withdrew. I couldn't deal with all that, but I didn't let people see that I'd withdrawn. I was outgoing on the surface, could put on a front and talk to anybody, but I was too embarrassed about what was happening with me inside to begin to let anybody know about that. I am good at conceptual work and can grasp structures so I majored in chemistry.

My own drinking really started in college, though it was occasional drinking. I drank to impress others. I had my worst drunk in college though and my first blackout.

After college I went into the army. The theme in college and in the army was that I had no desire to do anything significant, so I just did what I was told to do. I didn't understand where people got the desire to do anything. It was very important to me to be proper, to be good. After the army I got a job as a chemist with the same company I've been with for twenty years now.

Next came marriage. I had difficulty in meeting women because I always saw sex as a kind of aggressive act against women. I had been corresponding with a woman who was a missionary in the Methodist church at the time. I asked her to marry me because someone at work had made the comment that a man my age who wasn't married (I was 27 at the time) must have something wrong and because sex was so problematic for me. There was more to it than just that, but as I look back, I remember how uncomfortable that comment had made me, combined with everything else. Getting married was a way of making myself OK and securing easy sex on a routine basis.

I flew back South, my father married us, and we were the best of friends for eight years, but we never got emotionally involved somehow. After about a year, our sex life went down the tubes, and I started drinking more. When she started pushing away, I started hanging out in bars. She'd go to bed at 9:00 P.M. and I'd go to the bar. I was surprised that it was all right with her, that she didn't object.

During this time I saw that other people lived differently than I did, but I never connected my upbringing with what was happening to me in the present. There were two stories I told myself: that because I was black, I wasn't expected to do much, or that if I tried, society would hold me back. But by this time it was the early sixties and I began to see a lot of black men who were ahead of me and who exhibited a sense of self that I hadn't seen among black men when I was growing up. I was uncomfortable about that because it shot holes in my theory about blacks being able to make it in life.

Making it to me meant simply having a wife, a home, and living a moderate version of the American dream. I just wanted to be *Father Knows Best*. I had always told myself that I couldn't have what I wanted because I was black, but by now I was seeing black people with self-esteem. Then I knew that I was a coward and didn't have the self-respect that they did.

I was going to graduate school at this time. Somehow I blamed by wife for my lack of self-esteem. We separated for a while; I drank a lot that year. It was very hard to perceive myself as an alcoholic. I had a very high tolerance for alcohol. I could come home from work, drink a quart of Scotch, go downtown, and wander around until 3:00 or 4:00 in the morning, go home, get up, and go to work the next morning. There was little that happened to me physically to make me think that I was an alcoholic. I had to slow down from time to time, but I was not a falling-down drunk. I didn't pass out a lot. I'm only aware of having had one blackout during that time.

I was afraid of sex but I didn't think about anything else. I couldn't talk to anyone about it because I was embarrassed and crazed at the same time. My wife asked for a divorce. I was relieved that the marriage was ending.

I met a woman who lived in a house that was affiliated with Synanon, and I moved in. You couldn't drink or smoke there, and so I didn't for a year, to be with her. In the end they kind of threw me out, and I bought a bottle of Scotch just to get even, and that's when I hit the skids. I was sitting on a bar stool drinking, I stepped down, and the next thing I knew, I was in my bed and the sun was coming through the windows. I had had that blackout, and it terrified me. I didn't know what a blackout was at that time, didn't find out that that's what had happened until my first AA meeting. I went downhill fast. I drank all the time, now more than a quart a day, and took Librium so that I could hold myself together for work. I'd been taking Librium on a daily basis for two-and-a-half years, plus the drinking, and I was nuts.

I was scared of running out of Librium. I thought that the Librium was keeping me together. I would drink and take Librium. What was happening was that I had the alcoholic shakes, it was the alcohol that stopped the shakes, not the Librium, but I didn't know that. Finally, I got into AA and stopped all that. I don't think I could have lived another six months.

I took to AA like a duck takes to water. I went to meetings, I loved it. They said, "Don't drink," so I didn't. I wanted to please everybody. I had been trying to stop for two years unsuccessfully, but suddenly I could do it—no big deal.

I was physically sober, but there was nothing going on inside. I would tell people that I was on a pink cloud, that everything was great, that I felt wonderful. I did—the shakes had stopped. But I envied people who had relationships and were into their careers and really active. For me nothing was happening, and I was moving into a corner. The stuff people were saying in AA didn't make sense to me, but I said it because I thought I had to say it to be there. I was glad to be around people, but there was a wall around me. I could not do a Fourth Step, take an inventory of myself.

A friend of mine in AA told me that she was going to Adult Children of Alcoholics meetings. She talked about the "laundry list," the characteristics of ACAs, but it just didn't mean anything to me. I didn't think of my father as an alcoholic at the time, so it just didn't click. But as she kept going down the list of characteristics she mentioned one of them was being addicted to excitement. That I could relate to: my dad was addicted to excitement, I'm addicted to excitement; yes, I wanted to know more about that. I used to get upset at bars when they would close at 4:00 A.M. Where would I find any excitement? That's what got me into ACA, addiction to excitement. That was all I was interested in talking about. I was so relieved to find a place where I could talk about addiction to excitement.

Not long after that, there was an Al-Anon open house with meetings going on all day long, and I went to that. One couple did a workshop on sex. I walked in there, and it was so riveting and so open that it blew my mind. I found a Thursday night meeting which had the topics food, sex, and money, and I started attending that meeting regularly. I began to be aware how I used food as a mood changer, a mind-altering substance.

At that time, there were not daily Adult Children of Alcoholics meetings like there are now in a lot of places, but I went to every one that I could find. All the people were like me, it felt. I didn't go there to get well, I went there to feel good.

In meetings people talked about their childhood, and I would remember things that happened. Before I got sober I was in therapy, and if my therapist implied in any way that my parents were not perfect, I would get angry. I wouldn't accept the fact that my parents who had worked so hard to give me what they did might not have been perfect people.

In ACA meetings when people spoke negatively about their parents, it was really hard for me to deal with. I couldn't believe they were saying bad things about their parents. ACA is an anonymous program, so it's not like you knew who they were talking about, but still it was hard. I just built up another wall by telling myself that their parents had done really bad things to them and that my parents hadn't. It took me a while to begin to understand some of the damage and hurt I had endured. A lot of it was more subtle, not so blatant and obviously unacceptable, for example, how my mother used to tell me nasty things about my father, always followed by the statement "but I stayed with him so you all could grow up to respect your father." Though she had no idea of how that twisted or hurt me, it doesn't change the fact that it did, a lot. I just kept going back to meetings because people were talking about things I understood.

A couple of years ago I picked up a book called the *Drama of the Gifted Child* by Alice Miller. I had heard people in meetings talking about it, so I sat down with it at breakfast one morning and opened it up to read and started crying after the first page.

I read and cried, and cried and read, and for the first time really felt about what had happened to me. All of the sudden, even though I could still tell you all the wonderful things my parents did, I knew why my life hadn't worked, what had been missing. I was always trying to fix myself, take another self-improvement course, because I could never get the pieces to fit. Suddenly, I understood the abandonment that I had experienced as a child. My parents gave me some things, of course, but not what I needed as a child. Nobody had done that. I've spent my whole life trying not to let anybody see me because I'm so embarrassed about what's inside. What Adult Children of Alcoholics meetings began to do was help me acknowledge and own those feelings. I have a long way to go still.

Much of what is referred to as "dumping" in ACA has been very valuable to me. In AA when I heard people talk about recovery, I didn't know what recovery was—recover what? The only thing I could think of was sex and money. Character building? I didn't know what that was. Despite the fact that I grew up in the church and heard these people talking about these things all the time, I had no idea what it meant to have self-esteem.

My first AA sponsor gave me the Canadian Air Force book of exercises and that was a real gift. I was in horrible shape, but I did them and gradually built myself back up. It was the first thing that was mine. There had never been anything in my life that was mine before; my family always had call on it.

During the last couple of years of my drinking, I had become fascinated with computers, and I'm really developing that interest now. So between the exercises and the computers, I began to get some sense of what it is to have something of your own that's important, that you want to work for.

Now I'm beginning to get in touch with that kid inside, the one with all the feelings, and I'm beginning to at least think about taking the risk of getting involved in a relationship. When I read the newspaper, sometimes I'll glance at the obituary section and see someone who has accomplished something in his life. I want that now, and I see that the combination of work and service builds a meaningful life. I never understood that before. I had such an emptiness inside that I thought money or sex would fill, and you drank in between if you didn't have those. I never knew how to take care of myself in any meaningful way.

I didn't see that there are things that are meaningful to do for me. I only saw doing things for my parents, particularly my mother. If only I could make the pain go away for her, then I thought everything would be all right. Not long ago I realized that one of the reasons I couldn't have anything in life was that that would mean she would come and live with me. I'm not saying that's necessarily true, but somewhere that was a story I believed and used to keep myself down. I've always made more money than my brother or my father, but I've always lived like a bum. They all live in nice homes. I just recently moved and I was embarrassed to have the movers come in, for anyone to see how I lived. But that's all changing. Taking care of myself has begun to have meaning now.

I'm 48 years old now, and I'm excited. I think I've got a wonderful future. I'm starting a second career. I'll soon be retiring from the company I've worked for for twenty years, and by then I hope to have my own business going. I'm just turning the corner from how things have been. I never wanted to feel the pain of my life, and I also never learned to have fun or take responsibility. Somehow those things seem connected. I've got a lot more pain to feel, I know, but my only fear is now that I won't really open myself up enough to get in touch with my humanity. Other than that, I don't think there's anything that can really hurt me. The childhood I never had, I'm having now.

I'm permitting myself to have a relationship with a woman who is simply a friend. At first I was embarrassed because there was that aspect of the culture that I grew up in that maintained that it was a waste of time to talk with any woman you weren't going to sleep with. So the concept of friendship with a woman is one that I've had to work out for myself, based on what it means to me, not to someone else.

It took me a while to go to Al-Anon meetings. I saw it as something that was just for women, and it took a while to work through that. Now I go to get information, to hear certain things, like about not feeling guilty. AA stopped me from drinking, but even after I was sober for two years, I still had no reason to live. Now I have a reason to live, a concept of what living is about. If you just stay around ACA meetings and let it work on you, you will change, that's for sure. So now I go to one AA meeting a week and sometimes seven ACA meetings a week, with a regular Al-Anon meeting thrown in on the side. I'm working on being aware of the emotional abandonment I had as a child and how to heal those feelings, so that's the kind of mixture of meetings I need right now.

I've been very active in AA and ACA. These programs have shown me that I can do things. I can make mistakes and I'm not criticized. I can turn around and choose to do something well, and I've never had that experience before.

I was in a meeting not long ago, and the woman talking mentioned her concept of a higher power. I became aware that as I reach for the best there is in me, that there is a higher power within me that I can grow through. The speaker said that our job as men and women is to live our lives as though limits to our abilities didn't exist, as though we are limitless if we reach into that higher power within us. I'm just taking in that idea now, listening for tidbits like that and seeing how they fit for me.

10. Meredith T.

The earliest memory I have is of laying under my bed, shaking from fear. My father had gotten angry with me, and I was afraid that he was going to throw something at me. I was about 3 years old. My dad seemed to be angry that I was even born at all.

He was a surgeon, just beginning his medical practice, when my mother divorced him. I wasn't quite 4 years old when they got divorced. I'm 20 now, the second child of four by my mother's two marriages.

I remember sitting in a rocking chair and asking Mom when Dad was going to come home. That's when she told me. "Dad isn't going to live here anymore. Now if you want to cry, go ahead." But I didn't want to cry. I was so happy at the idea of not having to live with the fear I had when he was around. When I look back today, I'm pretty amazed that by the age of 4 I had been living in so much fear that I didn't care whether my dad came back to live with us. He was already using a lot of alcohol and drugs.

Shortly after my parents separated, my mom moved us out to my grandparents' ranch. While we were living there, my father had to be put in a private psychiatric hospital. It was terrifying to go and visit him at the hospital. I knew he wasn't coming home, but we were periodically taken to this strange place (the psychiatric hospital) and told that we could see him for half an hour, and then we'd leave.

The divorce was finalized and we continued to live with my grandparents on their ranch in the Northwest. My mom was in shock from the whole experience and the prospect of having to support my brother and me and my younger sister by herself.

We saw Dad on a pretty regular basis for about three years, but he was still very ill. I remember going to see him and some of the things that he would do. I could not have been over 7. My brother and sister were with me one night when he took us out to dinner and offered us wine to drink. I thought that was pretty neat at 7; I'd never had any wine before. It turned out that none of us liked it, so he grabbed all the glasses and sat there finishing off the whole bottle by himself. I distinctly remember the drive home after that and being terrified because it was pouring down rain. You could barely see to start with and he was bouncing the car off the curbs, weaving everywhere. When we got home, he couldn't put the key in the keyhole, he dropped the bottle he was carrying with him, and there was glass all over the place. Other times he would tell us that he was going to come see us, and then he just didn't show up or call. I was really angry when he'd do that.

He had a different girlfriend every weekend we were with him. I began to make up excuses for not having to see him. I couldn't stand to go down there. I knew that something was wrong, though I couldn't have told you what. I was 9 years old. Over a period of three years he went through two more marriages.

One weekend when I was in fifth grade, my little sister came home from a weekend with him terrified. She was 5 at the time. He had gotten really drunk, thrown his girlfriend up against the wall, and fondled her right there in front of my little sister. Then he took his girlfriend in the back room, and my little sister was just left there watching. I knew after that incident that I never wanted to go back to visit him again.

Unfortunately, I did end up spending Christmas with him and his family, and I did not like it. They lived in a small town a hundred miles or so down the road. My grandfather, his father, was also an alcoholic. He was very grumpy and demanding, and nothing could ever be as perfect as he wanted it to be. No one could live up to his expectations. In turn, I saw my father do to my brother what his father had done to him. He constantly pressured my brother to go to medical school as he got older. He told him that he could take over our dad's practice. There was even a hospital named after our family in this little town. My grandfather and great-grandfather had been doctors in that community as well. Dad was pressuring my brother to follow in the family footsteps just like his dad had pressured him. My dad had been raised in the community where he was now practicing medicine and was having to perform for a lot of people. Everyone knew us and knew that we were his kids. Finally, the visits with him diminished.

When I was 10, my mom came into my room one day and told me that Dad had had an accident and that he was very ill. He was in intensive care. I didn't really understand what was going on at the time, but, in fact, he had tried to commit suicide. There was some story we were told about how he had driven from the hospital to his home just before he was to go in for surgery. He went into the garage, was about to get sick, got out of his car, and left it running. He made it into the house where he supposedly got sick and passed out on his bed. Carbon monoxide "leaked" through the door, and he was in a coma for three weeks.

I honestly don't think anyone knew for sure at the time what happened. His parents didn't want to believe it was a suicide attempt. No one in his town wanted to believe it was a suicide attempt because Dr. Maxwell was such a great man. He was like a hero in his hometown. But that was the story they told and the way his accident was explained to me. I remember all of a sudden realizing that I could lose this man, having to rethink everything, wondering what am I going to do if he dies, how am I going to handle the situation? Miraculously, he survived. I was in the fifth grade.

I channeled all my frustrations academically and became an excellent student. I was very athletic as well and was a good soccer player. I was really driven. I wanted to be the best, score more goals. I compensated by overachieving. I became the family hero. When I got to be 11 or 12, I just decided that I was so angry with this man that I was going to be the best, so good at something that he was going to read about me in the newspaper someday. Then he was going to want to claim me as his child, and when he tried, I was going to turn around and say, "Who are you? Where have you been?" I said that to my girlfriend many times. I completely channeled my anger into achieving. I was going to be the best, and he would have to read about me in the papers.

My mother remarried and I remember thinking to myself, "Well, if I don't have Dad, I always have Bill." I was Bill's kid. I loved him. My sister and brother couldn't stand him. It always went that way: me by myself with someone or against someone, and my brother and sister on the other side. That created a lot of tension among the three of us. Bill was an alcoholic, too, but we weren't aware of it then. I was so overjoyed at having a father in the house.

My mother doesn't even drink and yet she married two alcoholics. She's really beginning to wonder herself if she came from an alcoholic family and never realized it before.

I bonded immediately with Bill. I thought he was the living end. Now I can see that he was a professional con. He was after my mother's money, both from my grandparents and from the divorce. My grandparents had bought Mother a nice home here, and he knew there was money in the family. I thought he was great. I didn't know much at that age.

He and Mom had dated for two years before they got married. Then one weekend they went to Las Vegas and came back, and I found out they were married. My younger brother came along after that.

Bill was in the apparel business and on the road a lot. I remember my mom talking to him on the phone saying, "Bill, where are you?" He'd say, "I'm in Boise, Idaho." Then she'd go down to the apparel mart and find his van parked in the lot, which meant he was in town and out with someone else. At least that's what she finally came to believe, or eventually found out.

He came in really drunk one night and started yelling at my mom. The next thing we knew, he had grabbed my baby brother, swooped him up in his arms, and said, "I'm getting out of here and I'm taking this baby with me!" I remember that episode so well because our maid went running right after him saying, "You bring that baby right back here!" Her name was Helen, and she was very protective of us, particularly my little brother, Jamie. She thought he was the living end. She was an older woman, a large black woman with a commanding presence. Bill brought Jamie back to her, but he scared the living daylights out of the rest of us.

My mother was home very sick from the flu, and Bill completely neglected her. He'd be out at bars shooting pool with his friends. She was very ill. Bill wouldn't do anything. Finally, Bill's brother-in-law came over. He was the meanest person I ever knew, and even he said that she needed to be in the hospital and took her over there right then and there. Bill never went to see her in the hospital. I was about 10 at this time.

While my mom was in the hospital, Bill started working on me to turn me against my mom, and he did a pretty good job. Even though he frightened me from time to time, I was the one who bonded with him, who had replaced my dad with him. I was Bill's kid. He knew that I had always wanted a horse, and he started telling me that I could have a horse if my mom would just sell the house we were in. He had these grandiose schemes about how we'd go out to my grandparents' ranch and build a house on the ranch. I thought it sounded great because I could get finally have a horse, which had been my dream. He'd say, "It's your mom. She's the only one holding us back. You'd better talk to her. I think you should have a horse. She's the only one saying no."

"It's you," I'd turn around and say to my mom. "It's your fault that I can't live out in the country and have a horse." By the time she came home from the hospital, I was just hating my mom. I couldn't understand why she wouldn't do it. I bought his story—hook, line, and sinker: Everything was great, and it was mom who was disrupting our whole family system because she wouldn't go along with Bill.

It was a very confusing time. I desperately wanted to trust Bill because I couldn't trust my own dad. I believed everything that Bill said. Yet he'd turn around and do things that really embarrassed my mother and me. In sixth grade I had some friends over, one girl in particular I thought was fantastic. I was so glad that she had come over to my house. It was a big deal to me. Bill came in drunk and just started yelling at me, being really abusive in front of these friends. He was so angry that he was throwing things, breaking stuff. My friends decided that they'd better leave. I was completely humiliated.

Mother divorced him. They had been married three, maybe four, years. Sometime after the divorce passed and my mom and I were talking one afternoon—I don't even know how the subject came up, but I mentioned something to her about the fact that lots of times Bill had come into my bedroom in the morning. I told her that I didn't think he kissed me the way fathers kissed and that he didn't touch me the way I thought fathers should. Since I'd never really had a father, I wasn't sure about how or what fathers did or what the difference really was.

As Mom and I talked further, it began to dawn on us that I

had been sexually abused. We realized that I was an incest victim for the entire time that my mom was married to this man, starting at age 10. I was 12 years old when we realized this. It was all very subtle, and it had never even dawned on me what was going on. I had never mentioned any of this to my mother. I had kept it all a total secret during their marriage. It was only after the divorce that this came out. He never actually had intercourse with me, nothing that blatant or obvious. The things he would do felt good. He fondled me, kissed me, caressed me, of course always when my mother wasn't around. Or very early in the morning or very late at night when everyone else was still asleep, he'd come in and get in bed with me.

I remember his saying, "Now stand back and let's see how much you've grown," and then he'd insist that I'd take my clothes off so that he could "see everything." That stuck in my mind. I felt very uncomfortable about that, but the other stuff was so subtle it didn't really dawn on me until my mother and I started talking that day, and she asked me a lot of questions.

We ended up taking him to court. Mom was really upset, and so was I. It was the most traumatic experience that I'd ever had. Here I was, 12 years old, in court, finding out that because I had trusted this man and thought that the way he treated me was normal, that it was OK, that it wasn't. All of the sudden I'm being told that it was all wrong, that he was actually very nasty to have done what he did with me, that he was a very sick, perverted man. I went to court because I was told that if I didn't testify, my little brother would become gay. They said he would sexually abuse my brother as well. It was a nightmare.

So I went to court. Bill was there too, standing in the halls. I was absolutely terror-stricken because I didn't think that the judge or anyone else believed what I was saying. This was several years ago, before people were talking about this stuff. And there I was in a judge's chamber with three men, trying to talk about what another man had done to me. You have got to understand this. I was a 12-year-old girl alone with these three strange grown men, having to confess to them that Bill had put his hand in my pants, and so forth, be really explicit about what happened. I was incredibly embarrassed.

They asked me if it had ever dawned on me that this was wrong. I tried to explain that I'd never known anything else, I'd never had a father before. I walked out of there with a terrible feeling; as far as I could tell, they had not believed me. Bill got full visitation rights with my brother Jamie. That meant they hadn't believed me. It was a horrible experience to go through. I had to go through all the various episodes with them. And Bill was taking Jamie to bars with him when he was only 2 years old. Jamie grew up in a bar. When it was all over my testimony didn't make any difference. Bill kept his rights despite everything that had happened and what he did to me.

Those were really bad years for me. Sixth, seventh, and eighth grades were very depressing. I was fat, overweight, did not feel good about myself at all. I was very studious, but not much else. In the seventh grade I did pick up tennis, and I played three to four hours a day. I got very involved in that and started playing tournament tennis. It was a very positive thing to put all my anger and frustrations into.

I hadn't seen my dad except maybe once in a couple of years. I think I had seen him when I was around 13 and then not at all for almost two years. Then one Sunday morning I walked out to get the paper and there was my dad on the front page with the headlines saying, "Dr. Maxwell Being Brought Before the Board with Five Malpractice Suits Against Him." I had had no idea where my father was; I didn't even know if he existed anymore. I got to read all about it. I found out that he'd been up in another mental institution and was back out again, that he'd married yet again and had another kid.

His name was the same as my brother's, and it felt so strange to see it splashed across the front page. He was going to be investigated, and his medical license was going to be taken away from him. There was a horror story about the people who had died because of my dad's malpractice. It came out in the article that my dad was really messed up on drugs. I had no idea. He was quoted in the paper saying, "I'm very depressed and I'm taking too many barbiturates." So here I am 14 years old, reading about my dad in the paper. Mom said, "I'm so sorry that you have to see it this way. I know that you didn't know what happened to your father. He was so intoxicated before he did one operation, either from drugs or alcohol or both, that he removed the wrong organ from someone and she died. Another person, he did something wrong to his bladder and he had to have a catheter the rest of his life." That scared me. He was a surgeon, he was delivering people's babies, and he was on call all the time.

I don't know what happened with all the malpractice suits, but after all that, his license was not revoked. He admitted himself into a hospital for treatment. Another four years went by, and I didn't see him or talk to him except for once when my brother was in so much trouble Mom didn't know what to do with him.

My brother was 16, smoked marijuana all day, and drank. He had so much anger toward Dad that he was dumping on our family. I was afraid that he was going to kill Mom. She had had to hide all the knives from the kitchen. She was going to throw him out of the house. He went to live with my dad, who at that point was as messed up as my brother was, so my brother decided that he wanted to come back with us. But Mom had had enough. She had bailed him out so many times before, she told him that he simply couldn't live with her and do the things that he did. She wouldn't let him come back.

By the time I was 16, I was a little mother. My mom had gone back to school for a master's degree and was working. I did the car pooling, all the grocery shopping, fixed dinner at night, and got everyone in bed. I'd fix my little brother's lunch for school in the morning. I learned how to take care of everyone at a very early age.

In high school I was overachieving so much that I didn't even know what an A was, and I was making all A+'s. My mom was worried about me because of the level at which I seemed absolutely driven to perform. I was trying to make up for the fact that my brother was in the same high school. People would say, "Oh you're——'s sister, aren't you?" and I'd say no—I'd deny it. I didn't want anyone putting the two of us together. I was going to be so smart and such a leader that no one would ever think that we were in any way related. He was acting out, skipping school, in the vice-principal's office all the time. I was so ashamed. I didn't want anyone to know that we lived in the same house.

I started dating someone who made matters worse. I got into a big ego trip. This guy would say, "Your family is really fucked up. You're the only one with a head on your shoulders. You're the good kid, the 'normal' one." So I ended up denying that I even had brothers and sisters for a while: "Yeah, that's my sister. She's really screwed up. Where's Dad? Oh, well he left us, but that's OK. I can do without him anyway." That kind of thing. I was going to be the kid who didn't have a father who made it anyway. I was going to be *it*, I was going to rise above this morass and be superkid.

I tried to please everyone. I never got angry at school. Among my friends I was known as someone who never got angry. I never could get angry because I always thought people would leave me if I got angry with them. I connected abandonment with anger. I was also very afraid of angry people as a result of living with my father and stepfather. As soon as anyone was angry, my automatic response was being scared. Inside I was still a little girl lying under the bed shaking, scared that someone was going to throw something at me.

I had a very hard time getting physical in relationships. Guys would be really frustrated with me. It was horrible. Whatever was supposed to be feeling good, to me was nasty, lowdown. I felt like a slut because of the way my stepfather had treated me and what had been channeled into my head from that whole experience with the court. Whenever anyone tried to touch me, I said no, this is wrong, this is nasty, perverted. It didn't matter even when someone was in love with me. I'd say, "I don't care. You're going to touch me and leave me. No."

I mortified some of the boys I went out with. I tried to explain to this one guy I really liked. "I've been sexually fondled by my stepfather, and if he had been around much longer, I might well have been raped. It scared me, and it's going to take a lot of time to get over that, and it's going to take developing some real big trust." He broke up with me. That was hard.

By the time my brother was 20, he'd been using cocaine for four years. I was 18 by this time. We had a family therapy session to confront my brother about his cocaine use at this point, and my dad showed up. He'd been to treatment himself and now he'd decided that he wanted to be part of our lives again. I was so angry that I just froze. I couldn't begin to say the way I was feeling. I had no desire to get to know him because he had never made himself part of our lives. I just sat there with my arms folded for the entire therapy session and didn't say a word. My brother was so angry at my father for never having been there for him that he just blew up and walked out of the session.

Later that summer, my brother decided that he wanted help and he went into a treatment program. Dad flew up for his family week, which was good. They finally started to establish a relationship, and my brother was able to get rid of a great deal of his anger. I still have never really established a relationship with my father myself.

My sister went into treatment for chemical dependency when she was 16. My dad came up for her family week as well. I flew out from college on the East Coast where I was finishing up the semester. It had been a miserable year for me, and by the time I got to the hospital I was really frayed. The therapist running the family group knew about my poor relationship with my dad and knew that it needed to be worked out. I was asked to tell him how angry I was that he had never been around. I was physically gagging when I said this because it had been stuffed down inside of me for so long. It made me sick to look at him and tell him how I really felt about him. I distinctly remember looking him in the eye and saying, "I hate you." It was incredibly hard for me to do that. That wasn't my way. I didn't want to be malicious toward anyone and yet I had to admit to my feelings. I was being confronted on all sides about my anger at his having left us, about having been his little girl and then being abandoned by him. I could no longer avoid or hide from my feelings. I wanted him to either stay in my life or get out of it for good.

Then I turned around and confronted my sister. She told me before the counseling session that she did not want to deal with her anger toward Dad that week. Once again I found myself in the middle. I knew how she felt about him. I had let her put me in the middle for years, telling me everything she did and telling me not to tell Mom. Well, for years I didn't tell Mom and that was part of my disease, but now she had ended up in treatment because I told Mom everything she'd done. I had stopped protecting her, covering up, keeping secrets. I already felt guilty about that. So the next session I said to her, "I'm not going to bear the brunt of your anger toward Dad the rest of my life.

You deal with it now, while we're all here and there's support for doing it, or I'm never going to live in the same house with you again. All your anger toward Mom and me and the boys is misdirected. It belongs to Dad and you know it!'' God, was that hard to do! It was the hardest three days of my life, but we got a lot aired and worked out. My sister dealt with her anger with Dad, just like I had done and that helped a lot.

I don't really keep up with my Dad. I got out what I needed to say to him. I told him that if he didn't want to call me or write to me that was OK. He'd never been a part of my life before so it wasn't going to make a big difference. But, on the other hand, if he did make a decision that he wanted to become part of my life, then he had to do it on a consistent basis and that I would not tolerate his hopping in and out of my life. ''You don't even know me as a person. You can't appreciate me or anything I've worked for, so much water has passed under the bridge and you've jumped in at such odd times. It hurts me that you've been gone so long, and I feel guilty telling you that I don't have much hope for the relationship because I can see you're trying, but that's how I feel.''

That whole second semester of school in my sophomore year was bad for me. I had gone through my brother's hitting bottom and getting into treatment the end of the summer before. I was there for the family week for him. I had gotten a lot out of his family week and had planned to go to Al-Anon for myself when I was back at school that fall. Turns out that they didn't have any meetings at the college I went to, and I had no way to get to the nearest meeting, which was forty minutes by car. I was at one of the top Ivy League girls' schools on the East Coast, and I'm sure I wasn't the only one who could have used an Al-Anon meeting, but I just wasn't able to connect.

The second semester that was so hard was when I broke down and told all the family secrets. That got my sister into treatment. I felt responsible, guilty. She was angry with me. I was so caught up with what was going on with my sister halfway across the country that I was just barely making it. I was constantly focusing on everybody else and worrying about their problems. I kept up a B average, but it was killing me. I put on twenty pounds, I didn't take care of myself, had absolutely no fun. Finally, I called my mother at Easter and told her that I wanted to fly home for three days and see a therapist that Mother knew who was really good with me. He was a person who would not let me feel sorry for myself. I was drowning in self-pity and I knew I needed to do something and do it fast. Three days was not enough to make much progress.

I was in the worst shape I'd ever been in. My upset began to show physically. I couldn't get up in the morning, couldn't make myself do anything. It would take me weeks to write papers that I could have done in days because I was completely burned out emotionally and physically. I was just miserable because my sister was in treatment. I called everyone when my sister got sent off to the treatment center, called all my Mom's friends and asked them to please take care of her. I was still trying to take care of my Mom from 2,000 miles away. I was still trying to be responsible for everyone, trying to fix everything, save everybody.

I had secured an internship in New York for the first half of the summer, and for the second half of the summer I was going to Oxford. Always focused on achievement. I was supposed to leave for New York right after family week at my sister's treatment program. But by the time I finished my exams, packed up my room, and was leaving the East Coast for the family week, I was contemplating suicide. Life seemed impossibly hard, and I didn't see a way out. Nobody needed to confront me by the time the family counseling sessions began at the treatment center. I was just spilling over with feelings.

After five days of family sessions as part of my sister's treatment program, I concluded that I needed to go home. I needed to get my own life together and start taking care of Meredith instead of everyone else in my family. It had never occurred to me for a moment that I needed to take care of myself. That's what my mom's therapist had told me during those three short days at Easter. Now it really sunk in. Summer was staring me in the face. I called Mom's therapist from the treatment center and told him that if I could see him twice a week for the next six weeks, I'd come home and give up my job. That was incredibly hard for me to do.

Jack said he'd work me in and to just get home. "I'm going to teach you how to take care of yourself," he told me. "You've never learned that in your twenty years." I felt guilty and very unprofessional about calling the man who had hired me, but I did it. Just called him up and said, "Look, I've got some family problems, and I just need to go home for six weeks and take care of myself." He was incredibly understanding.

When I went home at the beginning of the summer, I started meeting some of the people that Mom had gotten involved with over the past year in Al-Anon and Families Anonymous. Even though they were older, I realized that these were the people that I was going to need. I started going to meetings. Jack insisted that I do things that I enjoy, too, start playing tennis again, lose some weight, start running. He was all for the meetings I was going to because he said that I needed to learn about the behaviors I accumulated as a result of living in the environment of an alcoholic family system.

I thought it was very selfish to take care of myself. I thought it was self-centered. I had been going to Al-Anon for a while before I ever begun to really fathom *how* I was taking care of everyone else but me. I needed to take care of everyone else. One day Jack really helped me understand what I was doing.

"Your whole role in life has been to be a caretaker. Now what are you going to do if you don't do that anymore?" I burst into tears. I really didn't know what to do with myself if I wasn't taking care of everyone else. "You are dependent on your role in the family, the role of the caretaker, running around and fixing everything and everyone and cleaning everything up. Now your job is to be yourself and that's going to be hard, isn't it?"

He was so right.

Jack began to push me to talk about the sexual abuse in therapy. "You've got so much bottled up about how you feel about the man who treated you this way—you have got to start talking about it." It was the hardest thing I've ever done, especially since I had to talk to a man about it. It's still hard to talk about it today.

Child abuse, particularly the sexual abuse, is such a touchy subject. The press is just now starting to come out with the issues and only now are people beginning to be believed about what happened to them. After my experience as a child in court, there was always a fear in me, a question, like maybe I'm just blowing this all out of proportion, maybe it wasn't as bad as I thought it was. Apparently that's not uncommon to wonder like that. It can also be another form of denial, another way of not dealing with reality. In any case, I know for a fact that it affected my relationships with men later on.

I tended to drown myself in self-pity and would then want people to pick me up. It got to be a vicious cycle, particularly between me and my mom. The unspoken agreement was, ''I'll take care of you if you take care of me in return.'' I would take care of my mom 2,000 miles away, but when I was down, I expected her to pick me up and carry me too. I would call her up and be depressed and say, ''You make the decisions for me. I can't do it.'' I would fall into a place of helplessness where I didn't think I could do anything.

One of the women in Al-Anon took me to an Al-Anon Adult Children of Alcoholics meeting and I immediately clicked. The people were so open and honest, the issues were things that were happening to me on a daily basis. I remember that I had been having a hard time letting go of a relationship with this one guy I'd been seeing because he was the first guy I'd gone out with that I really trusted. But then I found out he was seeing other girls on the side, and I just let him do it. I was groveling. I was so scared of losing that relationship, of being abandoned, that I just clung on for dear life. I was so dependent on him that I completely stifled him. There was no room for him to breathe in that relationship because I was always so afraid that he was going to leave.

I walked into an ACA meeting one night when I was in the middle of struggling with this, and the topic was relationships. They passed out a three-page handout on characteristics of co-dependent behavior in the meeting. It was a list of everything that was me, all my dependencies. It pointed out how as an ACA we are often addicted to relationships with people who are chemically dependent, that we have dependent relationships, destructive relationships. That was me I was reading about—how I am dependent on people who were going to hurt me, that I would let people hurt me rather than risk facing my fear of abandonment. I identified with being addicted to excitement, to always looking for approval from others. I derived my entire sense of self-worth, my self-esteem, from other people. I didn't do things for me. I ran to keep skinny because I wanted to look pretty for boyfriends, because people would like me more. I held in anger because I didn't think people would like me if I got angry.

The characteristic on that list that hit home the most was the one of deriving my sense of self-esteem from others. That began a big turnaround in my recovery. I began to see how I clung to sick relationships, how when that person liked me, I liked me. If they weren't feeling good about me that week, then I wasn't feeling good about me either. I was on an emotional roller coaster. If something wasn't going well in my boyfriend's life, then it must be my fault. "If only" I had been a better girlfriend, he would feel better. I was in a sick relationship with that boyfriend. He could get angry with me, but I could never stand up for myself. I took whatever abuse he dished out, not physically, but emotionally and verbally, and just held on. ACA meetings helped me see that I tended to be attracted to people that I could take care of, people that I could pity, people that were addicted to the same kinds of unhealthy relationships that I was addicted to. I didn't become addicted to chemicals like my brother and sister, but I sure was addicted to behavior patterns that I'm now really beginning to see. These things don't change overnight.

I told people what they wanted to hear. I never wanted any chaos. I wanted to keep things calm. I didn't care about sticking up for anything I believed in or anything I might need because I was so focused on pleasing everybody else. I didn't even know what I believed or needed. I never got upset about anything, so everything was just sitting there under the surface all stuck inside me. It was just as dangerous to me as my sister's chemical abuse was to her because it brought me to the same place— wanting to commit suicide. There were days when I was in so much pain, that to slit my wrist would have just been a different feeling for me and that would have been good.

I overate to keep everything down inside of me. I ate to get nurtured and full, but then I felt horrible instead. Jack, my therapist, helped by refusing to feel sorry for me. He taught me that self-pity is the opposite of gratitude. He taught me how to pick myself up and helped give me the tools to go on. If I began to feel overweight, he told me to just touch myself and say, "Well, you are overweight. What are you going to do about it?

Are you going to change it, or are you just going to sit there and feel sorry for yourself?'' He helped me understand how when I feel sorry for myself, I would fall into the old pattern of depression, not talking about feelings, taking care of everyone else but me, keeping the focus on the outside, not getting angry with people when I needed to be angry, and so forth. The ACA meetings really helped me stick up for myself in a lot of situations and to keep the focus more on myself than always be zeroing in on everyone else.

When I go back to school this fall, I'm looking forward to getting a sponsor. I'm at another Ivy League school now but one in a metropolitan area where there are lots of meetings, every day. When I went to England for the rest of the summer, I went to Al-Anon meetings there and they were wonderful. I met some fantastic women there, one of whom is from the United States. Her husband was a visiting scholar there, and I'll be able to see here again in the States.

It was really hard when I first came back home, to work on all this. It's been very hard to talk to people my own age about all this, because the majority of them haven't been through this experience. They just aren't in touch with their feelings. They haven't learned to take care of themselves yet. I found myself hanging out with much older crowds when I first came home.

The denial in my home community is to the degree I haven't seen anywhere else. There are abusive, violent parents here, and the kids still say, ''Oh, we don't have any problems.'' It's a scary thing to watch because I see the suicides coming. No one wants to believe that their kids are using drugs. That's common. We did not want to believe that there was cocaine use in our family. It's like the elephant in the living room that everyone walks around and cleans up after, but no one acknowledges it's there. I felt so stupid about my brother. I had been away at school for a year. I just thought that maybe he was depressed and that was why he slept all the time, worked fourteen-hour shifts, and didn't have a penny to his name. I knew a lot more about what was going on with my sister, but I completely missed what happened to my brother with cocaine. I did not want to see it.

I hope to become a lawyer someday. This whole experience has made me want to practice some kind of law where I can defend kids who are in homes where they're being abused and they've committed a crime. Kids need to be believed, kids who say, "My dad was going to rape me again and I had to kill him." This stuff happens, and there are not enough good attorneys who will believe a kid. I didn't feel like I was believed. Take a look at the book *The Kid Next Door*, and you'll see what I'm talking about. True stories of kids who finally took matters into their own hands, in self-defense from rape, incest, beatings. Having been in court, having to tell my story and not be believed gave me a feeling of helplessness I'll never forget.

The past just doesn't go away. Just because I eat one more piece of steak, or you do one more drug, or just try to forget it, these things don't go away. I called my Al-Anon sponsor from school several times this past year, and she'd always say the same thing, "Meredith, until you acknowledge your feelings— the loneliness, the sadness—it's not going to go away. It's going to stay with you like a piece of luggage you have to drag around the rest of your life. You are never going to feel good about yourself until you deal with some of the old issues you've got stuffed way down inside you." I know she's right.

I love the ACA meetings here and I look forward to finding the ones at my new school. I'm going to get a sponsor there and then start working the Steps. I know they're the key to this process of recovery. At least I'm on my way.

A Conversation with Marion Woodman on Addiction and Spirituality

In the early 1930s, Jung worked with one of the alcoholics, Rowland H., whose sobriety helped lead to the creation of AA. Under Jung's care for a year in Switzerland, Rowland was able to stay sober, but as soon as he returned to the U.S., he got drunk again. He returned to Switzerland, and Dr. Jung told him that the only hope for him was a spiritual transformation. There was simply no "cure." Bill W. and Jung exchanged letters about this event many years later, in 1961. Jung pointed out that it was no accident that alcohol is also called "spirits" and said that the alcoholic's thirst for alcohol is equivalent to the soul's thirst for "the union with God."

"Alcohol in Latin is spiritus, *and you use the same word for the highest religious experience as well as for the most depraving poison. The helpful formula therefore is:* spiritus contra spiritus," *he wrote in his January 30 letter to Bill W., 1961* It's an alchemical formula. It takes spirit to counter spirit.*

Looking at alcoholism and addiction as a longing for spirit might mean that something very different is going on in our society. One might say that we don't have a crisis with alcohol and drugs as much as we have a spiritual crisis. Addiction is the perversion of spirit, our spiritual nature turned inside out, devouring itself. The epidemic of addiction can also be seen as spirit trying to re-enter our society. I went to Toronto to talk with the eminent Jungian analyst, Marion Woodman, about the nature of addiction, the symbol of the child, and her work.

RACHEL V: In your latest book, *The Pregnant Virgin*, you talk about how the healing has to come through the wound. That paradox reminds me of Christ's comments about how the weak will confound the strong.

MARION: The weak does confound the strong. The conscious ego may know exactly what it wants to do, may be moving right

---

*This letter appears in *Pass It On* (New York: AA World Services, 1984), p. 384.

along through life in a very strong, goal-directed, ambitious way, but the unconscious, childish side of the personality can bring the ego down. Indeed, it will bring the ego down unless it is recognized. The weak side is the addictive side, so that it is only in dealing with that childish/childlike side that the individual is ultimately able to function. The chain is as strong as its weakest link. It's that weak side that is involved with divinity as I see it. The childish part that is so uncontrollable, so demanding, so tyrannical is at the same time the childlike part that brings joy and creativity into life. It is the soul that will not be silenced. Buried in matter, it yearns for spirit. A longing for alcohol does symbolize a longing for spirit. Think of the Greeks with Dionysus, the god of the vine. Intoxication and the transcendent experience with the god were intimately connected.

Think about the symbolism in the Christian mass where the wine becomes the blood of God and the bread the body of God, spirit and matter. Alcoholics are longing for spirit because they are so mired in matter, but they make the mistake of concretizing that longing in alcohol. Maybe if they really understood what they are longing for and could go into the realm of the imaginal, the soul's realm, then something very different could begin to happen.

What is this terrible starving in an addiction? It's as though our whole civilization is feeding the hunger, not to satisfy, but to make us hungrier. There is this sense of "I want more, more, more of—something." In eating disorders—binging, anorexia, bulimia—you find the same drivenness. Addicts do their best to discipline themselves and they may do a very good job from 7 A.M. to 9 P.M. Then they go to sleep. Their ego strength goes down and suddenly their unconscious comes up. As soon as the unconscious with all its instinctual drive erupts, the ego loses control. Then the addiction becomes a tyrant. Its voice is that of a starving, lost, child: "I want, I want, I want, and I am going to have." There's another instance of the weak confounding the strong.

RACHEL V: I don't know that much about anorexia and bulimia except they seem to be akin to some kind of profound rejection of the body.

MARION: Yes, a profound rejection of matter. So often you find a syndrome that goes from obesity to anorexia to alcoholism. It may go into religious fanatacism. Addicts tend to move from one addiction to another. So long as they are in that addictive behavior, they are just substituting one addiction for another. The healing has not taken place. Think of AA members who remain sober so long as they are workaholics. The drivenness is still operating in the household. In such situations, the children will pick up the unconscious of the parent who desperately wants a drink and runs to food or runs to work or any other addiction as a way to keep off the bottle. The child picks up that unspoken yearning, that unlived life, and the compulsive repetitiveness that aggravates and expresses denial. The child in its own way tunes into what is absent in the parent and goes after it.

I think to get to the core of the problem, you've got to look at what we have done to the body, what we have done to matter in our culture. The Latin word *mater* means "mother." Mother is she who cherishes, nurtures, receives, loves, provides security. When Mother could not accept her child in its peeing, puking, animal totality, the child too rejects its body. It then has no secure home on this earth, and in the absence of that primal security it substitutes other mothers: Mother Church, Mother Alma Mater, Mother Social Insurance, even Mother Food, which it also cannot accept. A desperate love/hate relationship develops. The terror of losing Mother equals the terror of being buried alive in her. Without the security of the body home, the individuals must rely as best they can on these substitutes for the maternal security they do not have. More than that, if the body is rejected, its destruction becomes one's *modus operandi.* The fear of cancer does not make an addictive personality stop smoking.

In the absence of the nourishing mother, whether personal or archetypal, people try to concretize her in things, as if to make present what they know is absent. Ironically, what they capture is not a presence that they always experience as absent but the absence itself. Think of how people try to photograph everything, tape-record it, try to capture and hold an event in a static state. That's what I mean by "concretize." Like the evil witch who turns everything to stone.

I went to see the pope in Toronto, and after he passed by, the woman in front of me burst into tears, crying, "I never saw him!'' She had a camera and had been so busy taking pictures of him that she never "saw" the man she came to see. By concretizing the moment, she missed it. The person she came to see is caught in the picture, but the picture reminds her only of absence. She was absent from the experience.

Think of tourists jumping out of a bus at the Grand Canyon. They snap pictures, but they never arrive at the Grand Canyon. They don't open themselves to the experience. Inwardly they are not nourished by its grandeur. The soul in the body is not fed. It's like slides filed away in a box that no one, even you, wants to look at.

William Blake says that the body is "that portion of Soul discerned by the five Senses." I live with that idea. I sit and look out my window here in Canada and the autumn trees are golden against the blue sky. I can feel their "food" coming into my eyes and going down, down, down, interacting inside, and I fill up with gold. My soul is fed. I see, I smell, I taste, I hear, I touch. Through the orifices of my body, I give and I receive. I am not trying to capture what is absent. It's that interchange between the embodied soul and the outside world that is the dynamic process. That's how growth takes place. That is life.

Most people do not feed their souls, because they do not know how. Most of us in this culture are brought up by parents who are, like the rest of society, running as fast as they can, trying to keep up financially, socially, and every other way. There's a drivenness that the child is subjected to even *in utero*. In infancy the child is expected to perform. Often the parent isn't able to receive the soul of the child, whatever the little soul is, because the parent doesn't take time to receive or doesn't like what the child *is*. Many parents are too interested in seeing that the child will have dancing, skating, an education, and be at the top of the class. They are so anxious themselves in all they are trying to "give" to the child that they do not receive from the child. The child, for example, comes running in with a stone, eyes full of wonder, and says, "Look at this beautiful thing I found," and the mother says, "Put it back outside in the dirt where it belongs." That little soul soon stops bringing in stones and focuses on what it can do to please Mommy. The process of growth turns into an exercise in trying to figure out how to please others, rather than expanding through experience. There's no growth without authentic feeling. Children who are not loved in their very beingness do not know how to love themselves. As adults, they have to learn to nourish, to mother their own lost child.

RACHEL V: Marion, you've talked so much about the mother and the Goddess. I need to clarify that what I think we've been talking about *isn't* male or female, but different aspects of the human experience. These are not so much issues of gender as epistomology. We are straining the language here. The verbal shorthand of associating certain qualities such as receptivity with the feminine do us all a disservice and I think compound our difficulties. "Masculine" and "feminine" are <u>descriptions</u> of experience not the experience itself. "The map is not the territory," as philosopher Gregory Bateson said. We end up with a neo-Manichean split if we're not careful. The basic premise is that we are all, men and women alike, male and female, biogenetically as well as psychologically.

MARION: Yes, Rachel, I agree. This is not about gender, "male" or "female." These are principles I'm talking about.

RACHEL V: The denial of feeling and the emphasis on pleasing, keeping peace, and performing is not limited to alcoholic families.

MARION: True, but I think there is some addiction in most families; our culture is addicted. The addiction can cover a broad range of problems: parents that are involved with another partner, a relationship addiction, a food addiction, a gambling addiction, a sleeping addiction, a TV addiction, which is another way of going to sleep. I have analysands who go to sleep the minute I say anything they don't like. In five minutes, they come to. They cannot take confrontation. They cannot take pain, and as soon as they feel it coming, they fall into unconsciousness, which wipes out the possibility of growth. They cannot confront. Where there is real strength required in a spiritual confrontation or a real meeting of souls, they cannot even receive love. They are afraid of love because it makes them vulnerable. To take that further, what you're left with is an infant, an abandoned infant inside the body. The body becomes an immense cavity with this screaming little baby inside. There is the abandoned child. On a symbolic level we might say that this is the divine child. Sooner or later that divine child starts to scream and he's the weak one that brings down the seemingly strong parts of the personality. Thus the addiction in its own circuitous way may be trying to bring us back to the God within—embodied spirit—Incarnation.

RACHEL V: This idea of becoming like a child to enter the kingdom of God, do you know of other cultures where we find this image?

MARION: In the story of Persephone and Hades there is a child. Hades abducts Persephone, takes her into the Underworld, and in some versions of the myth, she has a child. In many of the myths, Leda and the swan, Danae and the shower of gold, for example, the human woman is impregnated by the god. In other words, matter is penetrated by spirit and the child of the union of matter and spirit is the divine child.

What is going on then in a person who is forced to surrender, to say, "Yes, I am an alcoholic, I am an addict, I am powerless over my addiction. I have to turn myself over to a higher power"? That person is surrendering matter to spirit. There's the union that can produce the divine child. The addiction has made receptivity possible. Many of us cannot understand how powerful femininity is until we are brought to our knees through addiction or illness.

I think it's important to recognize that on some level, in some peculiar way, we're all in the same mess, whether we're alcoholic, children of alcoholics, anorexic, workaholic, or drug or money addicted. Addicts are trying to run away from God as fast as they can. Paradoxically, they are running right into her arms. Consciousness makes them realize how the soul is trying to lead them into the presence of the divine if only they can understand the symbolism inherent in the addictive substance and addictive behavior.

Take food as the addictive object. The biggest problem in dealing with an anorexic is that once she starts to eat, stops fasting, and breaks the euphoria caused by the fasting, she turns around and says, "If this is what life is, I'm not interested. It's dull, boring, not worth living." Eventually, she has to recognize that rejecting food is rejecting the reality of being human, and her addictive behavior is the acting out of her tyrant child determined to control or escape the tyrannical parent, whether that parent is inside or outside. So the anorexic, and this is true for all addicts, has to come to a new way of life.

If you live day by day, in touch with the world around you, just even a minute a day, as Blake says, then that's the moment in each day that Satan cannot find, it's what you need to keep the soul alive. Because you are in touch with the eternal, you hone into Home. Then you can *see* the bronze blue morning; you can *hear* your child's silence. Then life is never boring. Too many people never take that moment in the day, so they run around trying to find it, outside. That's the problem: they try to do it outside themselves and that hurls them into the addiction.

All the running is away from the tragic fear that we are not loved. Unless we perform well, we are not lovable. That terror leads to self-destructive behavior. It can also lead to global self-destruction. Addictions may be the Goddess's way of opening our hearts to what love is—love of ourselves, love of others, love of the dear planet on which we live.

Lots of people are trying to find spirit through sexuality. Through orgasm they think they can be released from matter, and for one brief moment, they hope to experience this extraordinary union of spirit and matter. But if they can't bring relationship into sexuality it's just a fly-by-night thing. Eventually it just becomes mechanical, and then they become frantic. "I've got to have it. It's got to work. It's not going to work. It's my fix." Sexuality without love is matter without spirit. People who are unable to love may be addicted to sexuality and be driven over and over again to try to find love. What they are projecting onto sexuality is the divine union that they so desperately lack within themselves.

Jung said the opposite of love is not hate but power, and where there is love there is no will to power. I think this is a core issue in working with addictions. Sooner or later, the feminine face of God, Love, looks us straight in the eye, even when that love manifests as rage at our self-destruction. She's there. We can accept or reject—live or die.

I don't know about muffins in the States, but muffins in Canada are numinous. A patient came in yesterday, a woman with an eating problem and she was crying. "I don't know what to do," she said. "You tell me that I have to recognize my feelings. Most of the time I don't do anything I want to do because I don't feel it would be right. I was driving here, and I had a desire to bring you a muffin. Then I thought you wouldn't want the muffin. But I know you would love a muffin, but no I won't buy it. You don't take your analyst a muffin. But then I got into such a state, I was just sweating, because I wanted to get the muffin so much. I stopped the car, went back, got the muffin, and I have the muffin in the bag, but I don't know whether to give it to you or not. I feel such a stupid child, but I don't know what to do."

"Well," I said, "I want to receive the muffin."

I broke the muffin in two and gave her half. Because of the love that was in the muffin, and because she had been received, it was a communion. It's a simple, simple story, but I tell you, people at that level of feeling are so terrified of being rejected that a muffin can bring out the rejection of a lifetime. In outer reality this woman is most competent. She's very professional, highly respected. Everybody thinks she is very mature, and she is except for this rejected child. Here's the weak again. The little child says, "I want to take Marion a muffin." If that child has been rejected and rejected and rejected, it goes almost into a state of nonexistence. It experiences loss of soul. The person becomes disembodied. That's the point of vulnerability to an addiction. It is also the point where the god or goddess can enter.

At the heart of it is the religious issue. Our soul is our eternal relationship with God. The soul's language is the language of dreams. As I see it, every dream is a communication with God. We have an inner dialogue going on all the time. At night we experience it. But I think if we stop to daydream during the day we drop back into the dream. Periodically, we come to consciousness, then we drop back. The dream gives us symbols, images, but because we're so concretized we don't understand the symbols. We say dreams are crazy, silly. We have cut ourselves off from the world of the imaginal, and so we have forgotten the language of dreams. Thus we make the mistake of assuming that if we're uneasy, insecure, it is food that we want. Thirsty? We have to drink. Feeling a little empty in the gut? We need sex or whatever other concrete thing we can get hold of. But it is the soul that is calling out in dreams and the soul communicates through symbols. If we meditate on these images, they reach us on all levels: imaginative, emotional, intellectual. Our whole being, including our body, resonates. We feel ourselves whole. The images of that eternal world are the images of the bread-and-butter world—food, drink, sexuality. That's where the two worlds meet. That's why we have to be so careful interpreting dreams. A sexual dream, for example, may be the soul's way of expressing a need for union of spirit and soul—a creative act in the imaginal world—dance, painting, writing. Alcohol as a symbol may be a need for spirit. Gallons of ice cream cannot bring sweetness to the soul, nor can gallons of gin float you into the presence of God.

Our own inner child has to be disciplined in order to release its tremendous spiritual power. If we identify with its childish side we say "I was always a victim. I will always be a victim and it's all my parents' fault." Then we can go around with a hangdog look the rest of our lives. If on the other hand we identify with the childlike part we say, "My parents were the victims of a culture as were their parents and their parents. I will not be a victim. I will take responsibility for my own life. I will live creatively. I will live in the *now*." To be childlike is to be spontaneous, able to live in the moment, concentrated, imaginative, creative. Because most of us have forgotten how to play, we have forgotten the joy of creativity. Without joy, we find ourselves running away from pain. Without creativity, we run away from emptiness. The faster we run, the more severe our addictions. We cannot face our own nothingness. Nothingness is the ultimate anguish of childish people who live their lives knowing who they are not rather than who they are.

In the New Testament when the divine child was born, Herod the King ordered the killing of all the babies in the kingdom. That's what happens when our own inner child is born. Herod represents the collective, conventional attitudes that will be destroyed if new life thrives. As soon as our inner child comes alive and says, "This is who I am. These are my values," all the terrified Herods in our environment rise up and say, "You are a fool." If the baby is not protected, it will be killed. It takes immense courage to find out the values of our own divine child and even greater strength to live those values. Addictions drown it, starve it, drug it, kill it. Ironically, they keep us in touch with it as we run round and round the hole where it is lost.

Lucifer and Christ are very close together in many addicts who yearn for a "high." A fast high. They want to be gods in control of a perfect world in which they are perfect. They long to be like Lucifer, the morning star, the brightest star, the first son of God. And like Lucifer, their pride brings them into collision with God. They cannot accept their own human imperfection. They cannot live in a universe they cannot control. When they stand in their own desert, their inner Lucifer faces their inner Christ and says, "I will give you all the power and material goods you want if you will bow down to me." Addicts are trapped in illusions of their own power, illusions that rob them of their human life. They are driven by a voice inside, "I have to. I can't. I've got to. I won't." They long for a paradise not of this earth. They don't want to be here, but they are. Their bodies are driven, their muscles so tight they cannot relax. Some addictions overcompensate by allowing the body to fall into stupor. On a Friday night, for example, if the body is armored and tense, a woman may be saying to herself, "I will not drink. I will not," but another voice says, "I'll explode if I don't let go. I've done everything everybody wants me to do all week. No more. I'll show you who's boss. I'm going to drink and I'm going to drop out of consciousness. I don't want to feel anything." Trying to be a god all week can flip one into being an animal all weekend. There is no *human* balance in the addict.

RACHEL V: Are we ever free from an addiction?

MARION: In AA, however many years you are dry, you still say, "I am an alcoholic." How many people do you know who fell back into their trap after one drink or one cigarette? The unconscious is like the ocean: the obsession can fall deep into the ocean floor, but a crisis can bring it charging up from below. Life moves in cycles, consciousness expands. Each time we are faced with new truth about ourselves part of us dies and a new part is conceived. In the fullness of time we have to move through a birth canal and birth canals can be dangerous. In any experience people tend to repeat their original birth trauma each time they attempt to leave the warm womb they have cuddled into. If they were Caesarean births they may hesitate to confront; if they were breech births, they might go at things backwards; if their mother was drugged, they can tend to find some anesthesia (drugs, alcohol, food) to throw them into unconsciousness. These points of transition where we are called to stretch into new maturity are the points where the addiction is most liable to resurface. Changing the habitual behavior is extremely difficult because it is the only behavior the individual knows and it is interlocked with the unconscious behavior of one or both parents. If you are convinced that at some point in a relationship you will step into an ambush and fall into a dark hole, then that becomes your habitual behavior and you can be sure you will land in that ambush. You are in it before you know what is happening because it is your unconscious reaction. If you can pull consciousness in and say, "I don't have to fall into that trap," then you walk at a more precarious gait and foresee the danger. With this steady perceptive awareness, I think it is possible to reach the point of stillness that is free of the addiction.

Our culture is not geared to process. It values security and status quo, and because we are living under the shadow of nuclear war and annihilation we try to hang onto whatever permanence we can. The pain of leaving the old life behind and facing the new without any real understanding of who we are becomes unendurable. Some cultures have rites of passage that give meaning and companionship to people in transition. Most of us experience total aloneness. I see it in dreams where the dreamer comes to a border crossing in pitch dark confronted by fascist customs officials or has to cross a rickety bridge that spans a river of whirlpools. Addicts tend to be loners; their dark intuitions take them out of their bodies. In an ungrounded state, sheer terror can drive them back to the addiction.

Intuition can be a blessing and a curse. People who are intuitive are never quite in their bodies. They are confounded by possibilities and driven this way and that exploring what might be. They are rarely in the present, never quite in their bodies. Their bodies then become vulnerable to all the pain in their environment. Through osmosis they pick up other people's unconscious garbage. When the load becomes too heavy, they escape through an addiction. (Think of this dynamic between parents and children.) Again, it is the problem of absence. The soul is hiding somewhere in the gut; it isn't animating the body. You feel that when addicts hug you. Their children sense it, and while they can't articulate it, they are haunted by emptiness. They feel they are living in an illusion in which nothing is quite what it seems; the left hand doesn't know what the right hand is doing. Dad is charming; Dad is vicious. Mom dresses like a model; Mom is a slob.

Transitions are hell. Your beloved dies or goes away and you are left alone. That is hell, it is also an opportunity to grow. Alone, we dialogue with our own bodies, our souls. This wisdom is exactly what we need for our own wholeness. It makes quite clear what is real, what is illusion. It strips off layers of false pride. This wisdom make us human. What a relief to be a human being instead of the god that Mom and Dad projected onto us!

Each hell burns off more illusions. We go into the fire, die, and are reborn. To put it in Christian terms, we carry our own cross, we are crucified on our own cross, and we die and are resurrected on a new level of awareness. We find our balance on that plateau for a while and then another phase of growth is demanded and a new cycle begins. Addiction, like illness, can bring us into our bodies. Healing comes through embodiment of the soul, the soul living in the here and now. The body is. The soul in matter is what I think the feminine side of God is all about. The agony of an addiction can break the heart open to the love that is present in all creation. It is that breaking point that is so important — that edge where addicts tend to live—annihilation or apocalypse. Our technological age pushes us so fast that we annihilate what is happening to us. We pass by the moments of soul. We move from incident to incident without being there. An anorexic in a euphoric trance can move to the edge of death without any awareness of what is literally happening. If I say, "Look, you're going to die," she looks at me in bland astonishment. Unless an incident is made conscious, it does not happen in the soul. It has to be thought about, written about, painted, danced, made into music. In other words, it moves from literal to metaphoric if it is to be assimilated into the soul's flowering.

That's what analysis is about. As analyst, I become the mirror to reflect back to the patient what is being said, what the body is saying, what remains silent. Without a mirror, we cannot see ourselves. But one doesn't need an analyst for reflection. Keeping a journal can provide an opportunity for reflection, for example. Parents who are locked in their own narcissistic need cannot provide a mirror for their child, and therefore their child cannot develop an individual identity. Take the small incident of that muffin. Had we not taken time to reflect on the need and the love and the faith epitomized in buying that muffin, we would have committed soul murder. Such a tiny interchange seems like nothing until you remember the moments in your own childhood when you hoped and you loved and you gave your all and nobody received you. That's death.

My first analyst, Dr. E. A. Bennet, taught me a great lesson in the healing power of love. I thought analysis was a very serious business and so I went to every session with my dreams carefully recorded, with associations and amplifications. We worked rationally together for six months. Then on December 24 I received word that my dog had been killed in Canada. I had a session scheduled for five o'clock that afternoon and I told myself I must not waste it talking about my dog. The doctor would not be interested in a dog being killed. So I went and spent the hour telling him about my dreams.

Then Dr. Bennet said, "What's wrong?"

"Nothing," I said.

"Well, you haven't been here," he said. "I wish you hadn't come."

"My dog was killed," I said.

The tears welled up in his eyes. I couldn't believe it. This great doctor, 74 years old, could weep for my dog.

"How could you care about my dog?" I asked.

"Your dog was a soul connection for you," he said. "You can't bear to bring that feeling out and so you come here and waste Christmas Eve."

Then I was able to cry. His love recognized my soul. God was in that moment. From that point on, I was present in my analysis.

It happens again and again with my analysands. Their pain is so deep that it takes a very long time for the real feeling to surface. People are ashamed of their "childishness," but those blocked feelings cannot mature if they have no one with whom to interact. So long as we are determined to move at our swift, logical pace, the child remains hidden. The natural rhythms of the body are slow. The little soul-bird that was put away in a dark box in childhood needs time and silence to learn to trust again.

Marion Woodman is a well-known Jungian analyst, lecturer, and author. She received her training at the C. G. Jung Institute in Zurich and maintains a private practice in Toronto, Canada. She is currently working on a new book on the nature of masculinity and femininity and is the author of *Addiction to Perfection* and *The Pregnant Virgin*.

11. Nicholas K.

I was born in Alaska in 1953. I am full- blooded Tlingit Indian. Alcohol has been in my family for a number of generations. When I first heard of Al-Anon's Adult Children of Alcoholics meetings, I really identified with the concept, but I had some trouble with the name. I feel like I'm an Adult Child of Alcohol because even if I had been raised in a family that didn't drink, the whole village that I was raised in was slowly being destroyed by alcoholism. There is no way I could not have been deeply affected, whether my own family or I had ever taken a drink of our own. But we drank, too, so I was affected from inside the family as well. I was particularly affected by the alcoholism of my uncles on my father's side. That's what I remember the most.

In the village where I grew up, alcohol was wide open. It was in almost every house. My earliest memories were of people committing suicide, murders going on in the village, whole families being destroyed. The alcoholism in my family wasn't unique; it was in every house that I knew.

I was brought up in a very large family with traditional Tlingit ways. There were nearly a dozen of us. My father drank a lot. He always provided for us; we always had a home. But when I was 8 years old, my father died from an alcohol-related boating accident, and it tore our family apart. That was a turning point in my life. I made a pact with myself and said I was never going to be like him. I was going to be the last one that anyone in my family had to worry about. So many of us that are raised in homes with alcoholism say that. When he died, I stopped crying. I never cared anymore. I told myself that I was going to make it in this world, no matter what. I was the youngest of the boys. I have three sisters younger than I am.

My brothers were at an age where they started going to the military, and they left me at home with my sisters. My uncles were still living in the house, and their drinking was much worse than my father's. They became loners. They stayed in their rooms all the time, talking to themselves. Mother didn't let them drink in the house, but they always came home drunk. You could hear them through the door. I always wondered what they were trying to say. They withdrew from the whole family, and it put a lot of strain on us kids. My mother was very traditional and couldn't take it anymore. She had my uncles removed from the house and took over the land and the house for us kids to be raised in. That was very hard on her.

I started using alcohol not long after my father died, when I made this pact that I wasn't going to feel anymore and care anymore, or cry anymore. So at 9 years old I started hanging around with other guys that were probably going through the same thing that I was, so we started drinking. The village that I grew up in was surrounded by a town of non-Native people, and in the village we had a gang of kids that everybody considered to be lost causes. People thought of us as lower-class types, and even other native people who lived outside the village considered us kids of the lower class, poverty-type people, and so that kept us together as kids. We formed a gang, and we hung out together. People, our elders, would call us good-for-nothings, said that we would never amount to anything or come to any good. We believed that. We believed every word they said. We said, "We're no good." Even the natives that lived outside the village were afraid of us because we had this stereotype that we were no good. That just made us stick together all the more. We acted out that role, using more drugs, glue, gasoline. Anything we could get a hold of, we started using. We built forts in the woods to just use our drugs. We got into old army dugouts and made forts out of them so we could store the booze and drugs that we stole from the warehouses around town. By the time we were 10 years old, we were thieves. We had become very good at stealing things: liquor, cigarettes, candy. We filled up whole rooms with stolen goods. People were dying. I have an uncle who at 16 years old hung himself. I'm saying alcohol was in every house and home and family. He was drunk when he did it. He hanged himself, and I remember as a kid, looking up in the trees and seeing his body. It's left a permanent imprint on my mind, that body hanging up in the tree. I was too young to really know what was going on, but it's there. I still have nightmares about it. So I went through a lot of tragedy as a kid. I've seen a lot. I got to a point of not caring, not having any feeling toward anything that died anymore or anything. I just lost so much.

My first experience at being a pallbearer was when I was only 8 years old, the same year my father died. A friend of mine hanged himself, and he was only 9. He was using alcohol. Everybody in his family drank like crazy. Everybody says that they don't know why this young boy took his life the way he did, but I know it was the alcoholism in his family. We used to talk about it, and he was one of my best friends. Because he was one of my best friends, I asked his father if I could be one of his pallbearers.

I don't know how the community took seeing a whole bunch of kids carrying this coffin down the street, because it was all kids that carried the coffin. We were all children. It's just the way we were back then. We accepted death so easily. All us kids had no feelings toward death; it was happening all around us.

I was raised around a bunch of older guys. After I got into this gang, they were wearing black leather jackets, their hair was greased back, and they started teaching us how to be like them. The gang was fifty to sixty strong, of guys that were involved in gangs and fighting the non-Native people, the coast guard, and the students. We were pretty rowdy back then. The first things we learned as a kid is how to run away from cops and people of authority. When they were running from the cops, they would give us kids all the weapons in case they got caught. That way they'd be clean, and if we got caught, they couldn't do anything to us because we were such young kids. So when they were running from the cops, all the weapons, knives, chains were given to us. That was one of my jobs as a kid, hold on to these weapons and run.

When I got a little older, one of the real young kids that hung out with us killed himself. He was only 7 years old. He was always a very happy kid. He kept a lot of us going, us older guys. He was kind of like our mascot. He was always doing things for us, more than willing to do whatever we asked. He was well liked by all the rest of the kids. He wouldn't ever say anything about his family, never talked about what happened at home, kept it all inside. A few days before he died, he was crying. He was resenting something that was going on in his family. He was crying about it. We tried to let him know that we cared about him and and told him, "Hey look, we are village kids, and we have to hang together. As a part of this gang, for better or worse, we hang together. We *have* to hang together." We were all Natives.

The morning they found his body, we were going up to his place, and his father found him lying in bed. He had tied a rope around his neck and the other end around a post to the bed and turned over. His head was off the bed and his body was just down, was lying on the bed. He was just hanging up there. It was a very slow way of dying for a little kid. But that's how they found his body. His parents were all drinking, everybody in that house was drinking, and he was the youngest of the house. Apparently they got drunk the night before, and he was real hurt about it. Apparently he was abused at home. That's how they found him. Everybody was in denial. They said, "This kid was happy. Why him? Why did it have to happen to him?" They never connected it with alcohol.

During the fifties and early sixties, the village I grew up in was very large. It used to be 1,500 to 2,000 people, and every house had a large family, including grandparents and extended families all living in large houses. That's how I remember it. But alcohol destroyed almost every house in the village, to the point where the village is now almost gone. It's not much more than an empty parking lot. The alcohol had been around for generations, at least 300 years or so. So I saw the tail end of the village life. It was being destroyed from within by alcoholism and chewed away on the outside by development interests. The community around the village was getting larger, and the village was getting smaller and smaller, and now what used to be a beach is now all industrial property.

My uncles' alcoholism continued to get much worse. I hung out with them all the time as a teenager, and my drinking was getting a lot worse too, even though they were out of the house. I was always around the older crowd. I started using LSD and all the other drugs because, like I said, we had warehouses full of drugs, alcohol, cigarettes, and candy. Anything we ever wanted, we stole. Marijuana was coming into the village more and more, and we were getting access to it. I started using it because it was easy to deal with marijuana. We were getting wilder and wilder as time went on, and my uncles were already wild. It was an accepted way of life—to be drunk and crazy. We adopted the way we saw them treat women and became sexually active at a very young age because of the alcohol. We watched the older guys and just did what they did. The Native women didn't have a chance. We were too wild toward them. They were getting really abused. You often wonder why Native women don't marry Native men and it's probably because of the way we abused them. There was a lot of physical abuse, rape. We really abused the native women, just to put it mildly. I was a alcoholic by the time I got into my teenage years. Not much good happened to me in my teenage years. It was always marijuana, alcohol, and drugs. We had a little bit of cocaine, but mostly speed: speed and pot and alcohol and LSD.

My older brothers' friends and my friends were all drinking too. We had the same friends. Our patterns of drinking were the same. We got so used to losing people. That's a terrible thing to get used to. When we were 13 years old, we were getting into sniffing glue, and the only thing that stopped us from sniffing glue was that one of our friend's turned yellow. He died from sniffing glue. When we came out of that glue sniffing back to reality, we had this guy laying in the fort, and he was dead. His liver apparently gave out on him—too much glue. That stopped us from using glue.

The whole family was involved in alcohol and drugs, pretty much except my mother and my sisters. She was real strict with my sisters. She felt that it was kind of too late for the boys, but she could save the sisters. I really love my mother today for what she did. She was a very traditional, strong woman. By the time she started having us kids, she had quit drinking and had very little alcohol since then She felt that her kids were more important than alcohol. She sort of set the pattern. Alcohol was never allowed inside the house as we were growing up. If we were going to drink, we had to do it outside the house like she did with my father and my uncles. Same rule for us, and it's still a rule today. When my uncles and my father drank outside the house, they would always come home drunk. I never went home when I drank and used, so as a consequence, I hardly ever went home. I was always going to the party houses and staying there, and sometimes I'd be gone two to three weeks at a time or a whole summer, just out partying around some place.

Because our family is traditional and I was getting to be 15 to 16 years old and my father was gone already, the old people got together and lined up a husband for my mother. In the old way, when somebody like a provider dies, my father's clan would get together and line up another clan member to marry my mother. My mother had one of the last traditional Tlingit marriages in our village. When my stepfather came into our lives he was an alcoholic, too, but he was very traditional and was considered a very strong leader. Very traditional. He knew the old ways, and he was very strict. The very first thing he told us when he came into our house is, it's too late for us boys, we're too old. "I can't teach you anything," he said, but, in fact, he tried. I didn't like him at the time. I hated his guts, and it's a natural reaction for a kid to hate his stepfather. I tolerated him because he was good to my sisters. He taught me how to hunt and fish. I still hated him. I didn't realize at the time that he tried to love us. It was hard for him. But he said it was too late for us: "You'll have to go out in this world all on your own." So my brothers went into the service, and I moved in with my grandmother.

He taught me the traditional ways of hunting. But that was during a time when I was really heavy into drugs, and I wouldn't go hunting on drugs. He knew I was sick. He would look at me and condemn me and tell me I was good for nothing. He tried to get me off the drugs, and he'd get meaner and meaner and meaner about it. Like if I was stoned or something, he would know. He was getting mean about it because he didn't know how to approach a kid who was so heavy into drugs and alcohol. So finally, I just stayed away from the whole family. The last thing he told me was, "What are you going to do when you find out who you are?" Those words have stuck with me.

I moved out and stayed with my grandmother. I was always very close to my grandmother. She was the only one out of everybody in the family who stuck with me. She prayed for me. I thought everybody was against me because I was getting wild—not just my family, but the village, too—but she always stuck with me. I was always close to her. She always stuck with me, no matter what. She didn't know how to speak English. I was really raised by her. From the time I was very young until the time she died, I always felt I could communicate without speaking words to her. She and I had a link of some sort. I always knew what she wanted. I was just very close to her. She never gave up on me. She always prayed, and maybe that's why I got sober today, because of her prayers. I think about that sometimes. Because today I still do things that I think she would like me to do, so I still feel very influenced by her. I think I'm living the life she would like me to live.

After my grandmother died, I got out of high school and went on to college. I was the one they call the "lost child" in the family. I just removed myself whenever there were problems. When disruptions happened, I would go off someplace, off in the woods. I would withdraw, I wouldn't say a word. Still, it's in my personality today, I still disappear into the woodwork, I ignore the whole thing and hope that when I come back, that it will go away. I really have to work on that attitude. That's one of the things I've come to understand in my recovery as an ACA, and that's hopefully begun to change. Things don't go away, like feelings and memories; they just get buried. Sooner or later, in one way or another, they will make themselves felt. I have a choice now, thanks to recovery, of facing these things myself and being conscious about who I am and where I came from. If I don't get conscious about my past, it just runs me without my even knowing it, especially in my relationships with other people. That's where it really shows up.

I got into college, and my drinking and drug use got worse. How I made it through my first year of college, I don't know. Some good things began to happen to me though, too. That first year of college showed me that I was actually a pretty smart guy, not the good-for-nothing village kid that I used to think I was. I was starting to be around other people like myself. I was first exposed to Alcoholics Anonymous and the Twelve Steps in college. I still thought drinking was somebody else's problem, not mine. Still I knew that something was wrong.

I started realizing that I was always doing things halfway, never completing things. I was always doing things just to get by. I was getting C's and B's in my classes, and I'd never study. It began to occur to me that if I could get C's and B's without effort, maybe I was smart. Maybe with some effort I could do even better yet; maybe I could amount to something after all. I started taking on leadership roles. I started making some real effort to find out what my potential was. I started by coming fully aware of being Indian, the positive parts of being Indian. There were 500 of us going to college at that time. I got involved in Native politics and became president and held office, became involved in the politics of the community as well. There was a lot of regional prejudice going on at that time. Racial tension was high. We were fighting an eye for an eye, and we just succeeded in making things worse. Our sense of "Indianness" got more perverse. We organized a group, and the only way you could get into this group was if you were full-blooded Indian. There were about a hundred of us. We called ourselves "the master race"; it was really distorted. Alcohol and drugs started coming in more and more and destroyed the whole thing. There was no tradition at all, it was just a party and just a radical group of people. The elders started holding conferences, and they started working with us. They started inviting us into their meetings because they were worried about us, because we were getting worse and worse. They started telling us that this is not the way to go. "Treat everybody the same, no matter who you are or where you came from. This is the traditional way, this is the way of our people," they said. The traditional way of Native people is not the way of prejudice and racism. We were just as bad as the people we were accusing of being racist toward us.

I dropped out of college my second year because I chose to drink rather than go to school. School was getting in the way of my drinking and drug use. My priorities were switched around somehow, and I was using. We used to go into bars. I'm a very good pool player, and we used to go into bars where there were Puerto Ricans, whites, and blacks. We'd play pool for a while and start instigating fights. I was very good at pool, and I knew how to get people mad and into fights. So the whole bar would just blow up into a big fight. I really enjoyed the excitement of it. It wasn't until I heard somebody talking about being addicted to excitement in an ACA meeting that I began to understand what I'd been doing all that time. And in an alcoholic home, it can be plenty exciting—usually pretty negative, but excitement nonetheless. I wasn't sure anything was happening unless there was some kind of conflict going on. Serenity? Never heard of it before AA and Al-Anon.

When I got 18, 19, and older, my attitude toward women started changing. It began to shift. I felt like I had two different personalities. There was a wild side that looked on women as objects, and there was a side that I'm living now today that respects women and sees them like my sisters and my mother. That split in me just got bigger and bigger. It was really hard for me to get close to women, to become really intimate. I've never allowed myself that, and I've never been married. All the women I picked in the past were alcoholics. That's something I've really had to work on in recovery and just practice learning how to be friends with women. As I grow in my recovery, my ability to get close to people grows too. It's all changing as I work the Steps over time. There's no shortcut for me.

There's a good side of me that cares about other people, that wants to help. That first year in college I was into Native studies, archaeology, and social work. And when I quit, I was still part of this Native movement that was going on, so much so that I was asked to be the youth director of one of the Native associations. They didn't know that I was still using alcohol, still using drugs. Eventually, I drank my way out of that job, but in the meantime, I got exposed to AA. The seed got planted.

When I was director of the youth program, part of my job was to set up self-help groups for young people. I didn't know how to do that, so I went to AA to learn what that was about. I was always trying to help other people. It's tricky. That can also be a characteristic of the co-alcoholic too. Though I wanted to do good, at that time focusing on helping other people was a way of avoiding myself and hiding from what was happening to me. Still, I have always wanted to help my fellowman. Anything I had I would give away. I also got some training as a counselor and learned a lot about group dynamics. I hired a drug counselor, an alcoholism counselor, and youth workers. I was supervising eleven people and administering the grant. I kept thinking alcohol was always somebody else's problem. I started missing work, and I started drinking during lunch and disappearing and sleeping in, and finally I just never went to work. I'd go to the bars. AA started screwing up my drinking. I even put a little note in my desk saying that "I quit alcohol," and I'd open it up and look at it. That's when I started realizing that I had an alcohol problem. But I never did anything about it at that time, so I lost the job because of alcohol.

I got into trade school, and after that my drinking got worse. I used more drugs and more alcohol because I made more money. It was a very good trade, an electrician. I spent 3½ years as an electrician apprentice, and my income tripled. It went from $20,000 to $40,000, then to $60,000, then to $80,000, but my alcohol and drugs and women and legal problems made my habits go up. If I was making $40,000, I was spending $70,000. If I made $80,000, I was spending $120,000. There was never enough. The more money I made, the more I needed to support my habits. During that time, I was really getting into cocaine heavy. I was giving my money away. I knew more lawyers than friends. The union at that time was also paying for my lawyers because I was in an apprenticeship and I was an investment to them. It got to the point that I was no longer an investment to them. I was beginning to cost them money. They got tired of sending me to jobs in remote areas where there was no alcohol. They got tired of bailing me out of jail and got tired of my drinking. So they dropped me out of the apprenticeship program the first chance they got. I lost everything because of alcohol and drugs.

I came home suicidal. What's the use? Relationships, school, jobs, I couldn't keep anything. I always left or got fired because of alcohol. There was never enough alcohol, money, drugs, sex to fill the hole inside of me. I drank for the next year, getting worse and worse, and tried to kill myself twice. I was a full-blown alcoholic at 25. That was my bottom. I had no job, no home, no people. I was losing friends, and I finally tried to commit suicide with a .38 Smith & Wesson. The last thing I remember was pulling the gun up, pointing it to my head, and getting ready to pull the trigger. And I blacked out. When I woke up the next morning and found that gun next to me, I grabbed it and ran down to the docks and threw it in the water.

I had just broken up with another girlfriend, and I remembered that her mother was in AA. She was Indian, and I went looking for her. I started drinking again and was drunk by the time I got to where she was listening to some AA speaker. I was in a blackout and finally passed out again. When I came to, I was in a van and this priest was in there with me. It was

Father Joseph Martin, and the guy driving the van was director of the local alcohol program. I went into treatment not long after that.

I thought only alcohol was my problem, and so I continued cocaine and marijuana. It wasn't until nine months later that I stopped using marijuana and cocaine. Things were happening to me. AA was beginning to set in because I was going to meetings all the time, and more and more meetings. All these people were expressing love to me. I couldn't handle love at that time. I couldn't handle all these people smiling and saying they cared for me. Things were happening to me. I feel that the higher power was there because I was being attracted by all these AA people. They had something that I didn't have, and I wanted it. It was their love. I was always running from that too. About nine months later, for the first time since my father died, I cried, for the first time. I had to go back into the woods because I was raised not to show my feelings. I was told to be strong. I went back into the woods and spent three days back there. I sat three days in one spot. I didn't move. For my first day there, I could just feel this lump in my throat. That night at about 2:00 in the morning, it all came out. The tears came, and I just sat there and cried and cried. The third day about noon, I stood up and walked away from that spot, and the farther I got away from that spot, the better I felt. I was running, smiling, felt like I was right on top of the world. I could hear the birds. For the first time I experienced life at that moment. I loved life, I wanted to live. That's when AA came in to my heart.

So I started reading books, AA books, the Big Book. I started reviewing films from the alcohol program. I started doing part-time work for the alcohol program. I worked on the film library and put together a library of all the books, films, and cassettes. I was a sponge. Any information that I could get on alcohol and drugs, I went for it, anything. I put it all into this library. I was willing to do anything. I read everything. I've seen over 350 films on addictions, and I started looking to people, developing people resources, finding people who were involved in Fetal Alcohol Syndrome (FAS), Children of Alcoholics, anything related to alcohol. I started singling people out who were good in certain areas and started doing community presentations.

With others, I set up a lot of self-help groups in town.

There's now Al-Anon, Hope for the Children. We started teen-age groups, went to schools. I started working with Native students especially. I developed a list of things that life doesn't have to be like. It took a lot of work to really get back into a life, to really get out of my suicidal tendencies, and to really want to live. When I shared that with other students, telling them that they don't have to go through what I went through, that these are signs you have to watch out for, these are things that are going to happen, then good things started to happen.

I didn't realize it at the time, but the old people were watching me, the elders. They started coming up to me and saying there was a time that you couldn't have lived up to your name. There was a time when we turned our backs on you, which they did, but now we have watched you and know you are serious about what you are doing. So I started recording elders on videotape and started recording stories and legends and anything that had anything to do with alcohol and Native people. I met one of the elders who had a legend that predicted the coming of alcohol before the white man, and he let us videotape him telling the story. We have it in our language and in English. I can't say too much about it without the permission of that man's family, out of respect for him, because he is no longer with us. He died when he was in his 90s, a respected elder of our community.

What I can see from this tape is that it's the Twelve Steps and Twelve Traditions from our people's perspective. Our people look at this tape like it's a prayer. Symbolically, it depicts the suicides and deaths that have happened to us as a people. It puts everything into a spiritual perspective, and it's seen as a prayer. So I am honored to be a carrier of this tape. The first year we had this tape in our program, I had to go all over this part of Alaska and present this tape to the elders to get their opinion of it. Our people believe that one person cannot speak for everyone; I have to talk about my family and my clan only—that's the way we are. So I had to go to all the elders and present the tape, because it talks about everybody, and get their permission to present it to the public. So that was my introduction to more of the elders. I got their permission. I presented the tape the way it was told to me to present it, and I asked their permission and also got their opinion on the tape. Every elder said, "Yes, this tape tells the truth. Yes, show it to the young people." So I did. I started showing it to programs in schools. It's done in such a way that they can see that there is hope. This legend was very important for me as a recovering alcoholic because I had heard people, so many people, say that Alcoholics Anonymous does not work for Indians. Watching this tape and being a part of the recording of it, I realized that that's not true. The story is hundreds of years old, and yet somehow it has the spirit of the Twelve Steps in it.

The man who passed the legend down to us is from the family that originated it. He was one of the descendants of the story, and the old people who saw this tape know this man to be a descendant of that legend. So they know that this man had the right to say it. So this legend is true to fact. There isn't an elder in this area who will say any different. They said it's true to fact. They said I should share it with the younger people, which I have done.

This legend has been passed down through generations, on and on. It took a while to really pick out the Twelve Steps and Twelve Traditions in this story, but as the years went by and as I was presenting it and hearing it over and over, every time I heard it, I got something different out of it. I present it in such a way that it is a prayer. I've seen what this legend has done to other people, to other villages. I've seen the results of this legend. Very positive results.

I am looking to my own people for answers, where in the past, I've always looked outside. For the first time in my life, I see my people. That's where my program is today. I'm looking for answers within my own self and my own people, incorporating values that were passed on to me from my own people—like "Treat people with respect, don't judge people"—values that missionaries tried to push on us and didn't realize that we had all the time. We believe in one God. We're not totem worshipers like people say we are. We have a religion that is comparable to world religions, as far as I'm concerned. That's my impression.

I've been around some of the elders, and I've seen them heal. At ceremonies I've seen elderly ladies in their 80s who have probably been in wheelchairs for twenty years, and I've seen them climb out of their wheelchairs and dance because the

Spirit is so strong in that room. I've seen that. I've seen the healing go on that natural healers can do. I've seen cancer victims come into the hospital where doctors tell them they have two weeks to live, and a traditional healer from our people would come in, and those cancer patients would have two years added to their lives. I've seen all that, and I know my people. I walk around here now, proud to be part of my people. There are things that are part of traditions that should be held on to. I've seen it. I feel it now.

The ACA meetings have really helped me see that I had to take time out for myself. I had to learn to work my program for me instead of always doing things to help other people. I was so enthusiastic about the program that I shifted out of being the "lost child" in my family when I was drinking into being the "hero" when I got sober. A lot of people in the alcohol field in Alaska treated me like I had some answers because I was Indian, young, sober, and free. I was traveling all over the state to the villages, trying to set up youth programs after I was sober awhile. Well, I ended up going to a village that had the highest suicide rate in the nation, and the suicides were all teenagers. It just showed me that no one person can take on all these problems, and no one person has the solution. It really showed me that I'm only a part of a movement, and it takes a group of people to come together to attack these problems. We don't need heroes anymore; we need the group consciousness. No one person, a hero or not, can take care of these problems. We burn people out all the time. That's what happened to me. I got so overwhelmed by the deaths and suicides that I had nothing to offer. Nothing. That's when I realized that I had to take a break or get drunk. I took a break.

I had to really take time out for myself, and for myself only. I had to finally get this program back to me. I was very fortunate when I first started going to ACA meetings that I had a few years of AA first. It took having a solid base in sobriety to really begin to look at what happened. What they were saying in ACA really hit home, made me realize that there are still things I have to work on, like my relationships, self-esteem, how I relate to my sisters and brothers. Getting clean and sober isn't all there is to sobriety. In ACA I've learned that I have to work on more intimate things, my feelings toward other people and my acceptance of how people express themselves to me.

One of the characteristics of ACAs that I really identified with was the tendency to not complete tasks. That was something I was still doing after I got sober. The other side of that coin is being an overachiever. That's another kind of compulsive, characteristic ACA behavior that I've been prone to fall into. The meetings helped me see that these are both kinds of behaviors that help me hide from my real feelings. The goal is balance, not these extremes.

Because of my job with the state, I visited over ninety villages, and I was able to listen to many people. People would talk to me about the problems with alcohol and drugs in the village, and I listened. I was looking for what was still intact in the culture, what people had within their own village. I knew all about the incest, rape, child abuse, all the horror stories. I just pushed that aside because I knew what I was looking for. My belief was that the answer to alcohol and drug abuse was something that kept the people together, something from our own traditions. Then I heard about a program in another region where the elders had stepped in and were taking over the leadership. There had been so much suicide that in 1983, the elders, along with some others, started a program called the Spirit movement. I was able to go and attend one of their Spirit camps. They are bringing together the elders and the children, to pass on the values from our culture. There were also young people like myself who were coming back from the cities, were getting out of prison, and people who wanted to come home. They were finding that more and more people wanted to return to their village. In the Spirit camp they try to blend the best of both worlds, AA and the traditional ways of our people. They shared their story and the stories of our people. They've gotten some very positive results. It was very exciting to see. Villages have begun to start turning around. Alcohol abuse is beginning to stop in places where people have been involved in the Spirit camps. Now these camps are being set up around the state. We're seeing lives turned around. In some places it's the young people who are standing up in front of their own people and saying. "I'm proud of my people, but there are some things I'm not proud of, and alcohol is one of them." Teenagers are beginning to stand up to their elders and shaming them. The teenage suicide rate is so high in some villages that it's teenagers themselves who are taking action, not the elders. I can see that we're on the road of recovery now as a people. We have tools, we're going in the right direction. For so many years, we wrung our hands about the problem of alcohol in the villages. Now we're talking and beginning to live out some of the solutions. There is a solution, and for me it comes from a blend of the best from both worlds, the Native and the non-Native. For a guy like me that used to be so prejudiced, who hated white people, it was a big eye-opener to see that we need to know the resources that are available to us outside our culture, like AA and Al-Anon. It was equally important for me to realize that I also need to know what my own culture is, my own people's traditions. I have to use both worlds; they complement each other and for me, that's what works.

There's a program that we brought in from Canada called the Four Worlds Development Project. They're looking at the traditions of all people—red, white, yellow, and black—and how we can bring them together. Our culture is based on respect. And there is a great need to bring out that part of our tradition, or we cannot recover. I know I can't. Alcohol blends in with prejudice and hatred perfectly. The tradition of respect for all people, for the Earth, for all creatures, needs to be cultivated. The Spirit movement is based on this idea and gives me hope today for our people, as it blends in AA and Al-Anon. My father died because of alcohol; my friends and family died because of alcohol. I finally realize now that it does not have to be that way. We have tools now. There is another way of life out there, and it's beautiful.

12. Mark K.

I was born into an Irish immigrant family in the Northeast. Both my parents were immigrants and spoke with Irish accents. I'm the oldest son. We had a big family. We grew up as a lower middle-class family in a middle-class neighborhood, full of Irish, Italians, and Germans. My father was a fireman. He had completed six years of a grade school education in Ireland and then went to work in the fields, as a child. My mother had completed maybe seven years of schooling before she had to quit to help at home. Both my parents' fathers died when they were very young. My mother came from a family of thirteen children and my father from a family of fourteen with only a widowed mother and grandmother to raise all the children, so everybody had to work. I always had the idea that they grew up in very, very poor conditions, but I found out a few years ago when I first went to Ireland that my mother grew up on a beautiful farm that anyone would have been proud to live on. There were just too many of them. My father grew up on a smaller place in a neighboring county, but a lovely one as well. They didn't meet until they got to this country.

I'm practically convinced that there's alcoholism in every Irish family. My father had a least one brother who was an alcoholic. He was the only one of the brothers to come to this country, so I don't know about the rest of them. My mother had several brothers as well, and all the ones who emigrated to this country were alcoholic, too. I became an alcoholic as well, though I've been sober in AA now for almost fifteen years. I'm 56 years old.

We all knew, even as children, that there was something wrong with our family. My father drank and occasionally got drunk, which terrified my mother. She would be very upset and do everything she could to hide it from both the children and the neighbors. As a child I didn't understand much of this. I just remember hearing her say, "Mickey, you're going to have to stop drinking because it's affecting the children." We lived in a very small house, and we could hear everything that went on.

I don't recall the drinking being a large issue until I was 9 or 10 and my father was caught drinking on the job. That created a huge family crisis. He was suspended from work and told to report to the Civil Service Board for a hearing. With five children to feed, we needed the money desperately. I remember his getting dressed up in his uniform to go before the board. He was a big, handsome man. We all went to the hearing with him. They ended up putting him on probation, but he was able to keep his job. Not long after that, the whole family—mother, father, kids, all of us—went down to our parish church and my father "took the pledge" to never drink again. It was a common enough thing then, to take "the pledge" in the Church. There was a priest, altar boys, lighted candles. He swore before God that he would never drink again and he didn't, not that I ever saw.

He had what we call "white-knuckle sobriety," and he was not a happy man. Putting down the bottle is one thing—that gets you dry—but sobriety has to do with changing your life, with serenity. He never got that.

I was very afraid of my father as a child. He was physically abusive toward my brothers and me. If we did something he didn't like, he'd take off his belt and beat us, sometimes to the point of drawing blood across our legs. Apparently I had been the object of some of this, more than I could remember until my brother filled in some of the gaps in my memory. One of my brothers is also in AA. He's an Irish cop, and we've become very close over the past ten years. On several occasions when we'd visit, he'd ask me if I remembered Dad doing such and such, and I couldn't remember. I had blacked out huge areas of the physical abuse. Once when Dad caught us having been around a fire and we lied to him, he beat both of us badly, but my brother assured me that I'd gotten the worst of it. He couldn't believe that I had no memory of the episode at all. It had frightened my brother terribly, but I had no recall.

The last time he came to visit, we went to an Adult Children of Alcoholics meeting together. It was the first one he'd been to, and I had just discovered ACA myself. On the way home he said that it was one of the greatest meetings that he'd ever been to. "I got more insight into what's bothering me today than I

ever got in AA." I had a very similar reaction when I came
to ACA.

I got tremendous relief from doing my Fourth step in AA
thirteen years ago. I got a great sense of forgiveness for my
father without really thinking of what I was forgiving him for.
It was just a comfortable feeling, that whatever it was that
caused the separation between us, I forgave. But when I started
going to ACA meetings and hearing other people have the courage to talk about their childhood, I got more of a breakthrough
of real feelings than I ever did anytime in AA or regular Al-
Anon meetings.

I was a very good student in school. I enjoyed studying and
was successful at it. The nuns in Catholic schools thought that
I was bright and gave me as many opportunities as they could.
There was one nagging problem; my father resented it. I didn't
know to call it that at the time. I only knew that if I came home
with all A's, he would say, "Well, I expected you to get that.
How come you're not playing football or baseball?" I never could
please him, no matter what the hell I did. It wasn't a daily
occurrence, but I was conscious of it all the time, my inability
to please him. It's very important for a young boy to please his
father. My brother, who wasn't a particularly good student,
couldn't please him either.

I had a very close, happy relationship with my mother. I
could always talk to her, and it's because of that, I think, that
I've always had a good relationship with women. Always felt
like they were a group of people I wanted to be friendly with
and knew how to do it. My mother was very understanding of
my desire to be successful in school. I'd always wanted to be a
doctor, from the time I was 9 years old. I'd read her poetry,
things I was reading in school. She loved it. My father wanted
none of it; he wasn't interested.

My father was very tender toward my sisters, but not toward
us boys. The boys got beaten, the girls didn't. Our family was
not demonstrative or affectionate as a whole, though my mother
was very careful to tell us how much she loved us.

Life was sort of schizophrenic with my father working twenty-
four hours on and twenty-four hours off for the fire department.
When he was gone, I was the hero, the apple of my mother's
eye; when he was home, he took over being the boss and I

somehow went down in stature. I resented him for that; not only resented him, but had feelings of how neat it would be if there were a big fire and he became a hero, but got killed. I wanted all the other kids to say, "Gee, I heard your dad was a hero, too bad he died," but for God's sake, die. My brother had the same sort of feeling, but he outright hated my father. When he got to be as big as our father, he would just say, "I hate you, you son of a bitch!" I never said it out loud.

My father and I were never able to talk about anything except the weather. I don't think he knew the name of the college I went to; he was that separate from the most important part of my life.

When I was in the seventh grade, I started talking to my mother about sending me to a private high school. I knew that was the way into college, but we couldn't afford it. I kept pushing, and finally she took me to see our parish priest. He looked into it, talked to the nuns, found out how well I was doing in school, and talked to the priests at the private school. My father was never involved in any of this. I was accepted. The parish priest paid for my first year. They gave my mother an envelope for each month that said "tuition" on the outside. If she didn't have the money, she was to fold a piece of paper into it so that I wouldn't be embarrassed by not having an envelope. They were very great men. I did well and, in turn, they got me three full scholarships to college. I was on my way to becoming a doctor. I'll never forget them.

I discovered in ACA that I have had emotional blackouts for long periods of my life. One of the things that I had just gone unconscious about was the fact that I was ashamed of the fact that my father spoke with an accent, so I didn't invite many boys home from school, except those I was extremely close to. It was like showing them something secret. I felt good about my mother, but I thought of her as naive and uneducated, so I hoped that my friends would just say hello, sample her Irish bread, and not get too deep. But that wasn't really fair to her, and I knew it and I suffered for it. I was ashamed of those feelings about my parents, really mixed up about them. I knew those kids weren't even good enough to wash my mother's feet. When I went off to college, I was very homesick and I shed many bitter tears over my sense of shame.

I had a one-track mind. I was going to be a doctor, no matter what the hell happened, no matter what it cost or how I had to get there. I know that's tied into coming from an alcoholic family system and my issues as a co-dependent, always focused on someone else, trying to fix everything, save someone to avoid myself. It's a rather elaborate form of denial that looks very acceptable and good from the outside, but it's inside that counts, the motives.

I thought of medicine at such an early age as a way to save people, to be a savior. My mother's favorite brother was an alcoholic. When I was about 9 years old, he died in our home at the age of 26. He had gotten drunk, taken a fall, and laid out in the zero-degree weather of our midwestern winter. He died of pneumonia. He had just come over from Ireland, a handsome, redheaded man. The disease of alcoholism will kill you and not fast enough. It took about ten days for him to die in our house. My mother was crushed. I think that's when I decided to become a doctor. The doctor came every day to see my uncle, with his little black bag full of things to fix people with. I was going to save people. It would also give me the hero status in my family. I didn't understand it that way as a child, but in looking back as an ACA, I see that as the niche I carved out in order to survive.

We are now estimating that 80 percent of the people who go into the alcoholism treatment field do so because of their own unresolved issues of co-dependency, whether they're ACAs, Al-Anons, or AAs. In the last four to five years, the consciousness level about all this has skyrocketed. I think the Adult Children of Alcoholics program has allowed that to happen. It's OK now to be an adult child of an alcoholic with issues that go back to your childhood that are twisted or sick. I'm discovering a lot of issues that I've had buried, didn't even know they were there because they were mostly unconscious. I never mentioned them until it was OK to be an ACA.

When we haven't worked through what happened in our childhood, those issues are sitting there ticking away like a bomb ready to go off; for example, trouble with intimate relationships, authority figures, just to mention a couple. I have often wondered why I felt certain ways about various authority figures in my life. It puzzled me; to be specific, bankers have always terrified me. They have the money, and I come to borrow it and end up feeling just like I felt when I would go to my father and ask him for money or the car. He'd belittle me. "How dare you ask for the car? It's my car. What the hell do you need a car for?" And so on. It became too painful to ask, so I depended on other people to have cars. If I needed money, he'd say, "Don't you know that your mother and I don't even have enough money for ourselves with all you children?" He wanted us to be sure and know that he had no extra money. So somehow I ended up construing bankers as authority figures who also felt the same way; "How dare you ask for money! We're going to keep the money. . . . "

This wasn't true of all authority figures, but some. Again, it's important to understand that I didn't *realize* that I felt this way. I just knew that it was very hard for me to go to a banker for a loan. I was very uncomfortable, though I didn't know why until I got into ACA.

For years, priests were something that would engender a fight in me. As a kid I remember that there were some things that never come up in an Irish family and one of them is sex. It's dirty, nasty, you don't talk about it, and you save it for the one you love. What a mixed message! That was actually the message we got from the nuns. From home we got the message that it's never mentioned, as though it's not something that occurs in this family. I was very naive about my relationships with women. If I started dating a girl and went out with her a few times, then I thought you should probably get engaged, get married, and have a family. The first girlfriend that I ever broke up with, I felt terribly guilty about, really suffered.

My problem with men centered mainly around authority, though I had another problem with men that was different, and that gets back to what I said about priests engendering a fight in me. There was one priest who really terrified and embarrassed us. As he was talking in class, he would find the younger and more naive boys and put his hand down inside a boy's shirt, sometimes all the way down to the abdomen. It was very embarrassing and frightening. Some of the kids knew what he was doing, but most of us didn't get it. The object of his attention would be frozen with terror and couldn't say anything. We went on a school trip; the debating team and I got put in a room with this priest. I didn't know what the hell he was going to do, and I was terrified now. Of course, there was only one bed for the two of us to sleep in. In the middle of the night he starts feeling me up and trying to engage me in sex, and he scared me to death. I jumped out of bed and raised hell and told him that I was going to go to the principal and get the other priests. He said that he hadn't meant anything, that he'd just been asleep, but I knew that was bullshit. By standing up for myself, he never bothered me again, in or out of the class-room. I thought to myself, Why hadn't I done this a year ago as a freshman when he was putting his hand down my shirt? Once I knew what to do, I told all the other kids at the time, "If Father X ever bothers you, just tell him you're going straight to the principal, and he'll run away."

Though nothing happened, that episode disturbed me. It introduced an element of doubt about my sexuality. It made me wonder if there was something about me that attracted him. Did I look like I would go for it? Why was he attracted to me? I was maybe 14.

I finished high school by the time I was 16 and left the next fall for college on a scholarship. I got drunk the first time I drank, and I drank abnormally from the beginning. I could drink more than the others. I had a very high tolerance from the beginning. Not only could I drink more than the others, alcohol did more for me I know now. I assumed that it had the same effect on everybody else, but I know differently today. It affected me the way I hear people who are manic depressives describe the experience of being manic: Everything moves faster, colors are brighter, everything is better. That's exactly what alcohol did for me. The whole world turned brighter; all my problems were solved; I felt really normal, super. But I couldn't afford to drink. I was concentrating on grades and school, and drinking was strictly in second place. No money and no time; I was too busy. I graduated Phi Beta Kappa from undergraduate school and went right into medical school. Once I got away from home, I had very little contact with my family. A long period of separation began.

Medical schools are breeding grounds for alcoholics, no ques-tion about it. I drank mainly on the weekend and graduated in the top 2 percent of my class. I was in the national honor medical fraternity. Obviously I wasn't a hopeless alcoholic at that point, but I was an alcoholic nonetheless. I generally got drunk whenever I drank, and I would set out to do so. It was all carefully planned. I knew that I had to sober up on Sunday and start studying by noon, and that's what I did very methodically. That's the only way to get through medical school and drink. I only drank once the year of my internship, and I got drunk. I didn't drink the rest of the time because I knew that if I did, I'd get drunk and blow it.

After medical school I married a good Catholic, 100 percent Irish girl I'd gone with all during medical school. That relationship was based on the movies, more or less: You fall in love across the room with eye contact, you stay in love, don't date anybody else, you get married and live happily ever after. Very naive. I had had maybe three girlfriends before that. She was a co-dependent, seeking out the dependent. Our issues tied right together.

We had eight children. The marriage was probably over before the divorce finally came. No one in my family had ever been divorced. I had two affairs during that marriage and that tortured me. My neighbor used to have affairs going in two to three towns, but he could shrug them off. I couldn't. Guilt and remorse come with your mother's milk in an Irish-Catholic family like mine. Yet I was terrified of getting a divorce after twenty years of marriage.

It was funny, odd, how all that time that Colleen and I were married, she didn't like my family because they weren't well educated, they spoke with an accent. All the feelings that I had had as a child, she had as an adult. And did I resent her for that. They brought out another side of me, which was to "Leave the Irish alone." That's a famous Irish statement, and boy I felt it. It was OK for me to be angry with them because they spoke with an accent, but no one else. She didn't want to visit them, so I withdrew even further. Fifteen to eighteen years went by when I might call a couple of times a year, send a Christmas card, but I was really out of touch. My family was very hurt. My sisters would write to me and say, "We haven't heard from you. What's the matter?" and I wouldn't answer. I wasn't even in touch with my mother. The longer the time went by, the guiltier I felt and the less I wanted to be in contact.

So there I am married, with all these children, and I was very successful early on with my medical practice. By the time I was in my early 30s, I was chief of a department at a major Catholic hospital in one of the biggest cities in the country. That's when I first began to grapple with my alcoholism.

I was at home, drunk, on a Sunday morning. The last place doctors drink is at the hospital; I never did that. But a friend of mine who knew all the powers that be at my hospital came by to see me that morning at home. Colleen and I had just had a big argument. The children were all terrified by the yelling and shouting. They were all downstairs, and I was upstairs in my bedroom, pissed off and drunk. Jack came in and said, "If those nuns find out that their bright, young, Irish-Catholic depart-ment head is drunk, you can pack up your 5.5 kids and leave town. They just won't put up with you." And I knew that. Deep down in my heart, I knew someday that someone was going to pat me on the shoulder and say, "We know all about you. You're a secret drunk, get out."

I suffered with that, and yet here was my friend telling me that. But I loved Jack; he was the father I never had. He was older; we were friends. I said, "What the hell can I do?" He didn't know about AA and neither did I. He was a great Catholic and went to Mass and Communion every day. He said, "You and I will go to Communion every morning and ask God to keep you sober. I'll quit drinking, too, until you feel comfortable being sober." I said, "OK, I'd do it." We went to Communion every morning at 6:00 A.M. for seven years. I'd meet Jack, go to Communion, ask God to keep me sober; we'd go to work. It lasted for seven years.

I was very uptight. I was redoing what my father had done. I was "white-knuckling" it. The family had to walk on eggshells around me. I didn't ever beat my kids, but if I were taking a nap in the afternoon, everybody better tiptoe around because I got really pissed off if you woke me up. I thought the world owed me a living and goddamn it, I'm doing all this for you, and being such a nice guy. I'm successful, and you'd better be nice to me. I was too busy for my children, had no time for my family, no time for anyone, and I resented anyone who could drink. But I was as dry as a bone.

Finally one night we're having a party around our new

swimming pool and I'm serving drinks. I had been in the service and had been promoted to commander in the reserves. There were a lot of navy and marine officers there that night. Everyone's having a great time, it looks like. The women were very attractive, the men handsome, my marriage long since dead, and so why, I ask myself, can't I have a drink? Here I am serving drinks to everyone else; I should join them, I told myself. I'm sure by now that I can drink sensibly. After all I have a position in the community, I'm successful, and so the story went in my head. Well, I got so drunk that night that I made a pass at a woman who had just lost her husband in Vietnam the year before. It was completely out of character for me. Talk about a change of personality; I made one, complete with a crude pass. I woke up the next morning feeling like I'd rather be dead. Most of the evening I had gone through in a blackout, but I could remember that something happened with her. I felt terrible.

I drank for the next seven months. I was drunk every night, and I practiced medicine every day. I had left the hospital and was back in private practice. I would leave the office at 4:00 P.M., drinking on the way home. I didn't care who knew. I damn near died of alcoholism that time. I knew that I couldn't keep on drinking. I was losing weight, had gotten myself in terrible shape.

I went to see a friend of mine, who was also a physician, and told him that I needed his help. He asked me what was wrong and when I told him that I couldn't stop drinking, he couldn't believe me at first. "You don't drink," he said. That was the word on me—"he doesn't drink"—and there I was dying of alcoholism. I told him my story and that I had been drunk every day now for over seven months. It was 2:00 in the afternoon, and I was already starting to shake. He said that he would help me and ended up giving me Librium to get off the stuff. I went from alcohol to Librium to all kinds of tranquilizers, all kinds of sedatives, and ended up getting into pills heavily. That was my last drink of alcohol though, 1968. No alcohol. Now it was just pills. Later this doctor who had "helped" me died of alcoholism himself at 42.

Another doctor friend who knew I was an alcoholic asked me if I was still drinking. He'd seen me at some point drunk. I told him that I had quit. He asked me what I was doing to stay well. I said, "Nothing." I didn't tell him about the pills. He said, "Why don't you and I go to AA together?" I assured him that I could not go to AA: "What if somebody sees me?" He said, "If somebody sees you there, I'll tell them that you're there to study the disease." I was so phony, I bought his story. I went with Paul to my first AA meeting and found out that it was all right to go to AA. They weren't a bunch of old farts with skinny legs and big bellies. They were normal people. I stayed.

Not long after I got sober, a friend of mine asked me what I was doing about the other doctors who were still out there drinking and using. I said, "What other doctors? It's just Paul and me. We're the only ones in AA in town." He assured me that there are a lot of doctors out there suffering from this disease, which I know well now. He suggested that I go see them, the ones who I heard were in trouble and just tell them my story, talk about what happened to me. I've learned that often if you wait for a doctor to wake up to his or her alcoholism, they'll be dead, so I've been involved with Impaired Physicians ever since it got organized, on a state and national level. It's simply AA meetings and education for doctors.

When it came time for me to do a Fourth Step, to take a moral inventory of myself, I saw how resentful I had been toward my family, toward my father and the fact that he was Irish. My sponsor pointed out to me how I had resented my family and yet "probably the greatest asset you had was your beautiful Irish heritage." Way down deep I knew that, and I burst into tears. I had wanted to be able to say that all my life, and I never had. I really appreciate my Irish heritage, and I can say that now.

I was sorry for the way I had resented my father, thrown out the baby with the bathwater. He was dead by this time. He died at 82, having become a gentle, white-haired, old man. I didn't really know him then. I had gone home for his final illness and realized that I had missed the change that had taken place in him. On that last visit I had with him, he was sweet, he put his arms around me, he had changed totally, his hair was completely white. It was a great loss to me not to have seen him. My brother assures me that I didn't miss a hell of a lot, that he still had that fire in him about I'm the father and you're the kids. Still, I felt like I'd missed everything.

Many things changed once I got sober in the program. I got

divorced finally. I remarried. I got back together with my family and the past healed. I've told my mother about my alcoholism. My second wife, Nancy, loves my family, and we visit once or twice a year or they come to our house. I've refound my family and refound their families, and they've refound me. It's been an incredible gift.

Nancy has been in Al-Anon for years herself and also in ACA because of the abuse in her family. Her parents weren't alcoholic, but there was physical abuse. Her grandfather probably was an alcoholic. She said that she doesn't know if she fits ACA, but the ACA meetings sure fit what she's feeling. She started going at least a year before I did. She goes to one to two Al-Anon and ACA meetings a week.

My wife tried to point out to me that many of the blank spots of memory, blackouts from childhood because of the beatings, were addressed in Al-Anon meetings. I told her that I didn't have time for any more programs; I was going to four AA meetings a week and anyway, AA addresses everything.

Well, I found out that that's not true, at least for me it's not. AA does not address Al-Anon issues, the issue of those who are in relationship with an alcoholic, whether practicing or recovering, dead or alive. Not surprisingly, as this disease goes, two of my own daughters are alcoholic, and one was actively drinking at the time Nancy kept trying to get me to go to Al-Anon. Finally I did, and it saved my sanity. I was going crazy over what was happening to my daughter. So then I kept on in Al-Anon and eventually heard about ACA. Nancy had already started going. I kept putting her off, telling her I'd go with her "one of these days." One evening she was starting out the door to her ACA meeting, and I said I'd come along rather than go to AA that night.

I was amazed at the meeting. Suddenly I realized that they are talking about things that I had been waiting to hear about for years. It's not that you can't talk about anything and everything in an AA meeting; it's just that I didn't feel like there was permission to talk about certain things. I'm not one who would dig up a subject that's painful that I've never heard talked about at an AA meeting before and put it out on the table. I'm not that advanced. I know there are brave souls that can do that and they helped me immensely in doing so, but I'm not one of them. I tend to wait until I feel like it's reasonably safe to bring something up, and then I'll talk.

At the very first ACA meeting I went to, I was able to say that though I don't know what the issues are, I can't put names on all these feelings, but God, have I got them, and I'm grateful to know that ACA is here. I've gone regularly since, in addition to AA. Since I introduced my brother to it, he's going regularly. His wife, who's been in Al-Anon for years, said that she didn't think he'd ever do something like that. He was one of those people that thinks AA is the answer to everything, and he could barely tolerate Al-Anon. Now he's going to Al-Anon's ACA meetings as much as he goes to AA.

Another issue that I identify with an ACA is that sense of a lost childhood. Everything in my childhood was serious, especially me, from the time I can first remember. I've gone back and looked at family photos at my mother's, and I see that I'm very serious, never smiling. My sister standing next to me in the photo is smiling, and I look like the breath of doom. I remember that as I was growing up, someone would say to me, "Why are you frowning?" and I'd tell them that the sunlight bothered me. I was not a happy kid, and I lived in fear of my father. So often we repeat the mistakes of our parents, and although I didn't beat my children, I did repeat one thing that my father did to me. I've only got one son out of all my children, but he couldn't be good enough for me. That was bad, really bad. I've since made amends to him over this, but I did it just the same. When he'd come home with his grades, I'd always tell him he could do better. I gave him the message, "You're not measuring up to my idea of what a son of mine should be." My daughters could do no wrong. I now have eight girls; Nancy and I have just had one of our own. I never told any of my girls that they weren't doing well enough, only my son.

There are still a lot of issues that I have to work through and resolve. I can see that the fear of my father was translated to men in general. Again, this is all unconscious materials that I'm just now beginning to see and grasp. Until this point, I was just at the mercy of it; now that I see it, I can do something about it and change it. It's not that I'm afraid of men especially, so much as sometimes I am really afraid of loud arguments and anger. If I get into a discussion with somebody and they begin to get angry, I'll tend to retreat, withdraw, back away, end the discussion, rather than stand my ground and tell them that I'm not going to put up with their anger and get right back into the discussion. I don't like myself for that, for retreating rather than standing up for myself. Sometimes I compromise myself, and I don't like that. I'm not blaming my father for this. He may have made the initial wound, but now that I'm aware of it, it's my responsibility, it's my problem. There's no one to blame now but me.

I did my Fifth Step at my father's grave, on my knees. That's when we admit to ourselves, our higher power, and another human being the nature of our wrongs. He was long dead, but somehow I felt like he was there, that he heard me say, "I forgive you, and please forgive me." He didn't have the benefit of AA. He did the best that he knew how with us, just as I have done the best I could with my own children. I realized that I fed into his sense of intellectual inadequacy. There's a lot of respect for doctors in the Irish community, and in the old country it's almost more for doctors than for priests. I played on that I realize now, made sure I let him know how well educated I was.

Now I see more since I've been going to ACA. I have more of a forgiving attitude toward him. If he'd known what he was doing to his growing son, he would not have done it. He had the same background, I'm almost certain, the same experience of being beaten by his father. Most people who beat their children do so because they were beaten, not because they get pleasure from it but because they're frustrated.

Though I feel like I've expiated most of my feelings about my father. I'm finding other areas that I've never looked into, such as my sexuality and the negative impact my childhood had on that. But I'm willing to look at it now, to get all the way into it, whether it requires addition psychological counseling or not. I'm ready.

I want to get into these issues because since I've learned to just get into the knots in my life, I've gotten much happier, more contented, more serene, so I want to get into them all. Recovery is an ongoing process. I don't care if I'm 75 years old, I still want to do it because it's so valuable to me. So exciting, this whole experience of recovery, painful sometimes, but exciting and totally liberating.

13. Beverly B.

I was born on the Midwest, the youngest child of an upper middle-class family. My father was a very prominent lawyer, a local hero. My mother was a housewife. Both my parents were alcoholics. I'm almost 40. I had an older brother and sister, both of whom had left home by the time I was 11.

I was surrounded by alcoholism as I grew up, though, of course, as a child, I did not realize this. Two years ago I started reading about Adult Children of Alcoholics and began to connect that with what wouldn't work in my life. That's when I began to think about my background and realize how much alcohol had affected my life. I'm a good example of what they mean when they say everybody gets the disease, whether you ever pick up a drink or not.

My mother is a twin. Her sister was an alcoholic as well and married an alcoholic. My sister married an alcoholic, who is now in recovery. My brother is an alcoholic and, unfortunately, not in recovery. He lives with a woman who's a cocaine addict. And, as I said, both my parents were alcoholic. I say *were* because I'm not sure what's going on now. They're pretty old, and he's had a stroke and is severely incapacitated. He can't drink anymore, at least not on his own.

My father was a lawyer; my sister became a lawyer; my brother's a lawyer; my sister married a lawyer. My mother and I are the only ones who are not attorneys in the family. I got a degree in psychology—I was going to figure it all out—and then went for a master's in business.

All I understood as I was growing up was that my parents didn't get along. I did not put the alcohol together with all the friction. Though we had a lot of real estate, my father came from a very poor background and never got over it. So we lived in a very small house during the school year and had an enormous summer home on an island that we owned, which he loved. It was an odd arrangement. They were forever arguing about real estate. I don't know what that had to do with anything, but it was a great source of conflict nonetheless. Mother would be drinking by the time he got home from the office and would start arguing with him the minute he walked in the front door. He would start drinking as well and may have had some on his way home. They would quarrel, and so generally dinner was late or burned.

I went to a very strict Quaker school. It was a good school, and I had to work hard. For many years I shared a room with my mother. My parents had separate bedrooms ever since I could remember. My brother slept with my father, I was with my mother, and my sister, the oldest, had her own room. I had no space to escape from their arguments is what it boiled down to. I remember once being especially frightened. My parents were screaming and yelling at each other more than usual. My sister had left for college, and my brother had taken over her room. I was pounding on the door of my brother's room, begging him to let me in. He would not. He kept his door locked and told me to go away. That's how he coped.

There was no place to hide, to get away from their constant bickering. That was terrifying. I was constantly afraid that someone was going to get hurt. I always felt like I had to be available to save my mother in case he tried to hurt her, so despite the fear, I tried to be close by, like on the upstairs landing. I was always in conflict internally.

Sometimes I would hear him chasing her around downstairs, but he never caught her. Once, though, I found her on the landing, passed out. He was bending over her. I don't know if he had hit her or if she had just passed out. I think he was trying to get her to come to as I came out of the room. I was about 8.

Since I shared a room with her, I was often regaled with stories of what my father had done to my mother, such as trying to strangle her, trying to rape her, or going out with some prostitute. That was all preteen and pretty hard to take.

I remember once writing in my diary that I would like for the town that revered my father so much to see what he was *really* like at night. It was so strange the way he was revered by the community and then to be at home with him.

My sister was my father's favorite. She would sit up in his room at night for hours, talking about politics or law. It's not surprising that she became a lawyer. My brother was my mother's favorite. Being the youngest by over seven years, I may well have been a mistake. In any case, I couldn't fit it or find a place. I was fortunate to have a couple of friends whose families sort of adopted me. One family in particular, a Jewish family, really took me in. They never asked why I was always coming over; they just took me in. They were marvelous people, warm, loving, and caring.

My father and I never talked. I was petrified of him, hated him for years. I stayed away from him. I can remember coming in at night sometimes and he'd be watching television in the living room. I would tiptoe through so that he wouldn't notice me. I tried to melt into the woodwork whenever I could. Sometimes when I wanted to go to a friend's house for the weekend, I would write out what I wanted on a piece of paper and draw little boxes for him to check yes or no beside. Then I would slip it under his bedroom door. He would hand it to me, checked off, the next morning on his way out the door.

I felt as though I didn't exist in that house. Apparently things were different for my brother and sister. They were quite a bit older. The disease had progressed a great deal by the time I was the only one left a home. I was 11 then. I used to like to get sick because my mother would pay attention to me then. She'd bring me soup in bed, give me an alcohol rub, take my temperature. I thought that was great. Sometimes she took me out someplace special, like the ballet or the zoo, but that was rare. My father never took me anywhere. The odd thing about all this is that I don't remember my mother. She was always there, but I just don't remember seeing her. It's my father who made such a powerful image in my mind.

I remember a time when they were fighting, and my mother called the police and then left. My father went up to his room and went to bed. I was left to answer the door when the police came. They were very nice and just kept asking me if everything was OK. I said, "Of course, it's OK." I didn't know what else to say. My parents had completely vanished from the scene. The police drove around the block a few times and then went away. That kind of thing happened more often than I like to remember. I was about 11 that particular time.

I never knew what was going to happen once I got home from school. I learned to read people's moods very well. I became hypervigilant, as do many ACAs. When they would be downstairs fighting and I was upstairs trying to do my home-work, my attention was always split. Some part of me was always listening. At night I would lie in my bed frozen, wide awake, waiting until I'd hear one or both of them go to bed. Then I could relax and fall asleep.

I was a B student nonetheless, and it was a tough school. My father was big on our having a good education and going to the best schools. He'd worked his way up the hard way, and he didn't want us to have to do that.

I don't know what kept me from developing a problem with alcohol myself. I've gone through periods where I wondered about it, but it's not an uncontrollable part of my life, thank God. My mother was a very spiritual person, and I think I got some of that from her. It gave her a special kind of strength she passed on to me.

I have never married. I've had terrible relationships with men and find that I've got some tremendous anger that comes up for me with men. I've really begun to work on this since I've been in recovery with ACA. I've gone through periods of softness, acceptance and even thought that I was in forgiveness, but the old anger comes back. The rage wells up so often that it's energy-draining, and it takes me away from being productive in other areas of my life. I feel like a prisoner of this rage sometimes. I've never said it like that before, but it's true. That's what it feels like sometimes, a prison. I want to break out of this!

When I first left home and went to college, I went nuts sleeping with boys. I felt like I was getting a lot of approval, something I'd never gotten before from men. But I never had an orgasm with a man until I was 28. The men I've had relation-ships with in the past, I knew from the beginning that there was something I didn't respect about them or something I felt was wrong. I knew it right from the start, but I would still get into a relationship with them and then just pour out all my anger and disgust and disappointments from the past. I was horrible to them.

Need I tell you that I didn't realize that this is what I was doing. I didn't have enough self-esteem to take my initial feel-ings seriously and stay with my sense that the relationship wasn't right in the first place. So, of course it never worked, and of course I was angry, but it was with myself. I went into individual therapy to take a look at all this, almost four years ago. I think that I was unemployed and depressed on top of it all. There I was 35 years old, with two degrees, and I didn't know who I was or what I wanted to do. It took me a good year to trust my therapist enough to begin to tell her about my family. She was the one who pointed out that I was an adult child of an alcoholic and suggested that I get in contact with a nearby clinic that had groups for ACAs. They were full, it turned out. I couldn't get in, but they sent me the literature, and when I read the list of characteristics of adult children of alcoholics, I completely identified. I saw myself: the low self-esteem, the inflated sense of responsibility, the trouble with intimacy, my inability to trust, on and on, down the list. I must have read it a thousand times.

I was finally able to get into a group with some private therapists, and it was wonderful. We met for eight weeks. Since then I've done some ACA workshops, weekend experiences, day-long seminars. It's been incredibly helpful. I'm signing up for another ongoing weekly group run by some excellent ACA therapists. I've gone to ACA meetings, the Twelve-Step program kind, and I had a hard time there. I like the therapy group myself.

I went into Al-Anon because of my brother, who's still using. It was very helpful and showed me how to disengage, with love. Not easy. But I can't stop his drinking and using, nor can I be responsible for him. The ACA group really addresses the issues that are up for me at this time.

It was so great walking into a room with people and discovering that you're not alone. Whether the experiences were just alike or not, the feelings were the same. I got a tremendous amount of strength from the group and a lot of self-acceptance. I was always beating myself up in my own mind, making myself wrong or bad, but the therapists showed me how the very behavior that may be giving me trouble now was just what I needed for survival when I was a kid. The important thing for me now to do is to learn to recognize those behaviors and learn new ways to respond instead of just getting set off into old patterns. To be specific, I'm now in a relationship with a wonderful man who's twenty years my senior. It's imperative that I sort out my feelings about my father, or they just get projected all over the relationship. A lot of times anger or rage will come up, and I've begun to see, it's not with him, it's with my father. It's been an incredibly hard love affair for me, heartbreaking; we've broken up, gotten back together, off and on. And yet I've gotten more love and warmth and security from this man than I've ever had in my life, so I know that it's worth the work. He's Jewish, like my surrogate father was, so I mix him up with the good stuff too. Now I'm really committed to getting into a long-term ACA group and working out this stuff. I've wanted to think, "Oh, I've worked on this. Everything's complete now. I'm well." This relationship has brought up so many feelings that I can no longer pretend that that's true. I've been obsessed with this relationship. Now I want to say I need help. It feels good to admit I don't have this all worked out. I know I can't do this alone.

One of the neat things about recovery is that I'm coming to appreciate some things about my father. He started telling me a long time ago to go into my own business. I ignored him, and I have come to regret that. It's so good to be able to remember some good things now, which have come up since I started in ACA recovery. I've finally begun to follow that advice and just recently started my own business, doing just what I always wanted to do, work with animals.

Given that I came from this family of lawyers, it was assumed that I would complete graduate school, which I finally did. My father told me never to learn to type because I would be forced to use it. Just because he said that, I went out and signed up for secretarial school. I worked as a secretary for years. I remember that my mother had worked as a secretary and had fond memories of those days. I think it was because she liked to work and couldn't stand being confined to the house, as she was after she got married. I don't have such fond memories of secretarial days. But that's what got me going to night school, taking business classes in accounting. It took me a long time to get that degree. I finally quit my job, took out some student loans, and went full-time to finish up the MBA. Then I worked for a real estate firm before I decided to pull up stakes and start my own business. I have a letter that I wrote to my mother ten years ago talking about getting into this business that I've finally started, working with animals.

That's been another gift of recovery, starting this business. When I was a kid, we always had dogs and cats. On the island where we spent the summer, I had no friends, so I'd walk in the fields with the dogs and cats. I talked to them, cried on their shoulders. I cried a lot, and they always seemed to understand in that funny way that animals have. I have a lot of love for animals, and I communicate with them well. I'm very spiritually attached to them.

The outdoors is a very spiritual place for me. I really need to get out to the beach or go for a walk in a forest. I can't stay in the city too long. And I love to take animals with me. It's uncanny the way everything connects: the animals, the forest, me. The forest binds us all together, and I'm able to sense that I'm part of a much larger whole. It's a lot like walking with the dogs and cats when I was a child. It's such a relief to be part of the whole rather than a single part. I get something of that feeling too when I'm in ACA groups. I feel connected, a part of a larger family that we all belong and I feel at home.

14. Leon S.

I was born in a small town on the East Coast. I never knew what was going on with my life until I started going to Adult Children of Alcoholics meetings, which was after I got sober in AA.

There was a huge piece missing after I got sober. I got into Al-Anon and AA almost at the same time. I went to Al-Anon because I was living with someone, and I was fixated on what *she* was doing wrong. Mind you, my own life was falling apart, but I was focused on her. Then someone at a party described another person's behavior, and it was similar to an incident I'd had with my girlfriend a few weeks before. From that conversation I decided that my girlfriend must be an alcoholic. This woman said that she was going to Al-Anon, so I decided I would too. Within two weeks, I realized that I was the one who needed to be in Alcoholics Anonymous and I joined AA.

I don't think I could have gotten into AA any other way. I was so isolated, and my drinking was so totally underground that no one would have even known to put me in a detox unit. I would have gone straight to the Bowery. No one knew what was going on with me. The people in my life at the time thought I had a mental breakdown when I joined AA. They didn't even know that I drank I was drinking so secretly. I drank with them, but I was so controlled, so discreet that they didn't think that I was a drinker.

The fact that alcohol can affect your behavior was a great revelation to me in terms of my girlfriend. Then when I discovered that I was an alcoholic myself, that was an even bigger revelation, but there was still something missing.

When I found out there was such a thing as Alateen, my reaction to it was that I can't wait to be sober long enough to be able to sponsor an Alateen group. I knew there was stuff I needed to talk about besides my drinking. I'm not sure I could have told you what it was that I needed to talk about so much, but I was sure there was something for me in Alateen, and I wanted to sneak in.

I had come into AA through the back door of Al-Anon, and now I was going to sneak into Alateen. The feeling of not being entitled, of being ineligible, permeated my life and gave me an overriding sense of not fitting, not belonging anywhere. The idea that there was someplace that I could go to get what I needed directly never occurred to me. Then I found out that there were meetings for Adult Children of Alcoholics.

I started going to ACA not long after it started here on the [East] Coast. It started out of a Fourth Step workshop with AA people who were also Al-Anon members, people who had been sober a minimum of twelve years. Some of them, many more, like one of the two fellows who started it, I think, had been sober twenty years at the time and in Al-Anon twelve to thirteen years. These were people who were still more miserable than they thought they were entitled to be after so many years of sobriety. There are two old-timers who provided a lot of leadership and organized the first meetings. They sort of discovered by accident in these Twelve-Step workshops that they were focusing on their childhood and their parents. As I understand it, once they realized this, they gave themselves permission to take their parents' inventory, which was a big no-no in both Al-Anon and AA. It was a beginning of uncovering something for themselves, a beginning of understanding the importance of your own childhood.

In my own sobriety I found that I simply could not do a Fourth Step. It was like being constipated for six months. The Fourth Step tells us that "we made a fearless and thorough moral inventory of ourselves." I wanted to do a Fourth Step in the worst way, but I couldn't stay in the seat to do it. I tried every method I ever heard of. I had all sorts of different sponsors, and I even made appointments for a Fifth Step. That's where you sit down with another person and go over your inventory. Then I tried to do a Fourth Step so I could keep the appointment, but what I came up with wasn't even a good beginning.

Finally, I got a sponsor who was a cop. He had done a lot of homework on child abuse and the effects of child abuse. He said to start writing down the ways in which you have been hurt. That unlocked it. I couldn't begin with what I might have done to someone else; I had to begin with what had been done to me.

It's important to know that not all alcoholic parents treat their children the way I was treated and the way a lot of people were treated. In fact, there's a deeper issue in my opinion. Alcoholism is just one manifestation of the problem, as evil as alcohol is. The phenomenon that's underneath it is much worse. My mother probably wasn't an alcoholic, but she was much more damaging than my father, who was the alcoholic. Alice Miller talks about it in her book, *The Drama of the Gifted Child*, as the incredible ego, the insatiable need of the people who are empty inside and have to turn everything in the room into their audience and their object. That's what my mother was like. On top of that she was totally unstable so her needs were constantly changing. Growing up in that house was terrifying. That was the main feeling.

My father always drank. I never knew anything else, so it was a total shock to me at the age of 32 to be informed that drinking had something to do with being unhappy. When my friend told me that her boyfriend was behaving in the crazy way he was because he was drinking over a quart of booze a day, it was like discovering electricity. It was unbelievable. When you live next to the waterfall, you can't hear the water.

I was born into alcoholism, although I didn't know it. It was there, and it had been there for generations. I had been given the usual cover-up stories about my parents' parents. I found out after my father died that as bad as my childhood had been, it looked like Walt Disney compared to his. His father was the kind of drunk who never brought the money home. One of my father's jobs as a kid on payday was to find out what bar his father was in and try to get some money from him before it was all gone. They lived in a town of 10,000 people, and they moved every six months because they could never pay the rent. That's the way my father grew up. He had to quit high school to stay home and take care of his mother, because there was no money. Yet the story that I grew up with was that my grandfather was supposed to be this wonderful, gentle man who was active in politics and was supposed to be this nice guy. That's the story I grew up with.

My father's alcoholism was in full swing well before I was born. When my parents were engaged, my father had a bad automobile accident and hit a bridge while stone drunk, wiping out one side of the car altogether. My mother would have been killed if she had been in the car with him. He was a mess even back then, and they were married seven years before I was born.

On the other side, my mother's father was always described as a tragic figure who had come to this country with nothing. He opened up a restaurant, did well, and ended up owning quite a bit of property, including some apartment buildings, a big car, and a chauffeur. He was this jolly, wonderful man who traveled to the city for the opera with crates of live chickens tied on to the roof of the car because he felt sorry for his city cousins who never got a fresh chicken. Then a terrible thing happened: A truck jumped the curb and killed him when my mother was 12.

But many years later, I found out *another* story and discovered that that grandfather had been an alcoholic too. His oldest son, my uncle, had been sent to medical school to become a doctor. He was supposed to make the family respectable. When my uncle was ready to come back home and practice medicine, my grandmother told my grandfather that he was a bum and that it was time for him to sober up. He was crushed by this statement and apparently died right afterwards. Whether he had stopped drinking and was just dazed, whether he stepped in front of the truck on purpose or never saw the truck or some of each, I don't know. I've been in that kind of shape myself. I didn't have the guts to kill myself, but there's something inside that's leading you to destruction anyway. So I had alcoholism on both sides of my family.

That son, my uncle, who was supposed to save the family, ended up a suicide himself about a year or so before I was born—drugs, alcohol, pills, money, you name it. He was a doctor who was sleeping with his patients. Women were making appointments to see him. Total craziness. But I was told that he was a wonderful man when I was a kid, and I never knew him. I was told he had been done wrong by some awful woman. It turns out that the woman was a pretty nice gal who split when she realized that was going on. It's so hard to describe all this because nothing that was supposed to be real was real. It feels like a life's work to put what I know together, and I know almost nothing.

The house I grew up in was a haunted house. My uncle had

just committed suicide in that house, and my parents were living in the house at the time. It may be no coincidence that I wasn't conceived until after his death, his influence was so strong. I was born in his house, and I always felt like there were unspoken expectations of me, that somehow I was supposed to fill his shoes, yet nobody told me what the shoes really were. I slept in his bed; his furniture was there. The house was full of undercurrents.

The whole family lived in that town. There were seven siblings, and they all still lived there. Everybody in town knew what happened to my uncle, and yet they were still pretending that it didn't.

It's the alcoholic family story again with my father's drinking. His needs overpowered everything and everyone else. My father's need was so great that when he died, it was a relief. Oh, I grieved horribly, but when I got done crying, I said, "I'm so glad that son of a bitch is dead." I realized later that a lot of my tears were for what we never had. That he was dead was a relief; it was the best thing he ever did for me. Of course, he didn't do it for me, and, in fact, he would have been dead long before that if I hadn't kept him alive. I didn't even know that that's what I was doing.

I grew up keeping him alive. That's what we all did. We kept my father alive. He was the only one who brought any money into the house. He kept us alive by bringing the money home, and we kept him alive so he could bring it home. By the time I was 7 or 8, he was so bad, he was diagnosed as having polyneuritis, which is a disease only alcoholics get. It's an affliction of the central nervous system. In the early stages you can hardly put one foot ahead of the other, you're very wobbly in walking, or you're paralyzed and can't walk at all, but then your walking comes back. Then he was sent to the hospital to have the diagnosis confirmed. But by the time he went into the second hospital, he had straightened up a bit, and they decided he had multiple sclerosis. So he spent the next twenty-five years or so "dying" from multiple sclerosis. He used it as an excuse to drink with abandon.

I took over the responsibility for the household. I did the chores. I remember struggling to keep that house, and in the end we lost it. There was a huge lawn, and I thought that I had to do all the painting and upkeep. The worst part was no one ever said, "You don't have to do this." I was 8 years old.

This sense of being threatened went on for years. My father was just an ordinary working man. He never graduated from high school; he worked in a factory doing piecework. He couldn't keep a doctor's house, so we moved to a smaller house. After we lost my uncle's house, there was always the fear of not being able to keep whatever home we had.

When we lost the house and had to move to a much smaller one, I went from the master bedroom to having to share a little room with my brother, and no one knew what was going on.

I never knew why we had to move. I thought it was my fault that we lost the house. "If only I had . . . then we wouldn't have had to leave." I never knew what was happening to my father. I just knew that he was sick, and nobody would say what was wrong with him. For many years, I didn't know that he was supposed to have multiple sclerosis, which he didn't have anyways. What he had was alcoholism for the twenty-five years.

All I knew was that I had terrible feelings of shame and guilt, and, of course, I felt terrible for feeling this way. I wasn't supposed to feel anything. I'm sure my mother and father felt them too. It was a big defeat, not being to keep that house. Then there was this illness hovering all the time, to make matters worse.

My father started making beer at home when we moved. He also threw his sister out of the house, who was living with us at the time. He never just *did* something. First he got roaring drunk and kept the family up all night screaming, and that's how he asked his sister to leave and get her own place. She was a lot older than he was. She had been engaged to be married to an alcoholic for years and years. Finally, he died, and there she was with us. That's just another crazy story.

My dad would get violent when he was really drunk. He would also join in with my mother in being violent with me. My mother was more violent than he was with us. They were both pretty violent. When I got to be as big as he was, which fortunately was fairly young because he wasn't that tall, he hit either me or my brother—I don't remember which—and I told him that if he or Mom ever hit either of us again, I'd kill them both. I had to do that, but it scared me terrifically. I was about 11 or 12. It was necessary, absolutely necessary. It was one of the smarter things I ever did. At a minimum, they would have killed our spirits. I was old enough not to have put up with that shit any longer. If hitting was included in the rules they were playing by, I was finally big enough to win the game. But they were still my parents, and the taboo was strong.

My mother beat us up, it seemed, gratuitously. It was always because we did "something," but what we did had no relationship to the violence. She would just go crazy. She would turn into a monster, and she would be foaming at the mouth. She could be sweet on the outside, but underneath was a volcano. She would just erupt, beat us and beat us with a strap or a hanger or a hairbrush, or just her bare hands. I have this image of myself, cowering in a corner, trying to cover up while she beat me because we were making too much noise or jumping up and down the couch or something. There's a lot I remember in the old house, before I was 8 years old. She could be in the middle of beating us, and the phone would ring, and she'd pick up the phone and say, "Hello. No, I'm not doing anything. No, you're not interrupting anything." She would go on to have a nice conversation and then hang up the phone and start hitting us again, or sometimes she would walk away after the phone call. It would be as if what preceded it had never happened. I really don't think she knew the difference. I think she was probably just that crazy.

I want to say that she didn't drink, but I can't say that. Alcoholism is such a strange disease. It could be that the people we diagnose as alcoholics are only the tip of the iceberg of what an alcoholic is. I think she was probably a barbiturate addict, and she was definitely a food addict. She was always tremendously overweight and had everyone convinced it was an affliction, that everything she ate turned to fat, that she couldn't breath without gaining weight. But in the middle of the night, I would discover her eating out the refrigerator, just standing there with the door open. But I never realized that my mother was probably an alcoholic and certainly a barbiturate addict. She had a huge bottle of phenobarbital of my uncle's, and she was always taking it to sleep. I never realized that that was serious stuff. I had to get sober and hear about it before I realized that

that's not candy. She could never get out of the bed in the morning. But she may have also been too sick to be truly addicted to any of these things. Because their focus is elsewhere, I think some people can be too crazy, their obsessiveness too global to have *a* specific addiction. They can sort of take or leave in huge quantities things that other people become totally dependent on.

I had a terrible time in school. I was very bright and considered special. When we changed towns and I left the school I was going to, the nuns cried. There was talk that I should be a priest. At home there was always a double message: "You should get an education, go to college, make something of yourself," and yet my father especially hated people who had an education. He even resented the foremen in the factory who wore a white shirt.

What my father put out was "Get yourself a sheepskin, and you'll never have to work again for the rest of your life." His resentment of people with an education was total, and yet he would tell me to become like them. As for my mother, even if you brought home all A's, she'd say, "That's good, but when are you going to learn to clean up your room?" Nothing was ever good enough. In fact, the better it was, the more she'd find some way to lower my esteem, because she couldn't stand people who could really hold their face up to the light, because she couldn't herself. In fact, neither of them wanted me to be any better than they were.

My own drinking started when my father started making the beer. I was 8. It was there; I needed it. I was supposed to help him make it; it was a family project. I joined the Cub Scouts and started making beer at the same time. That's what my father and I did together. The Cub Scouts were a drag. The beer was wonderful. It was exactly what I needed to feel a part of that family. The only time that it seemed like we had a happy family was when my parents were together with other relatives and friends, and they were drinking. But I never would have said that it was *because* they were drinking. I thought it was because they were together with relatives and friends. In other words, the problem was children—the problem was my brother and me. They were unhappy because of us. They didn't have to say that. It was obvious. When they were with grown-ups, they were happy. When they were with us, they were miserable. We never knew the difference between being hung over and drunk. I mean that's what it amounted to, but we never knew that. I could not wait to join the party. I hated being a child. I wanted to be grown up. That was the only goal I had. I wanted to be grown up. That's what I wanted to be. When I was sneaking those drinks, I knew how my parents felt. I was whole, I was real, and I belonged. I also was invulnerable, and I'd never felt that before. I had a nervous breakdown that year, too.

I remember wanting to get away from everyone. There were crawl spaces in the house we moved to, in the back of closets, and I would get in one of them as far away from everyone as I could get. It was the only place I wanted to be. I cried all the time. I was still only 8, and when I would go to school, I was convinced that everyone was talking about me, making fun of me. This is after I started drinking, after we moved, and after I started a new school. It was the combination of things. I couldn't adjust, and I couldn't handle alcohol at 8 years old.

They sent me to a psychiatrist and a psychologist, at least I think that's what they were. I had to make drawings for them. I don't know who the hell they were, and I would only do stick figures. They wanted me to do different kinds of drawings, and I wouldn't. I had had an aunt who had had a nervous breakdown and had shock treatments. I thought they would give me shock treatments. They were talking about putting her away. Pretty soon, I was sure they were talking about putting me away too.

A parade of people came and tried to talk to me. No luck. Finally, they decided to take me to the family doctor. I felt like he was my last chance. I had to make it with him somehow. He took the attitude that "there wasn't really anything wrong, was there now?" I said, "No." He said,"Well, this has all been a mistake then?" and I said, "Yes." He said, "Some kind of temporary confusion?" I said "Yes," and that was it.

I went back to school and pretended like nothing was wrong, except, of course, I knew there was something horribly wrong. And I kept on drinking, secretly.

All through school there would be horrible things that happened at home, and often on the days things had happened the night before, I couldn't recite the pledge of allegiance. I remember standing there with a lump in my throat, mouthing the words so that no one would know that my heart was in my throat. So by the age of 12 or 13 I'm going around pretending like nothing is wrong, not telling anybody what is going on with me. That's the message that I got when I was 8, loud and clear: you don't do that; you don't tell anybody that there's something wrong. So I just went on. I was lost.

At home I had taken on the role of the family hero, the one who was supposed to take care of everything. My father was always having a medical crisis and operations, which I now realize were all related to alcoholism. But nobody knew that then. Everyone just thought that he was the most unfortunate man, "your poor father." There were two phrases I heard over and over: "Your poor father" and "Don't upset your mother." That was the way they talked about each other to us. "Don't upset your mother" applied to everything. She could do anything she wanted to and you weren't supposed to say a thing, because it would upset her.

In high school, my own drinking accelerated terrifically. I was drunk at least a couple times a weekend and during the week too, usually. I didn't know what I wanted. The only goal I had was to be 18, because you could drink legally and nobody could tell you what to do. I wanted to be free, that's all I wanted. First things first. You can't decide what you want to do with your life when you're in prison, and living at home was like being in prison. I wanted out, but I couldn't get away.

I went to the local community college, and I was living at home. I was bright enough that I could have gone to any school, but I never applied. I talked about getting my own place, but my parents were totally offended that I should be going to a local school and not living at home. "What are you trying to do to us?" What would it look like? What would people say if I wasn't living at home? So at first I stayed. They were still having crazy parties with screaming and yelling and carrying on until all hours, and I couldn't study. I would say something about that and get a hostile response. So I just came home one night and told them I'd gotten this place to live, and I was leaving. My mother became completely hysterical, my father got drunk and started screaming and carrying on, and when I left, they called the cops and had me arrested for stealing the car. The car was my car. I'd bought it out of my own savings. It was in my father's name for insurance purposes, but it was my own car. I was totally blind with rage at them and at myself for having trusted him. And I was furious with myself for crying at my age. My father had called the cops because my mother was upset. When I complained to my mother about it, she told me not to be so hard on my poor father. Somehow I bought it. I moved out, but we went on as a family. It was unbelievable.

I flunked out of college. I kept drinking and spent all my time reading novels instead of doing lab reports. I ended up working in the same factory as my father. Flunking out of school was a tremendous defeat. I was horribly guilty; I hated myself for it. I worked in the factory nights and in a store during the day, and I drank and I drank and I drank.

I began having a dream where I was going down a spiral. I was 19 years old, and I said, "No, it's too early for this," so I went back to college. I was able to control my drinking enough at that point to go to college nights and make good grades. I got back into school full-time but still local. I just couldn't leave. That's the sickest part. I couldn't fucking leave. I just couldn't. I'd have to go home again and again. I was still trying to get what I never had from them. There was something missing, and I kept going back to find it. It was never there. Mostly, I had transferred from the home to the local bar. I'd keep coming back to that bar. I was always trying to find bars like home. Drinking with older men. They were like what I wanted my father to be. My father had been very much the milque toast. These men were like the father I didn't have. They were like him in that they were alcoholics, but he was on the passive side, and they were on the aggressive side. They were a combination of my mother and father, and the bar was home. I never got along with people my own age, with the exception of the handful who drank like I did.

After I graduated from college, I got into drugs. A whole bunch of us that had left for school came home, the broken-winged little birds. We all came back home to this little town and dropped acid together, instead of living our lives. I can remember being in this little apartment with twenty to thirty people stoned on acid. Not only did I know them from childhood, I knew their mothers and fathers and their aunts and uncles and their grandparents, and they knew the same about me. They were all alcoholics, all from alcoholic homes, and a lot of them are dead today. We were trying to create a family, trying to get from each other and from drugs that we never got at home. There's not even anyone to talk to about those days, because none of them made it. They are either dead or among the missing. The loneliness of this disease is unbelievable.

I got into drugs very heavily. That scene got very, very bad. I took acid; I tried smack and everything that there was. I ended up back in my parents' house dealing drugs. I was making them pay. That's what I was doing—I was making them pay. I went to law school after college, which was another horrendous mistake, and two months after I left law school, I was dealing drugs. I was getting grass in the mail from Vietnam and hiding it in the cellar. My father found it or saw me do it or something, and he said, "What do you think you're doing?" and I said, "Why don't you have me arrested again, old man? Go ahead and have me arrested again," that was my attitude. They were my prisoners at that point, in their own home. We had just changed it around. Finally, I left town for a while. I knew that I was being watched, so I joined a carnival. When I came back, the scene was even worse, and I stopped seeing almost everyone. Within a month, they had all been arrested. That's when I left town for good.

I decided that it was time to straighten up and fly right, so I went to a big city. I as totally isolated, trying to have one drink a week, which I never accomplished. No drugs, it took me two years to stop doing drugs. On the surface, I was getting better jobs, wearing a suit every day, was with a nice woman. I'd been in therapy and I was moving up the corporate ladder.

The woman I was with made more money than I did and was very sophisticated. I thought that I had arrived, that if I stuck with her, I'd be OK, because she drank more than I did, and she was getting away with it. She was the one who started acting crazy, but by that time I was in my father's role in the relationship: I was the passive one driving her crazy. In fact, she probably wasn't anywhere near as sick as I was. I pointed the finger at her, and that's how I got into Al-Anon, then AA, then ACA.

The Adult Children of Alcoholic meetings were unbelievably intense. There were only two meetings in the city where I lived at the time. They were small meetings, twelve people at one and six people at the other. I heard about them through other people in AA. People would talk about what had happened to them, and I'd go home paralyzed with emotion. I'd go to bed, and the dreams would be intense.

Then I started dreaming that I wasn't really an alcoholic. I went to ACA from January through the spring and started back on a novel I'd been writing. It was just flowing out of me. My emotions were so free, it was unbelievable. I just remember going to the meetings and writing my ass off, then having this dream that I wasn't an alcoholic and telling people about i:. They recommended that I leave ACA for the time being.

Leaving the ACA meetings was one of the hardest things I have ever done. I cried. It was like a very intimate relationship breaking up. I just didn't want to leave it, but I thought they were right. ACA itself was very new and fragile at the time. There weren't people who were newly sober in it. The people in those meetings had been sober for many years. So I left.

I focused on my AA programs at that point, eventually got into my Fourth Step, and went on to make amends to people. I went home one weekend to see my father and ended up staying ten days.

I wanted to make amends to him because he was dying. He was in the hospital. It was extremely healing for both of us. I know because his blood pressure and vital signs went up like thirty or forty points when I told him that I loved him and that I thought he had been a good father and that he'd done the best he could. I'm not sure that was entirely true, but I sure did feel for him and for what we would never have now. He couldn't talk, but he could hear me. He squeezed my hand, and I could see the relief go through his body. The release was unbelievable.

After I talked to him, he lived another couple days. That's the power of forgiveness. My father died after I got sober. I tried to get him to go to an AA meeting with me one night. He said he would go, and then when it was time, I said, "Are you ready?" and he said, "I'm not going." For the first time I looked at him and said to myself, "You're on your own." He was dead within two weeks.

My recovery began when I started going to those ACA meetings in January or February of 1979. I came into AA in August 1978. I went to Al-Anon thinking I was doing it for my girlfriend, because she was the one with the problem. So I read *Understanding Alcoholism* to help her. The second part of that book was a collection of AA stories. When I got to the part of the story where people found out they were alcoholic, I started crying, and I knew I wasn't crying for her. That's how I got into AA.

The truth is that my mother did her best as well, if you think about how out of control she was most of the time. That's what is so difficult about all this. There is nobody to string up, nobody to blame. There's nobody to get your pound of flesh from. My parents were not bad people. My mother still isn't a bad person. I don't think there are bad people anymore. There are just sick people, some much more so than others. When people commit crimes, you have to put them away. I know that, but I just can't hate anybody anymore. I know where that kind of pain and insanity comes from and how badly you can be hurt. Some people just never stop hurting back.

I hurt them was because I had to at the time. I didn't know any other way. You read stories about crazed killers who say I killed them "because I had to." I understand what they are saying, and that doesn't mean that they're not crazy. I understand what they are saying, where that kind of statement comes from. To them it was self-defense. It's especially self-defense when you're a young child, and the parents have all the power in the situation, and they are not giving you what you need. You've got no place else to go. I don't think that you can hurt anyone more than you can hurt a child in those circumstances. The fact that the same kind of thing was done to your parents, that they had it as bad or worse in their childhoods, means you can't really hate them. You can still hate what happened; you just can't hate them. There's a distinction that has to be made here: you don't always have a guilty party when there's been a horrendous miscarriage of justice. It just happened. There's nothing that can be done. And I'm not a kid anymore.

I can't go back. The more time I spend trying to go back, the longer I carry on what happened from the past right into the present. I have to let go of it. I have to just say it happened. I had a horrendous childhood; it was horrible. There are people who have worse and those who have had better. It doesn't matter—mine was horrible. I don't know how I got through, I deserve a lot of credit for just surviving.

Today my job is to give myself credit, because no one else understands what it was like. People who go to ACA and share what happened to them and try to put it behind them come close to understanding, but they weren't there. The only people who were there were my mother and father and me and sometimes my brother. I'm the only one who can see it for what it was. There's nobody to confirm my own perceptions of it. Even talking about it, I think, "Are they really as bad as I'm making them out to be?" In fact, they were probably worse, because I have a hard time seeing them at all. I have had a lot of trouble seeing people for who they are. This is especially true of my father, whom I romanticized. You always pick one. You have to have somebody on your side.

I thought that my father liked me because he took me drinking with him, because he asked me to help him make beer with him. He tried to be a father too, briefly, before he got too sick to care or to be able to do it. I knew that.

When I look back at some of those experiences that were so important to me as a kid, I now realize that it wasn't out of kindness to me as a kid that my dad took me into a bar with him. He'd put me on a bar stool and feed me orange soda with a cherry in it, while he got drunk with my uncles. Then when I was full of orange soda and sick to my stomach and wanted to go home, he would act like, "Kids. What a pain in the ass. Why can't you be a good sport? And don't tell your mother what we've been doing." I was the cover for him to go to the bar. I don't know if he did that consciously. I doubt it. He wasn't that sinister to sit around and think, "I'll just take the kid with me so that I can go drink." Alcoholics don't behave like that. They *have* to drink, and so they do whatever is expedient.

When I went home to make amends to my father, I thought I would make amends to my mother as well, but I didn't. It's taken me a lot of years to understand what "making amends" means in that situation. I began to perceive that, for me, there was an important way that amends are different in AA than in other Twelve-Step programs. I don't want anyone to hurt me anymore, and to the best of my ability I don't give them the opportunity. That was what I used to do with my mother, and it was a way in which I made her sicker. So as my amend, I both refrain from hurting her and I try not to give her the opportunity to hurt me. I'm not deliberately malicious to her. I make duty calls, I send her birthday cards, send her Christmas presents. But I don't have her in my house for Christmas, and I don't go to hers. That's too much. I've tried that, and it will make me very unhappy because she hasn't changed. She's not going to treat me any differently than she ever treated me because she doesn't know any better. So I don't let her do that. That's an amend.

I have changed my relationship to her. To the best of my ability, I'm not playing games anymore. This doesn't sound like the amends in the Big Book of AA, but that's OK. This is the best I can do today. It's as good an amend as the one I made to my father. I can't hold myself responsible for more. I try not to hate her today, and I don't let her visit her hatred on me, as much as I can. That's all that is left of that situation. The truth is sometimes worse than the fantasy. We'd like to have it be OK, but accepting the truth is harder sometimes, but that's the truth of it. I've had to let go of trying to change her.

My relationships with other people have changed tremendously. During the time that I stopped going to ACA meetings, I really worked the Steps of the program in AA, from the Fourth step on through the Tenth Step. One of the things I tried to do is not participate in my character defects, to let them go. That's an ongoing process, an attitude. To give you an example of what I mean and how things are different for me with relationships, I remember how I got involved with somebody very soon after I stopped drinking. She was involved with an extremely crazy guy, a total psycho. They were getting divorced, but the relationship between them was still raging with fire, and I'm right in the middle of it. And I thought it was heaven. The sex was great. She was beautiful, bright, talented, sensitive, but the sad thing is that this isn't what I loved about her. That's only what made it possible for us to come together, for me to rationalize the whole thing. But what really grabbed me was that she was severely damaged, like I was. She was a soul sister. She had the same pain inside her that I had in me, and that was the basis for what turned out to be a horrible relationship after I was "sober." I've heard a lot worse stories in sobriety. It finally ended when she told me she couldn't see any future with me.

A couple of days later, I went back to something I had

written about my father right after he died. As I recalled, it was really short, just some pages of scribblings. But when I opened the folder, I discovered a fifteen-page story, double-spaced, typed. A terrible rage came up, and I was literally blind from time to time that day. I could not get through the day fast enough to get to an ACA meeting. I knew that's exactly where I had to go, and I was totally ready for ACA at that point.

I had tried to go back to ACA meetings intermittently after my early experience with it, but it hadn't worked. I took everybody's inventory; I couldn't stay at the meetings. But after the breakup and reading that story about my father, I was ready. I went every night for a while. It was the only place I felt I could relax. Every place else I was just in a rage, blinding rage. I had been sober for four years, and I was in such a deep depression that I couldn't get out of bed in the morning.

I haven't been depressed since. I haven't had any of those rages since I went through that period and started back into ACA. I really got down to some of the core issues and began to see how I'd been hurt in a deeper way than I ever had allowed myself to see before, even in my Fourth Step. I finally got to where I was able to express my feelings and to understand why I was still getting into these sick relationships.

We were built to live. We are living creatures, and all of our coping mechanisms are life forces. They take us back to the scene of the crime so we can discover what happened. If we didn't go back, we would never figure it out. We can just keep reenacting these self-defeating patterns without any awareness and never get anywhere. But if we let ourselves go back in the context of recovery, with some awareness, we get more insight each time. The purpose is to eventually reach the point where we don't have to keep reenacting our sick family roles.

Today I'm married to a woman who I might not have looked at twice a few years ago. She's very attractive, she's fluent in several foreign languages, she's a writer, she's interested in art. In many ways she's a summation of all of the women I've ever been deeply involved with, except that she's not an ACA. She doesn't have that kind of abusive background. I really had to allow myself to get to know her. I was attracted to her, then I would think that I wasn't attracted to her. Because she didn't fulfill that sick need I had for chaos, I thought the intensity wasn't there. There wasn't that sick combination of sorrow, compassion, hopelessness, and fear in the pit of my stomach, which I had thought was love. So I really had to say to myself, "You're in recovery now, so if things are going to be different, they are going to have to be a way that you've never known before. See what this is about." Time and again, something would say to me, "This is bullshit. There's nothing here." And another part of me would say, "Give it a chance. Don't you enjoy being with her? Isn't it comfortable?" I wasn't used to that.

I was saying to myself, "Well, I think I'm in love," but I'm not throwing up, I'm not desperate, so how can this be a serious relationship?" I discovered that love is something else that can be pretty comfortable, and it works. She's steady and stable, and I'm pretty steady and stable myself these days. I have money in the bank, a life insurance policy, and we're about to have a baby.

I can't begin life as another person. I'm this person, but I can get detached enough from the past that I can be in the same situations and not act like I did before. Let's face it, the only way you can begin to recover, really, is to be in the same situation and act differently. I mean that's recovery—being in the same sort of situation that has triggered a reenactment of the past, and although at times you might want to fall back into that old pattern desperately, you make a different choice. To me, that's the Third Step. The purest instance of faith that I know of is when you act against everything that is in you, out of the belief that it's good for you. It's like going to the dentist and sitting in the chair and letting him hurt you, because you believe this is for the better, this is good for you. So much of recovery is exactly like that, having to experience pain, while you behave in a different way than you did before. We have to behave in a way that we've been told is away out of the pain, even though it doesn't feel like that at all. It feels like the old way we used to try to deal with the pain is the right way, but we only recover when we act differently.

This is as good a place as any to talk about the trap of ACA that I found. It's like the trap of AA: alcoholics can sit around together with other alcoholics and talk about their drinking. I used to do that. I'd say, "I am so glad I don't drink anymore," and then I'd go home. I'd feel better. There's a certain catharsis from that reenactment. There's a certain high you can get off of it, talking about the "war stories," the "drunkalogues." It's almost like sitting around a bar, reliving the night before on a Sunday afternoon. You can do that in AA and stay sober, if there's enough AA around, but that became a trap for me. On some level, I wasn't changing, that wasn't recovery for me.

In ACA, you can do the same sort of thing. You can go to ACA meetings, and you can wail, piss, and moan. You can recall one incident after another in all the gory details, and everybody else can do the same thing, and you can cheer each other on, and you can feel better for it when you go home. The next day, I found that you'll have to go to another meeting because you haven't learned a thing. You felt better, you got high off the emotions. I think one of the most dangerous aspects of recovery for ACAs, at least for this Adult Child of an Alcoholic, is the fact that these emotions are so intense, they trigger an endorphin release. I discovered that I can really get high off of them, that they can become addictive. If we're not addicted to chemicals, we're addicted to behaviors. I'm an addictive person; I'll get high off of anything. That high can become my reward for allowing myself to feel how awful my childhood was.

My recovery comes from just the opposite route. I acknowledge the past, admit it, stop denying what happened and how I felt about it. Recovery is slogging it out every day in the trenches. Recovery is action. In many ways, recovery is *not* allowing myself to feel those feelings. They can be a trap for me. In thirty minutes, I could be feeling everything I ever felt as a little kid. But why? The fallacy is the idea that you can get the emotion out, and it will be gone forever. That's a fallacy in my opinion. These are human emotions. We're human beings, and you never stop being human. It's tricky. I'm not suggesting repressing the feelings, just that there came a point in recovery for me when I discovered that I could simply make another choice. I could *choose* peace and serenity. When I feel myself getting away from myself into one of these old emotions, I work to get centered again. Number one—most important for me— is *not* getting the rage out. I think we're so afraid of being repressed. There's a difference between repressing a feeling and acknowledging it and moving away from it. Acknowledging it by saying, "Look at the way I feel: I can't sit still. I feel like I can tear down a wall. I better get calm, I better get centered, I better figure out what's going on here. I better stay away from that subject until I can handle it more rationally." That to me is recovery—choosing a different response to those feelings. I no longer have to say to myself, "I can't wait until I get to an ACA meeting so I can talk about this." Sometimes that happens and it's good, but sometimes I found that it can be a way of keeping the illness going rather than recovering. I've seen people up on their feet in a rage, defending their right to do so. Well, they are right. They have a right to rage; they can have all the rage they want. But I'll choose something else, thank you. As a kid, I would go into blinding rages. They scared me then, and they scare me today. It's still possible for me to have them. It's not as likely today. Rage is a human emotion, and it's available for all of us. But rage feeds on itself. Many things that happen today can become another instance of what happened way back when. That way of looking at life is available to us, but I can't recover that way. Recovery is when I don't live like that anymore.

There is much that happened that perhaps we'll never forget, but through recovery, we can let go of the grief. There's a tremendous amount of grieving that has to be done in recovery, but grief isn't neat. You can't just go to a meeting and grieve. We still try to package our emotions. When I was a kid, it was dangerous for me to feel. I wasn't allowed to have emotions. My father was allowed emotions when he got drunk and kept us up all night. My mother was allowed them all the time. Children were not allowed emotions, period. There was no appropriate time to have them. I remember the first time in recovery that I began to feel a deep ache, like a long-buried grief. I said to myself, "OK, feel this. Then you won't have to feel anything ever again." That was little Leon. That's what I wanted as a child. That was safety for me then—survival, *not* feeling. It's also death. It doesn't work. But in recovery we have to be careful of trying to process our emotions. The kind of grieving that I found to be effective comes out of a moment. The release is situational. For example, a lot has come up for me thinking about the fact that I'm going to have a child and realizing that this child is going to have a childhood that's not going to be my childhood. I have to let go of my childhood again. By being in recovery, I can give this child what I never had, but I can't think about this without underlining the fact that my childhood is over. That's a grieving experience. That's a reminder of a big loss. To the extent I allow it to surface, I feel more released from it.

I'm incredibly prone to addiction, and it has to be avoided at all cost. My ability to center, my ability to have a sense of myself is still very fragile. I still want to give myself away to other people. I want to drink coffee until I'm blind. I want to eat sugar until I'm blind. I want to work too hard so that I can get the high off the fatigue. You name it, sex, there isn't anything that I don't want enough of to numb me. Acknowledging that and realizing it, just accepting that this is the way I am is crucial. I gave up drinking a coffee that was 99 percent caffeine-free, not because I want to go to heaven or because I'm some kind of monk, but because I was *addicted* to it, because when the store ran out of it and I couldn't get it for two days, I went into withdrawal. That's how much of it I was drinking. I don't want to be addicted to anything anymore. I know that my recovery as an ACA is blocked by any form of addiction. I'm addicted to my past. I keep finding ways in which I am not in the now. I'm shocked, possibly because I'm newly married and expecting a child, to sense how my life is changing. But it changed a long time ago. I just never caught up with it. I'm nearly 40 years old. I'm getting gray hair, yet most of the time I think of myself as 19, at best. I have to constantly locate myself in the *now*. That's where I find my recovery.

15. Katie B.

Both of my parents were alcoholics. I was fortunate enough not to become one as well. I never had to take a look at myself until both my parents had died of alcoholism and I had divorced my alcoholic husband. Then for the first time I had to take a look at myself, and it was horrible. I didn't like what I saw. That's when I started to make jokes about renting an alcoholic. They're so handy to have around when you need somebody else to blame. I used to tell people that if you haven't got an alcoholic in your life, you should rent one. That way when people try to blame you for something, you've got somebody else to point the finger at.

My mother was an alcoholic when I was born, I realize that now. My father became an alcoholic later on in life, after he retired. He was always a daily drinker, but it was never out of control. He was a highly responsible and reliable person. In my eyes, he held the whole family together, because my mother was a very sick woman. But once she had died and he retired, it only took ten years for him to be dead from alcoholism too.

I had an older brother. There were just the two of us. He was five years older than I and somehow, whenever anything was going on at home because of mother's drinking, I was always right in the middle of it. He would be off in his room, reading a book. It was amazing. It was like he was never there. I'm sure he was affected too, but he handled it very differently. I was very involved emotionally.

I remember when I was very small, sitting in the kitchen where I could see the top of the bookcase in the foyer, where my father kept his hat. When I would see his hand reach up for that hat, I knew that he was going out and leaving me with this woman who was my mother. I would get hysterical and cry. Many years later, I realized that I just didn't feel safe with my mother. It was like being left alone to be left with her. When he left the house, I would be terrified. My father represented security. Nothing could touch me or harm me if my father was there. I was only about 2 years old at that time.

I remember lying in bed with the light on when I was a little older, and she would be alone in the living room. I remember knowing that something was wrong with her, but I don't know if I knew she was drunk. I just knew that something was wrong with her. She would just sit there talking to herself in the living room. She must have been tremendously lonely, but I couldn't see that as a child. I was just constantly afraid, and I began eating compulsively to cover up the fear. Of course, I didn't understand that when I was a child either.

I can't remember being unhappy before I was about 12, despite what went on with my mother. My father was such a powerful person in my life. He took me everywhere with him. I was very outgoing, friendly, and talkative. In fact, when I think about it, he took me places that my mother should have gone to with him. He and I became a team, and my mother was somewhere else. I looked at her as kind of weak, and I couldn't understand why she didn't want to be part of the family. She just stayed at home and drank. She prided herself on never drinking outside the home.

After I was 12 years old, there was a change. I went from being a happy child to being unhappy, and I became keenly aware of my mother's drinking. When I became a teenager, I dreaded coming home from school and finding her drunk or passed out on the couch. This began to happen almost daily, as the disease was progressing. But what did I know, I was just a kid, so I stopped bringing friends home. It was so embarrassing! Mothers just don't do this. I was terribly ashamed of her, and yet there was an extreme concern for her and a need to protect her—I never spoke to anyone about this, not even my brother.

Here was this woman who was our mother, laying on the floor, and we would just pick her up and put her to bed. We would never discuss this as a family either. Now when I look back on all this, it's terrible. The only time we would discuss what was happening with mother was when it would come to a crisis, like if she had gone across the street to the store and fell down in the store. I think someone phoned us to come get her. Then we would talk about it, but it seemed to take something that happened outside the house.

I remember coming home from school one day, and her belt had caught on the refrigerator door handle. She was drunk and must have passed out. Her leg was broken, and she was just caught there. That was a crisis that we talked about. It would take something like that, you see. Then my father would get really upset and angry, and we would put her in the hospital, like that time with her broken leg, and he would threaten to commit her, saying that this time he'd had it, he had really reached his limit. Then I would get hysterical and beg him not to, and so he didn't. He never did commit her.

Sometimes when he would come home from work, she would berate him verbally, chipping away at him as a person. He would get extremely angry. I never saw my father actually hit my mother. He would walk out of the room first, but one time he started to, and I jumped between the two of them and started yelling hysterically. "Please don't hit her. Please, Please . . . ," and then running around the house trying to find the booze that she'd hidden. That was a job I was always rewarded for.

Now that I was a teenager, my father would spend very little time at home. He would come in for dinner and then just go out again. My brother often left too, so it would end up just my mother and me at home alone. She'd would start rambling about my father being out with other women, following me all over the house talking to me. It was true. He was out with other women. I would just try to get away from her, because I was so angry with her. My anger was tremendous at this point. Sometimes I would have to lock myself in the bathroom to get away from her. What's amazing to me when I look back is that I never went out the door, I never left the house. I was about 16 years old at this time. I could have just walked out, but I never did. She constantly berated men, in general.

I was falling asleep in my classes at school, getting poor marks, and making it by the skin of my teeth. I got by because I was a clown. That was how I learned to get attention. My great distraction was humor and still is to this day. Whenever there is too much intensity for me, I will crack a joke. I have to do it, can't help myself. I have to take the focus off the intensity; it is very hard for me to deal with, to this day, so I sharpened my humor in school. I got in trouble with it, but not too much. I had a lot of friends and was very social, but I still didn't tell anybody about what was going on in my home. I knew my home was not normal. I went to other people's houses, and you know what amazed me was that their parents talked to one another, their fathers were there at night, and their mothers weren't drunk.

I went to a Catholic school, and the nuns would get really mad at me for falling asleep in class. Sometimes when I came to class, I looked like I'd been out all night, and I couldn't focus on things. I was not a bad kid; I was just in a bad situation.

At this point, I was angry with my father for leaving me there every night with my mother and going out with other women. Even when I was 5 years old and he would take me fishing, he brought along another woman. At that time, it was the woman from next door, because my mother never wanted to go. I never knew why I didn't like these other women; I just didn't. I was the cover; having me along made it look good. That's how he coped with all this. My brother aligned himself with my mother and developed a deep, smoldering hatred for my father, very quietly. That finally showed when he became an adult. He completely disregarded our father.

So that was high school. I ended up with a weight problem and some pretty bad grades, but I managed to graduate. I dated some, not a lot. When my friends would talk about how they wanted to get married someday and have children, I couldn't imagine. That was never my goal. I wanted to go around the world. I had a sense of adventure and curiosity. It was a good thing that my father was strict with me, loving, but a disciplinarian nonetheless. He would send us away for the month of July to a summer home we rented on the coast. I loved it there. He would come up on the weekends, and for some reason, mother never drank for the month we spent there. It was heaven to me. For one month somehow we appeared like a normal family. I hated going home because I knew it was going to change, and the drinking would start all over again. My father was now very rarely home, even for dinner, though he would come home at night. He would go away on vacations by himself or take someone else with him.

In my late teens, Mother got worse and would telephone my friends and ask them where I was and was I with a man. She would say horrible things about me and then not even remember that she had called them. Of course, they would tell me, and then I would get upset and yell at her and tell my father.

My brother left home to get married. Mother was so drunk at the wedding that she fell down. When I look at my brother's wedding pictures, I can see the deterioration of my mother. She had been a beautiful woman, but by then her face was bloated and distorted. She looked awful. I was 21 by now, and my mother was drunk most of the time. I can remember sitting across from her at the kitchen table and realizing that she was in pain, but I didn't know why. It seemed like she was in a tremendous black hole, and she was trying to grab me down into it. I spent all my time trying not to be sucked down into this hole. She was meek like a mouse until she drank, and then she had a mouth like a truck driver.

That same year that I turned 21, I got a summer home with a bunch of friends. It was the first time I had really left her house. At first I went away on weekends, and then I started to commute from work and not go home at all. She was calling my friends raving on, saying where was I, that I was a whore, a tramp. I was still a virgin at this point, mind you, so I decided that I was going to move out on my own. I couldn't take it anymore. My father was now dating a woman who had been a friend of mine, a year younger than me. I knew about this and felt sorry for my mother. I was furious with my father, and I hated the other woman. In the middle of all this, I moved out.

My mother was dead a month later. She was smoking a cigarette, and the house caught on fire. My father was across the street somewhere. I was filled with guilt.

I blamed my father after her death and severed my connections with the neighborhood. I imagined that people were blaming me. Less than a year later, I married the man who became the father of my son.

My views on men were very negative, as you might guess. Yet I loved my husband very much, in my own way, and I stayed in that marriage for five years. I knew he was a drinker, and I knew he drank too much, but I married him anyway. I was going to save him. He drank because he had so many problems. He needed me. That's what I told myself.

My son was born a year after we married. By the time three years had passed, we were both into heavy drinking. My husband would go off and drink for four or five days and not come home. We lived in a remote area and I knew absolutely no one. I was completely isolated and had no one but my infant son. He would cry, and I would cry. I didn't know what to do. My husband's alcoholism progressed. It is truly a family disease, in my opinion. I mean one person has a problem with drinking, and one person doesn't, but the effect is the same. Alcoholism contaminates and destroys everyone in its path. I can remember the feelings of wanting to destroy my husband, of wanting to destroy myself. I was filled with self-hatred, self-condemnation. I hated everything and everybody because I hated myself. I lashed out at everything. During those times when my husband would disappear for days at a time drinking, I could be found at home alone on the couch at two in the morning, obsessing about my death. I would picture myself laying in my coffin, dead, and people would be coming in at a wake to pay their respects. Finally, my husband would show up, not knowing what had happened until the very last moment when he walked up to the coffin, and there I was, dead. Overcome with remorse and hysterical, he would throw himself on my coffin, begging my forgiveness for all he had done to me. That was the end of my fantasy.

I think healthier people dream of killing their spouses rather than killing themselves, not that it's healthy to think of killing anyone. I was so angry that I turned it all against myself. I often wanted to commit suicide. I wanted to destroy myself. But I always reasoned my way out of that because I had to raise this child.

My husband was off on one of his drinking sprees. This time nine days had passed, and I'd even filled out a missing persons report, when he came home and said that he wanted to get help. I called AA. Where I pulled AA from, I'll never know. Two people came out to the house and talked to him. After that, he went to his first meeting. He had a slip after that and disappeared again, so I moved to the city. My son was a toddler.

I had no money. He would take whatever money we had and just drink it up. When he went on these sprees, he would fly somewhere and spend it all. I had to get back to something I knew because I felt like I was losing my mind. I was practically gone by that point. He followed me and went back into AA, and I went to all his AA meetings with him. That's when someone finally approached me and told me about Al-Anon.

I went to Al-Anon initially because of him. I had no concept at this point of how sick *I* was; I just had no idea. I thought that I had to learn about him, what he was doing, about alcoholism, and sobriety, and all that. I was in Al-Anon for two years before I realized that I was there for me. I didn't have a clue for those first two years that I was there for myself. People said it; I just didn't hear it. I can remember what a shock it was when I finally realized that. I was doing something for myself, and that was the breakthrough for me.

Before long my marriage fell apart, and I was in a terrible depression. When my husband left, all that grief came up over my mother's death. I was going through incredible pain. That's what came up, because I hadn't allowed it to come up before. I went into a terrible depression for about a year, and it was all around my mother. I continued in Al-Anon though; that was the only saving grace. That was about the only thing I did. I kept going to meetings and that got me through the depression. Then I went back to college, got my degree, and raised my son, who was still a very young child. His father dropped out of the picture completely.

Six years after I was in Al-Anon, I started to go to Adult Children of Alcoholics meetings, because I realized that a lot of the stuff that I was trying to sort through had nothing to do with my marriage whatsoever. My marriage was just a continuation of the saga of my alcoholic family. I had just played out their drama, so to speak. I realized that I had set my marriage up to fail. There was no way it could have worked. I didn't feel love as a child, so rather than go out and find it because I didn't even know what it was, like so many other adult children of alcoholics, we go out and find somebody else who will *not* love us, and then wonder what went wrong. I take full responsibility for my actions. Alcoholism is alcoholism, and it destroys everything in its path, no matter which end of the disease you've got: the obsession with alcohol or the obsession with the alcoholic.

My marriage broke up *after* sobriety. There was another woman. I had internalized my mother's negative attitudes toward men—they were no good. I wasn't even aware of this at the time, it was so unconscious. Once again, it appeared as if a man had destroyed a woman, just like it appeared as if my father destroyed my mother. What I hadn't seen was that she *allowed* herself to be destroyed by her sick love for this man. I had set my husband up to be my father, but instead of drinking myself to death like my mother had, the marriage ended, and I went the other direction. And that happened because I was in recovery. I chose life.

As I get older, I see so much of my mother in me. By the grace of God, I'm not an alcoholic. I say "the grace of God" because I don't know how it missed me; it's all around me in my family. Somewhere I chose life, but there's a great deal of my mother in me. I have a black hole in me just like my mother. There's a good deal of melancholy in me beneath the humor. There are tremendous fears that I see getting worse as I get older. And they didn't come to the fore until my father died.

After mother died, he remarried, and this second wife threw him out within two-and-a-half years. At the same time his marriage failed, he retired from his job and proceeded to drink himself to death. He was dead within a very short time. While he was alive, no matter what he was doing or what was happening, I always felt like I was safe; nothing could hurt me. Suddenly, I was vulnerable, and I had to feel it. I was afraid of things I'd never known I was afraid of. I really started talking about this in meetings.

It was in the ACA meetings that I got in touch with a lot of my fears, and the biggest fear was the fear of abandonment. Then I discovered how much I was afraid that I would be like my mother; that was a tremendous fear. I realized that if I looked at what I'd done with my life, I had never said I want to do this or that, I choose to go in this or that directions. What I had done, instead of working toward something, was focus on walking away from my mother. I would tell myself that if I go to college and get a degree, I won't be my mother. If I have a career and don't spend my time at home, I'm not my mother. So my whole life, instead of walking *toward* a goal, I had been walking away from my mother, doing anything I could not to be her. My whole life was about not being her.

I got in touch with that in ACA meetings. That was the first awareness I had of what I had been doing all these years.

The very first ACA meeting I went to, a woman was talking about abandonment. She said that in the past, if people weren't giving her their full attention, she just fell apart, and she didn't know why. She would just be embarrassed and couldn't figure it out. But after she came into ACA, she found out that it was the feeling of abandonment that would come over her when that happened. I had just walked in, and I started to cry. I couldn't stop crying. For the first time in my life, I felt like somebody understood me on the insides, and they didn't even know me. It was an extremely powerful experience. I had never understood what it was in me that happened if somebody didn't give me their full attention. I just couldn't deal with it. I was all over the place, especially with a man, and I never knew what it was before that night.

So then I started going to ACA meetings as well as the regular Al-Anon meetings, and I still go to both groups. I got a sponsor in Al-Anon right from the beginning. Turns out that she is an adult child of an alcoholic too. We talked on the phone almost daily when I first came into the program. I never could have dealt with all those feelings by myself.

My self-esteem was so low that I had to work on it like a course in college. Somebody in my Al-Anon group told me to look at it that way, like it was a class I was taking and I wanted to get an A. I had to work at it every day. They told me only to try things that I knew I could succeed at for a while, only be with people that affirmed me. It took me about four years straight, working on it every day, to begin to turn it around. That's how bad I was. But slowly I started to have respect for myself; I started to feel good about myself as a person. I began to see that I was intelligent, attractive, even pretty. I began to be able to make decisions based on what is good for me.

You must have heard the old joke about how you can tell an Al-Anon member: When an Al-Anon member is drowning, somebody else's life flashes before them. It's the same addiction as the alcoholic who is focused on alcohol, only we're addicted to the alcoholic. I had to learn to wrench my focus off the alcoholic. When I was married to my first husband, I was obsessed with his drinking. When he got sober, I was obsessed with his sobriety. When we split up, I was obsessed with what he was doing. It was insane. It was just like my childhood where my first obsession had been my mother. I worried about her all the time: Was she drinking, was she not drinking? When I came home from school, would she be on the floor or not? Should I risk it and bring a friend home or not? She, she she . . . my whole life had been focused on other people. I didn't know how to focus on myself. It's a great way to keep from ever having to look at yourself. I didn't even realize that I was doing that until I came into Al-Anon.

When I first began to look inside myself, it was frightening and painful. There was an emptiness that I've slowly filled now over the years, thanks to Al-Anon. I've been given so much. People in the program constantly affirmed me, showed me what love is. They kept telling me I could do it when I would say, "I can't," whether it was about going back to school, raising my son alone, or whatever was up. It's a wonderful place to create a good self-image.

It's sixteen years ago now since I first came into Al-Anon and ten years since I started going to Al-Anon's ACA meetings, and I'm still very active. After fourteen years in the program, I married again, and I didn't think that would ever happen again. I had been on my own a long time. I've been into a lot of things over these past several years. I'm always searching. I've been into Buddhism, done the *est* training, attended the Unity church. But the one thing that is always there for me, that I've never left, is Al-Anon. That's the one place where I've found a presence that I might call God. I see miracles in that program all the time. I see people come in, the newcomers, thinking that this is the end of the world, not wanting to live anymore. And then I see them walk out of that same meeting with a sense of hope because somebody at the meeting was able to say to them, "I've been exactly where you are now."

I met the man I'm married to now about eight years ago. And it was only because of this program that I was able to let myself trust another human being. I don't think I had ever learned that before. I learned how to love people without grabbing onto them and giving them no room. I learned to allow people to be who they are and not have to try to change them to fit my way. That's fear. He's much better at doing that than I am, but I'm learning.

Ironically, I was willing to be responsible for everyone's life but my own. I would be responsible for my mother's drinking, my father's behavior, a stranger on the street, anyone and everyone else's except for my own feelings and attitudes. I wanted everyone else to be responsible for my feelings, especially my mother and father. The relief I've gotten in Al-Anon is that I only have to be responsible for myself and for my own happiness. I didn't want it to be that way in the beginning because I'd rather blame twenty other people for my life. It was easier to blame everyone else than to take responsibility for myself. But with the responsibility of my own life comes tremendous freedom, and I like that. The two most beautiful things I've gotten from Al-Anon are the responsibility for my own life and self-acceptance. For me those two things add up to freedom. If you accept yourself as you are for today, that's freedom. I spent my whole life not accepting me or anybody else. I had to make them over; I had to make me over. It never occurred to me to accept anything like it was, you know, surrender. Change things, oh yes, but accept what you cannot change? Never. There's nothing I couldn't change—including the universe. Whatever it was, I was going to change it.

When we come into recovery, hopefully, we can finally break that cycle. My son is now 17 years old, and although he was too young to remember his father drinking or anything like that, I can see the effects of my part of the disease on him. I really can. I can see that my Steven has the same fear of abandonment that I have, that he has a need to control like I have, to an exaggerated degree, that he really has to work on the self-esteem. He's in much better shape than I was at his age, but I can still see the effect, see how the disease of dependency is passed down. I don't know how much he's aware of that. I share with him. He never went to Alateen; oh, once or twice, but he never got involved. I think that you just recreate whatever it is that you know. If you come from a healthy family, you recreate health. If you come from an unhealthy family, you recreate that too. Without some kind of change in awareness, I think we go through life trying to recreate what was, simply out of a need to just have what's known. There's comfort in what's known. Even if it's painful, at least it's familiar. The unknown is terrifying. We seem to endure all sorts of difficulties rather than face the unfamiliar. So when what is familiar is health, you recreate it. We all do this, not just alcoholic or chemically dependent families. It's just if all you know is disease, then, unfortunately, that's what you tend to recreate unless you get help.

It seems like the phenomenal growth of the Adult Children

of Alcoholics movement within Al-Anon over the past few years is a kind of living proof of that concept. It documents the human tendency to repeat our family patterns over and over again, at least through some kind of an oral tradition. Hearing people's stories in meeting after meeting makes it evident that left to our own devices, that's what we do, repeat. You don't have to be a sociologist to see that. What has become evident is the tremendous need for some kind of intervention to stop the process that goes on generation after generation. There's a point in the Twelve Steps that I got to, around Step Five, where I'd taken a moral inventory of myself, and now I was going to share that with another human being. I found myself with a tendency to want to take my parents' inventory, and I had to get beyond that if I wanted recovery. I can't keep pointing the finger at my parents. I found it helpful to remember that I am a victim of two victims. And so it goes all the way back. Nobody wants to have the disease of alcoholism. It happens to people, just like any other disease people get, whether it's diabetes or cancer or arthritis.

I still go to meetings after sixteen years, because today I know that I'm the problem in my life, not anybody else. It's not the alcoholics that did me in; it's my thinking back in perspective, and get on track with positive attitudes. But it takes more than positive thinking for me, it takes action; it takes constant action. Just an awareness is good, and it's a beginning, but it's not enough, not enough at all. Recovery takes constant action. That's what I found as soon as I do Step Three in the program I'm in constant action. In Steps One, Two, and Three, I am getting ready. Then there's a daily practicing of these principles: the daily mental "housecleaning," daily inventory, the program—what wisdom and vision!

I have to keep reminding myself that a higher power is in charge here. I'll call that God, for want of a better word. I've had a hard time coming to terms with that concept, but that's part of what I work on, am reminded of by the program, the Steps, the meetings. These things are all reminders. We have to constantly be reminded of who we really are. We have layers of appearances to see through, mask after mask to take off. They are so thick that knowing who we really are is almost impossible, I think, sometimes. That's why I keep going back, to be reminded. The program is a spiritual help, a way of reminding ourselves of who we really are. All of us, alcoholic and nonalcoholic or addict alike, we're children of God.

A Historical Note: Conversations with Lois W. and Bob S., Jr.

I spoke with Lois W. and Bob S., Jr., in July of 1985 at AA's fiftieth anniversary and international convention in Montreal. Lois is the widow of Bill W., co-founder of AA. She also helped to organize the Al-Anon Family Group. Bob S., Jr., is the son of Dr. Bob S., co-founder with Bill W. of AA.

Lois, 94 years old at the time, told me something about the early days of Al-Anon and AA. AA was started June 10, 1935, by Bill W. and Dr. Bob S. in Akron, Ohio.

I felt self-satisfied that I had done everything I could when Bill finally got sober. It never occurred to me that I needed any help myself, that I needed any growing and developing, I thought I was "it." I was just fine. I had no problem with alcohol. He had the problem. I joined the Oxford Group with Bill and went along for his sake.

Then came the famous episode when I threw the shoe. Bill said, "Hurry up, it's time for us to go to the meeting!" Well, I had a shoe in my hand, and I just threw it at him and said, "Damn your old meetings."

When I came to my senses and realized how I'd lost my temper, I thought, "Over what?" Over nothing. Why had I acted so violently over something so trivial? I began to think about myself. Then I realized that I needed to go to meetings for my own sake.

I told other people about the episode, and they told others in turn. From then on, when I went with Bill to talk, I would gather the families together afterwards, and we'd talk. There were wives, children, husbands, too, that came for those family meetings long before we got organized and had Al-Anon. Al-Anon started in 1951, but these family meetings had been going on for a long time before that, all over the country. I can't tell you the dates anymore. It just wasn't until 1951 that we had a central office for them to write to in New York. Then Alateen got started in 1957 by a young boy out in California.

Anne S., Dr. Bob's wife, and I had been working with the families all along. Then Bill encouraged me to get something more developed. That's when we started calling it Al-Anon. We realized long ago that alcoholism is a family disease.

Bob S., Jr. is the only person left alive who was present the day that his father Dr. Bob met Bill W. at Henrietta Sieberling's home in Akron, Ohio. That was Mother's Day, 1935. Stranded in Akron on a business trip, Bill wanted desperately to stay sober. He called a minister in the area to see if he could find another Oxford Group member who could refer him to an alcoholic to talk to. After several phone calls, he was referred to Henrietta Sieberling, a member of the Oxford Group and close friend of Anne S., Dr. Bob's wife. Henrietta and Anne had watched helplessly as Dr. Bob's disease progressed. When Bill called, Henrietta told him that she thought she could find him someone to talk to, then she quickly called Anne S. Dr. Bob was drunk at the time, so they arranged for a meeting the next day. What Dr. Bob thought would be a fifteen-minute conversation became a five-hour meeting on Mother's Day, during which Bob, Jr. waited, not so patiently, outside. He was then 16.

We lived in absolute poverty as the result of the Great Depression and his drinking. Lots of time we didn't have anything to eat at night but bread and milk. Anyone who's lived in an alcoholic home knows that it's bedlam, chaos from one day to the next. Dr. Bob was not an obstreperous drunk. He had the boys at the Central Garage trained to bring him home. The garage was under the house, so then the only problem was getting him upstairs. Mother, my sister, and I would get him upstairs, and he'd go right to bed so that he could get up the next day. He promised Mother many times that he'd stop drinking. Then he'd hide out in different hotels because if Mother caught up with him, she'd scold him. His medical practice went to almost nothing while he drank.

Well, after that meeting, Bill came to live at our house for three months. That's when the AA concepts began to be formulated, and they began working with other alcoholics. Times were so tough that they brought the alcoholics into our home to treat them. Dr. Bob was the only medical man involved at the time, and people didn't have the money. These were not just overnight guests; Arch T., who started AA in Detroit, was there almost a year. The change I saw in my father was one from despair to hope.

My father treated over 5,000 alcoholics personally without charge during his sobriety. He lived fifteen years after they started AA.

I've given a lot of thought to what being raised in an alcoholic home does to you. It makes it difficult to perceive normality. You have trouble adjusting because you've done things to counter the alcoholism as best you can. You can develop character traits that aren't good. I consider this Adult Children of Alcoholics movement a very positive thing.

I've been in Al-Anon a little over six years, and the way I got here was like everything else—I came when I had to. My wife is a recovering alcoholic, and I like to say that she drank my way into the organization. I drank for many years, it was never a problem with me but since my wife has gone into AA, I don't drink anymore. I don't have anything against it, but I like to keep our lives on the same plane so we're operating from the same place. I'm grateful for Al-Anon because it's enabled me to work on a quality of life I was never aware of.

It doesn't seem like it's possible that two people who've been exposed to as much alcoholism as my wife and I had been couldn't recognize it in our own home, but we didn't. She was the child of an alcoholic, too. She took her father to a drying-out center, and he became a member of AA back in the forties. I've always been kind of ashamed to admit that I was that stupid, but the denial of this disease is incredible. My wife didn't set out to be an alcoholic. Nobody does, you understand. We drank socially for many years; that's how it starts out. She was not an instant alcoholic, but if you've got the disease of alcoholism, sooner or later you're going to get to the point where you can't stop drinking or can't control it. Instead of you controlling the alcohol, the alcohol's controlling you. That's when we went for help. It's only a phone call away. All you've got to do is look in the phone book under A.

I was privileged to be the Al-Anon speaker at the first ACA

convention. I stayed long enough to take in some of the seminars. I got quite an education. It's really added to the sum of my knowledge. The only limitation to the growth of AA or Al-Anon is the growth of the individual members. Growth has to be due to the unselfish effort of members who are grateful for someone who took the time to present the program to them.

But a word of caution here. There are a lot of professionals in this field. There's a lot of money in alcoholism now, and people are jumping in right and left. I see a real danger in some of this, and I think we're going to see some pretty wild things for a while. Being raised in an alcoholic home can also be used as a cop-out to explain all the failures in life. That would be bad. There are some who don't get into Al-Anon, don't use the Twelve Steps and Twelve Traditions, and some of those groups are alarming. One has to use a lot of discretion in this area. All I can tell you is that Al-Anon's been a lifesaver for me.

APPENDIXES

Appendix 1.
If You Think You Have a Problem and Want Help

If you've identified with the stories and conversations in this book and realize that you grew up in an alcoholic or dysfunctional home and want help, you have several options. The first step might be to find and attend at least six of Al-Anon's Adult Children of Alcoholics meetings (see Directory below). Al-Anon is free and meetings are available most everywhere. They generally have a variety of kinds of meetings to choose from to fit your particular situation.

If you are from an alcoholic or dysfunctional home *and* are presently living with active alcoholism or addiction, whether it be in your partner, spouse, or children, you may want to go to at least six regular Al-Anon meetings as well as the ACA meetings.

If you're a younger person (12-19) and still in the home with active alcoholism or addiction, whether it's your parents or a brother or sister who have the disease, you can attend Al-Anon's Alateen meetings.

Therapists can also be helpful, provided they have an understanding and some experience with the Twelve-Step programs. Therapy combined with a Twelve-Step program can be very fruitful. But be careful. This is a new field. A therapist may have come from an alcoholic or dysfunctional home and not have recognized his or her own problems in this area. When considering therapists in this area, interview them, ask them if they are familiar with Al-Anon, AA, ACA, whether or not they've been to meetings, whether or not they have their own program of recovery or can support yours. There are no hard and fast rules to go by, just common sense and some caution.

Adult children of alcoholics often use other Twelve-Step programs, such as Alcoholics Anonymous, Narcotics Anonymous,

Debtors Anonymous, Cocaine Anonymous, Overeaters Anonymous, and Smokers Anonymous, just to give a few examples, to help address their issues as ACAs. The theory lying underneath this broad adaptation of the Twelve Steps is that people use many different substances compulsively. By substituting the words *money* or *food* or *drugs* or *tobacco* or *sex* and so on for *alcohol* in the original AA Twelve Steps and Twelve Traditions, the same program of recovery can apply. At bottom lie many of the self-esteem issues characteristic of children of alcoholics. Legitimate Twelve-Step programs have generally contacted and received permission from AA General Services in New York to adapt the Twelve Steps and Twelve Traditions. They are anonymous fellowships that do not charge and that use AA as their recovery model.

If you are trying to live with a problem drinker, you may be contributing to the problem instead of the solution without realizing it. If you think you have a drinking problem, chances are you do. There *is* help available, both for the alcoholic and for the family. Everyone in the family needs the opportunity to recover, not just the alcoholic. You can't stop someone else's drinking, but you can take action for yourself. There are many avenues of help available today in virtually every good-size town. In a dozen or so states, counseling is available through the public school system for students who are living in alcoholic families. Check with your school counseling office.

Many people feel that the alcoholic won't stop drinking until he hits a "bottom," an experience that is different for each person, so that there is nothing that can be done until and unless that person is ready to stop drinking or using. Others point to the "intervention" process as an avenue open to relatives and friends of an alcoholic or addict. Most major corporations and many businesses have Employee Assistance Programs (EAP) available through work for the employee who is seeking help or whom others recognize needs help.

Family and friends can take matters into their own hands as well. Over the last few years "intervention" has become used increasingly to get the alcoholic into treatment and family members into an appropriate recovery of their own. Intervention requires the skills of a professional intervention counselor who works closely with family members and friends to educate and prepare them to talk with the alcoholic about his or her drinking, lovingly, and with care. The goal of intervention is to get the alcoholic into treatment and the family members into their own recovery. Your local Council on Alcoholism can most often provide you with information on intervention. Interventions must be undertaken with a great deal of skill, cooperation, and care, and with an experienced intervention counselor. This is not something to try on your own or alone.

There are all manner (and costs) of treatment programs available today, depending on your pocketbook and your insurance coverage. Millions of people, including myself, simply joined Al-Anon or Alcoholics Anonymous; it works and it's free.

Al-Anon is for those who feel that their lives have been affected by someone else's drinking. Like AA, after which it is closely modeled, Al-Anon is a non-professional, self-help recovery program. It is an anonymous fellowship of men and women who come together to overcome the effects of living with or having lived with an alcoholic. By utilizing the Twelve Steps and Twelve Traditions, Al-Anon has grown since its inception in 1951 to become a worldwide organization with over 24,000 Al-Anon and Alateen groups registered around the globe. Alateen was begun in 1957 for young people 12 to 19 who are living in, or have lived in, an alcoholic home, whether the alcoholism is their parents' or a brother's or sister's. (It is *not* a program for teenage alcoholics. Teenage alcoholics go to AA.)

Al-Anon Adult Children of Alcoholics meetings have grown rapidly over the last few years, with over 1200 groups registering with World Services as of this writing. More groups affiliate every month. For information on meetings, times, and locations, contact your local Al-Anon organization by looking in your local phone directory or calling information or contacting your local Council on Alcoholism. Information on Alateen comes through Al-Anon as well. You can also call or write:

Al-Anon Family Group Headquarters, Inc.
P.O. Box 862
Midtown Station
New York, New York 10018–0862
(212) 302–7240

Adult Children of Alcoholics Central Service Board began in 1984. ACA is open to anyone who identifies with the ACA "Problem Statement." (see page 242), thus making the program available to adults who grew up in various other types of dysfunctional families as well as to those from alcoholic homes. ACA-CSB feels that there are many types of dysfunctional families that produce what is called the "alcoholic family system." "The focus is on healing the inner child and learning how to re-parent oneself through the use of the Twelve Steps and Twelve Traditions." ACA has nearly 500 meetings registered with half outside the state of California. Write or call:

ACA-Central Service Board
P.O. Box 35623
Los Angeles, CA 90035
(213) 464–4423

The National Association for Children of Alcoholics (NACoA) is a non-profit organization founded in 1983 to support and serve as a resource for children of alcoholics of all ages and for those in a position to help them. Its goals are to help create more effective services, to increase public awareness, and to provide training to those who want to help children of alcoholics. NACoA was founded by an interdisciplinary team of therapists, educators, authors, and physicians interested in developing a network of information and care for young, adolescent, and adult children of alcoholics everywhere. NACoA helps create a voice for all children of alcoholics by publishing a newsletter, sponsoring annual conventions, regional conferences, workshops, forming local chapters, and operating a clearinghouse of books on related topics sold at a discount to members. For information, write or call:

NACoA
31706 Coast Highway, #201
South Laguna, CA 92677
(714) 499–3889

The National Council on Alcoholism (NCA), founded in 1944, maintains affiliates in more than seventy cities throughout the

United States. A voluntary health organization, it can provide information and referrals about alcoholism on the local as well as national level. Their focus is on education, research, and service. A good source of information and publications. Contact your local council or:

The National Council on Alcoholism
12 West 21st Street
New York, New York 10011
(212) 206–6770

Children of Alcoholics Foundation, Inc. is a voluntary, nonprofit, public organization created to assist children of alcoholic parents. Estimates are that at least 7 million children (one out of every ten children under the age of 20) are still in alcoholic homes. The Foundation focuses attention on problems parental alcoholism causes for youngsters, as well as promotes and disseminates research. CoA Foundation sponsors conferences, seminars, public information and education programs, and encourages local, state, and federal agencies to respond to the needs of these children.

Children of Alcoholics Foundation
540 Madison Ave., 23rd Floor
New York, New York 10022
(212) 980–5394

Alcoholics Anonymous is a fellowship of men and women who share their experience, strength and hope with each other that they may solve their common problem and help others to recover from alcoholism.

"The only requirement for membership is a desire to stop drinking. There are no dues or fees for AA membership, we are self-supporting through our own contributions. AA is not allied with any sect, denomination, politics, organization or institution; does not wish to engage in any controversy; neither indorses nor opposes any causes. Our primary purpose is to stay sober and help other alcoholics achieve sobriety."*

---

*Reprinted with permission from the *AA Grapevine.*

With well over 42,000 groups registered worldwide and a conservative estimate of over 1 million members, AA is truly an international fellowship. Founded in 1935, AA originally formulated the Twelve Steps and Twelve Traditions that provide the basis for all the Twelve Step programs that have followed, starting with Al-Anon in 1951, to the myriad of anonymous Twelve-Step programs flourishing today.

Alcoholics Anonymous World Services, Inc.
Box 459
Grand Central Station
New York, New York 10163
(212) 686-1100

AA is listed in the telephone book, often in both the white and yellow pages. AA is free and it's everywhere. Some treatment programs are now offering treatment for family members in their own right (not in conjunction with the alcoholic/addict's treatment program).

Appendix 2.
The Problem: An Interim Statement for ACAs

Many of us found that we had several characteristics in common as a result of being brought up in an alcoholic household.

We had come to feel isolated, uneasy with other people, and especially authority figures. To protect ourselves, we became people pleasers, even though we lost our own identity in the process. All the same, we would mistake any personal criticism as a threat.

We either became alcoholics ourselves or married them, or both. Failing that, we found another compulsive personality, such as a workaholic, to fulfill our need for abandonment.

We lived life from the standpoint of victims. Having an overdeveloped sense of responsibility, we preferred to be concerned with others rather than ourselves. We somehow got guilt feelings when we stood up for ourselves rather than giving in to others. Thus, we became reactors rather than actors, letting others take the initiative.

We were dependent personalities—terrified of abandonment—willing to do almost anything to hold on to a relationship in order not to be abandoned emotionally. Yet we kept choosing insecure relationships because they matched our childhood relationship with alcoholic parents.

These symptoms of the family disease of alcoholism made us "co-victims"—those who take on the characteristics of the disease without necessarily ever taking a drink. We learned to stuff our feelings down as children and kept them buried as adults. As a result of this conditioning, we confused love and

Reprinted by permission of ACA Central Service Board of California, 1986.

pity, tending to love those we could rescue. Even more self-defeating, we became addicted to excitement in all our affairs, preferring constant upset to workable relationships.

This is a description, not an indictment.

Appendix 3.
The Solution: An Interim Statement for ACAs

The solution is to become your own loving parent.

As ACA becomes a safe place for you, you will find the freedom to express all the hurts and fears you have kept inside and to free yourself from the shame and blame that are carry-overs from the past. You will become an adult who is imprisoned no longer by childhood reactions. You will recover the child within you, learning to accept and love yourself.

The healing begins when we risk moving out of isolation. Feelings and buried memories will return. By gradually releasing the burden of unexpressed grief, we slowly move out of the past. We learn to reparent ourselves with gentleness, humor, love, and respect.

This process allows us to see our biological parents as the instruments of our existence. Our actual parent is a Higher Power whom some of us choose to call God. Although we had alcoholic parents, our Higher Power gave us the Twelve-Steps of Recovery.

This is the action and work that heals us: We use the Steps; we use the meetings; we use the telephone. We share our experience, strength, and hope with each other. We learn to restructure our thinking one day at a time. When we release our parents from responsibility for our actions today, we become free to make healthful decisions as actors, not reactors. We progress from hurting to healing to helping. We awaken to a sense of wholeness we never knew was possible.

By attending these meetings on a regular basis, you will come to see parental alcoholism for what it is: a disease that infected you as a child and continues to affect you as an adult. You will learn to keep the focus on yourself in the here and

Reprinted by permission of ACA Central Service Board of California, 1986.

now. You will take responsibility for your own life and supply your own parenting.

You will not do this alone. Look around you and you will see others who know how you feel. We will love and encourage you no matter what. We ask you to accept us just as we accept you.

This is a spiritual program based on action coming from LOVE. We are sure that as the love grows inside you, you will see beautiful changes in all your relationships, especially with God, yourself, and your parents.

Appendix 4.
An ACA Twelve Steps of Recovery (Interim)

This version of the Twelve Steps of Recovery is currently being considered by the ACA Central Service Board of California.* It will be at least 1988 before any final determination of adaptations will be made.

1. Admitted we were powerless over the effects of alcoholism and our lives had become unmanageable.
2. Came to believe that a Power greater than ourselves could restore us to sanity.
3. Made a decision to turn our will and our lives over to God as we understood God.
4. Made a searching and fearless moral inventory of ourselves.
5. Admitted to God, to ourselves, and to another human being the exact nature of our wrongs.
6. Were entirely ready to have God remove all these defects of character.
7. Humbly asked God to remove our shortcomings.
8. Made a list of all persons we had harmed and became willing to make amends to them all.
9. Made direct amends to such people wherever possible, except when to do so would injure them or others.
10. Continued to take personal inventory and when we were wrong promptly admitted it.
11. Sought through prayer and meditation to improve our conscious contact with God, as we understood God, praying only for knowledge of God's will for us and the power to carry that out.
12. Having had a spiritual awakening as a result of these steps,

---

*Author's note: These Twelve Steps are taken from the original Twelve Steps of Alcoholics Anonymous; see p. 256. Reprinted by permission of ACA Central Service Board of California, 1986.

we tried to carry this message to other Adult Children of Alcoholics who still suffer, and to practice these principles in all our affairs.

Appendix 5.
An ACA Twelve Traditions (Interim)

1. Our common welfare should come first; personal recovery for the greatest number depends upon ACA unity.
2. For our group purpose there is but one authority—a loving Higher Power as it may express itself in our group conscience. Our leaders are but trusted servants; they do not govern.
3. Adult Children of Alcoholics, when gathered together for mutual aid, may call themselves an ACA Family Group, provided that, as a group, they have no other affiliation. The only requirement for ACA membership is that one identify with "The Problem."
4. Each group should be autonomous except in matters affecting another ACA group, ACA as a whole, or another anonymous Twelve-Step program.
5. Each ACA Family Group has but one purpose: to help Adult Children of Alcoholics. We do this by practicing the Twelve Steps of ACA ourselves, by encouraging and understanding our alcoholic parents or caretakers, and by welcoming and giving comfort to other Adult Children of Alcoholics.
6. Our ACA Family Groups ought never endorse, finance, or lend the ACA name to any outside enterprise, lest problems of money, property, and prestige divert us from our primary purpose. Although a separate entity, we should always cooperate with other anonymous Twelve-Step programs.
7. Every ACA family group ought to be fully self-supporting, declining outside contributions.

Author's note: These Twelve Traditions are taken from the original Twelve Traditions of Alcoholics Anonymous; see p. 257. Reprinted by permission of ACA Central Service Board of California, 1986.

8. ACA Twelfth-Step work should remain forever nonprofessional, but our service centers may employ special workers.

9. Our ACA Family Groups, as such, ought never be organized, but we may create special service boards or committees directly responsible to those they serve.

10. The ACA Family Groups have no opinion on outside issues; hence the ACA name ought never be drawn into public controversy.

11. Our public relations policy is based on attraction rather than promotion; we need always maintain personal anonymity at the level of press, radio, TV, and films. We need guard with special care the anonymity of all members of all anonymous Twelve-Step programs.

12. Anonymity is the spiritual foundation of all our traditions, ever reminding us to place principles before personalities.

Appendix 6.
Al-Anon: Is It for You?

Millions of people are affected by the excessive drinking of someone else. The following twenty questions are designed to help you decide whether or not you need Al-Anon.

1. Do you worry about how much someone   Yes   No
    else drinks?
2. Do you have money problems because of   Yes   No
    someone else's drinking?
3. Do you tell lies to cover up for someone   Yes   No
    else's drinking?
4. Do you feel that drinking is more important   Yes   No
    to your loved one than you are?
5. Do you think that the drinker's behavior is   Yes   No
    caused by his or her companions?
6. Are mealtimes frequently delayed because   Yes   No
    of the drinker?
7. Do you make threats, such as, "If you don't   Yes   No
    stop drinking I'll leave you?"
8. When you kiss the drinker hello, do you   Yes   No
    secretly try to smell his or her breath?
9. Are you afraid to upset someone for fear it   Yes   No
    will set off a drinking bout?
10. Have you been hurt or embarrassed by a   Yes   No
    drinker's behavior?
11. Does it seem as if every holiday is spoiled   Yes   No
    because of drinking?
12. Have you considered calling the police be-   Yes   No
    cause of drinking behavior?
13. Do you find yourself searching for hidden   Yes   No
    liquor?
14. Do you feel that if the drinker loved you,   Yes   No
    he or she would stop drinking to please
    you?

15. Have you refused social invitations out of fear or anxiety?   Yes   No

16. Do you sometimes feel guilty when you think of the lengths you have gone to control the drinker?   Yes   No

17. Do you think that if the drinker stopped drinking, your other problems would be solved?   Yes   No

18. Do you ever threaten to hurt yourself to scare the drinker into saying, "I'm sorry" or "I love you"?   Yes   No

19. Do you ever treat people (children, employees, parents, coworkers, etc.) unjustly because you are angry at someone else for drinking too much?   Yes   No

20. Do you feel there is no one who understands your problems?   Yes   No

If you have answered yes to three or more of these questions, Al-Anon or Alateen may help. You can contact Al-Anon or Alateen by looking in your local telephone directory.*

---

*From *Al-Anon—Is It for You?* Copyright © 1983 by Al-Anon Family Group Headquarters. Reprinted by permission of Al-Anon Family Group Headquarters, Inc.

Appendix 7.
The Twelve Steps of Al-Anon

1. We admitted we were powerless over alcohol—that our lives had become unmanageable.
2. Came to believe that a Power greater than ourselves could restore us to sanity.
3. Made a decision to turn our will and our lives over to the care of God *as we understood Him.*
4. Made a searching and fearless moral inventory of ourselves.
5. Admitted to God, to ourselves, and to another human being the exact nature of our wrongs.
6. Were entirely ready to have God remove all these defects of character.
7. Humbly asked Him to remove our shortcomings.
8. Made a list of all persons we had harmed, and became willing to make amends to them all.
9. Made direct amends to such people wherever possible, except when to do so would injure them or others.
10. Continued to take personal inventory and when we were wrong promptly admitted it.
11. Sought through prayer and meditation to improve our conscious contact with God *as we understood Him*, praying only for knowledge of His will for us and the power to carry that out.
12. Having had a spiritual awakening as the result of these steps, we tried to carry this message to alcoholics, and to practice these principles in all our affairs.

Appendix 8.
The Twelve Traditions of Al-Anon

1. Our common welfare should come first; personal progress for the greatest number depends upon unity
2. For our group purpose there is but one authority—a loving God as He may express Himself in our group conscience. Our leaders are but trusted servants—they do not govern.
3. The relatives of alcoholics, when gathered together for mutual aid, may call themselves an Al-Anon Family Group, provided that, as a group, they have no other affiliation. The only requirement for membership is that there be a problem of alcoholism in a relative or friend.
4. Each group should be autonomous, except in matters affecting another group or Al-Anon as a whole.
5. Each Al-Anon Family Group has but one purpose: to help families of alcoholics. We do this by practicing the Twelve Steps of AA *ourselves*, by encouraging and understanding our alcoholic relatives, and by welcoming and giving comfort to families of alcoholics.
6. Our Al-Anon Family Groups ought never endorse, finance or lend our name to any outside enterprise, lest problems of money, property and prestige divert us from our primary spiritual aim. Although a separate entity, we should always cooperate with Alcoholics Anonymous.
7. Every group ought to be fully self-supporting, declining outside contributions.
8. Al-Anon Twelfth-Step work should remain forever non-professional, but our service centers may employ special workers.
9. Our groups, as such, ought never be organized; but we may create service centers or committees directly responsible to those they serve.
10. The Al-Anon Family Groups have no opinion on outside issues; hence our name ought never be drawn into public controversy.

11. Our public relations policy is based on attraction rather than promotion; we need always maintain personal anonymity at the level of press, radio, TV and films. We need guard with special care the anonymity of all AA members.

12. Anonymity is the spiritual foundation of all our Traditions, ever reminding us to place principles over personalities.

Appendix 9.
The Twelve Steps of AA

1. We admitted we were powerless over alcohol—that our lives had become unmanageable.
2. Came to believe that a Power greater than ourselves could restore us to sanity.
3. Made a decision to turn our will and our lives over to the care of God *as we understood Him*.
4. Made a searching and fearless moral inventory of ourselves.
5. Admitted to God, to ourselves, and to another human being the exact nature of our wrongs.
6. Were entirely ready to have God remove all these defects of character.
7. Humbly asked Him to remove our shortcomings.
8. Made a list of all persons we had harmed, and became willing to make amends to them all.
9. Made direct amends to such people wherever possible, except when to do so would injure them or others.
10. Continued to take personal inventory and when we were wrong promptly admitted it.
11. Sought through prayer and meditation to improve our conscious contact with God *as we understood Him*, praying only for knowledge of His will for us and the power to carry that out.
12. Having had a spiritual awakening as the result of these steps, we tried to carry this message to alcoholics, and to practice these principles in all our affairs.

Taken from *Alcoholics Anonymous*, copyright © 1939 by Alcoholics Anonymous World Services, Inc. Reprinted by permission of AA World Services, Inc. Throughout this book, the opinions expressed in interpreting the steps are those of the author. The interpretation accepted by AA appears in the books published by A.A. World Services, Inc., Box 459, Grand Central Station, New York, New York 10163. (212) 686-1100.

Appendix 10.
The Twelve Traditions of AA

1. Our common welfare should come first; personal recovery depends upon AA unity.
2. For our group purpose there is but one ultimate authority—a loving God as He may express Himself in our group conscience. Our leaders are but trusted servants; they do not govern.
3. The only requirement for AA membership is a desire to stop drinking.
4. Each group should be autonomous except in matters affecting other groups or AA as a whole.
5. Each group has but one primary purpose—to carry its message to the alcoholic who still suffers.
6. An AA group ought never endorse, finance, or lend the AA name to any related facility or outside enterprise, lest problems of money, outside property, and prestige divert us from our primary purpose.
7. Every AA group ought to be fully self-supporting, declining outside contributions.
8. Alcoholics Anonymous should remain forever nonprofessional, but our service centers may employ special workers.
9. AA, as such, ought never be organized; but we may create service boards or committees directly responsible to those they serve.
10. Alcoholics Anonymous has no opinion on outside issues; hence the AA name ought never be drawn into public controversy.
11. Our public relations policy is based on attraction rather than promotion; we need always maintain personal anonymity at the level of press, radio, and films.

12. Anonymity is the spiritual foundation of all our traditions, ever reminding us to place principles before personalities.

Appendix 11.
Books

Al-Anon Faces Alcoholism. New York: Al-Anon Family Group Headquarters, 1985.

Alcoholics Anonymous (The Big Book). 3rd edition. New York: Alcoholics Anonymous World Services, 1970.

Ariès, Philippe. *Centuries of Childhood: A Social History of Family Life*. Translated by Robert Baldick. New York: Alfred A. Knopf, 1962.

Black, Claudia. *It Will never Happen to Me: Children of Alcoholics as Youngsters, Adolescents, Adults*. Denver, CO: M.A.C. Publications (1850 High Street, Denver, CO 80218), 1982.

Black, Claudia. *Repeat After Me*. Denver, CO: M.A.C. Publications (1850 High Street, Denver, CO 80218), 1985.

Campbell, Joseph. *The Hero with a Thousand Faces*. Princeton, NJ: Princeton University Press, 1973.

Campbell, Joseph. *The Mythic Image*. Bollingen Series C. Princeton, NJ: Princeton University Press, 1974.

Cermak, Timmen L. *A Primer on Adult Children of Alcoholics*. Pompano Beach, FL: Health Communications, Inc. (1721 Blount Road, Suite 1, Pompano Beach, FL 33069), 1983.

Co-Dependency: An Emerging Issue. Pompano Beach, FL: Health Communications, Inc. (1721 Blount Road, Suite 1, Pompano Beach, FL 33069), 1984.

Covington, Stephanie. *Women and Addiction: A Collection of Papers*. Available from the author, 1129 Torrey Pines Road, La Jolla, CA 92037.

Demause, Lloyd. *Foundations of Psychohistory*. New York: Creative Roots, Inc. (P.O. Box 401, Planetarium Station, New York, NY 10024), 1982.

Gravitz, Herbert L., and Julie D. Bowden. *Guide to Recovery: A Book for Adult Children of Alcoholics*. Holmes Beach, FL: Learning Publications, Inc. (P.O. Box 1326, Holmes Beach, FL 33509), 1985.

Greenleaf, Jael. *Co-Alcoholic-Para-Alcoholic: Who's Who and What's the Difference?* Los Angeles, CA, 1981.

Hillman, James. *Loose Ends: Primary Papers in Archetypal Psychology*. Dallas, TX: Spring Publications (P.O. Box 22069, Dallas, TX 75222), 1975.

Jung, C. G. *Collected Works: The Archetypes and the Collective Unconscious.*, Vol. 9, no. 1. 2nd edition, Bollingen Series XX. Translated by R. F. C. Hull. Princeton, NJ: Princeton University Press, 1968.

Jung, C. G., and C. Kerenyi. *Essays on a Science of Mythology: The Myth of the Divine Child and the Mysteries of Eleusis*. Bollingen paperback edition. Translated by R. F. C. Hull. Princeton, NJ: Princeton University Press, 1969.

Kurtz, Ernie. *Not-God: A History of Alcoholics Anonymous*. Center City, MN: Hazelden Publications (Box 176, Center City, MN 55012), 1969.

McConnell, Patty. *A Workbook for Healing: Adult Children of Alcoholics*. San Francisco: Harper & Row, 1986.

Miller, Alice. *For Your Own Good: Hidden Cruelty in Child Rearing and the Roots of Violence*. Translated by Hildegarde and Hunter Hannum. New York: Farrar, Strauss & Giroux, 1983.

Moore, Jean, ed. *Roads to Recovery: A National Directory of Alcohol and Drug Treatment Centers*. New York: Collier McMillan, 1985.

"Pass It On": The Story of Bill Wilson and How the AA Message Reached the World. New York: Alcoholics Anonymous World Services, 1984.

Pinkham, Mary Ellen, with Families in Crisis, Inc. *How to Stop the One You Love from Drinking*. New York: Putnam, 1986.

Postman, Neil. *The Disappearance of Childhood*. New York: Dell, 1984.

Seixes, Judith S., and Geraldine Youcha. *Children of Alcoholism: A Survivor's Manual*. New York: Harper & Row, 1986.

V., Rachel. *A Woman Like You: Life Stories of Women Recovering from Alcoholism and Addiction*. San Francisco: Harper & Row, 1985.

Wegscheider, Sharon. *Another Chance: Hope and Health for the Alcoholic Family*. Palo Alto, CA: Science and Behavior Books (701 Welch Road, Palo Alto, CA 94306), 1981.

Woitiz, Janet. *Adult Children of Alcoholics*. Pompano Beach, FL: Health Communications, Inc. (1721 Blount Road, Suite 1, Pompano Beach, FL 33069), 1983.

Woodman, Marion. *Addiction to Perfection: The Still Unravished Bride, A Psychological Study*. Toronto, Canada: Inner City Books (Box 1271, Station Q, Toronto, Canada M4T 2P4), 1982.

―――. *The Pregnant Virgin*. Toronto, Canada: Inner City Books (Box 1271, Station Q, Toronto, Canada M4T 2P4), 1985.